Challenging Theory:
Discipline after Deconstruction

For Douglas

Challenging Theory:
Discipline After Deconstruction

Catherine Burgass

Studies in European Cultural Transition

Volume One

General Editors: Martin Stannard and Greg Walker

Ashgate

Aldershot • Brookfield USA • Singapore • Sydney

Published by
Ashgate Publishing Limited
Gower House
Croft Road
Aldershot
Hants GU11 3HR
England

Ashgate Publishing Company
Old Post Road
Brookfield
Vermont 05036-9704
USA

Ashgate website: http://www.ashgate.com

British Library Cataloguing-in-Publication data

Burgass, Catherine
    Challenging theory: discipline after deconstruction.
    (Studies in European cultural transition; v. 1)
    1.Criticism
    I.Title
    809

Library of Congress Catalog Card Number: 99-066608

ISBN 1 84014 680 X

Typeset by Pat FitzGerald and printed on acid-free paper and bound in Great Britain by MPG Books Ltd, Bodmin, Cornwall

Contents

Acknowledgements

This book was initially a PhD thesis and I am very grateful both for funding from the British Academy and for the help of my supervisors, Clare Hanson and Phil Shaw. I am also grateful to Martin Stannard for his encouragement. Peter Brooker read and constructively disagreed with an earlier version of Chapter 4. Earlier versions of Chapter 2 have appeared in *Euresis: Cahiers Roumains d'Etudes Litteraires*, 1–2 (1996) and *Romanian Review*, 351–2 (1998). I especially want to thank my parents, John and Christine Burgass, for their unstinting support.

General Editors' Preface

The European dimension of research in the humanities has come into sharp focus over recent years, producing scholarship which ranges across disciplines and national boundaries. Until now there has been no major channel for such work. This series aims to provide one, and to unite the fields of cultural studies and traditional scholarship. It will publish the most exciting new writing in areas such as European history and literature, art history, archaeology, language and translation studies, political, cultural and gay studies, music, psychology, sociology and philosophy. The emphasis will be explicitly European and interdisciplinary, concentrating attention on the relativity of cultural perspectives, with a particular interest in issues of cultural transition.

Martin Stannard
Greg Walker

University of Leicester

Chapter 1

Opposition and Difference

The 'first generation' of poststructuralist theorists were enthusiasts with a missionary zeal. These French intellectuals of the late 1960s believed that a synthesis of linguistics, literary criticism, psychoanalysis, and ideological critique would help to foment political revolution. Of course it did not, but the word has been disseminated widely and in Britain and America poststructuralism has been recruited in the critique of humanism, Enlightenment rationality, bourgeois liberalism, English literature and the discipline which endorsed and was endorsed by these values. For some, poststructuralism provided a fillip for a discipline which for decades had subsisted on a diet of close reading supplemented by pedestrian 'old' historicism. There has also been a strong negative reaction from disciplinary traditionalists, who rejected Continental theory out of hand and clung resolutely to a form of Leavisite criticism. There remains an anti-theory faction in many English departments today, but the old opposition between theorist and anti-theorist is breaking down. The assimilation of theory within literary studies is indicated by the fact that since the 1980s it has been the norm, even for older universities, to include literary theory on the degree course, often as a core element. For students of English literature, theory is now part of disciplinary convention and poststructuralism is no longer the iconoclastic discourse it once was but claims are still being made for its ethical and political relevance.

Although deconstruction ranges across disciplinary boundaries and has been transformed into a coherent method of literary criticism, it is primarily a metaphysical discourse. Derrida has repeatedly shown how conceptual oppositions, whether in the texts of philosophy, literature or politics, are not mutually exclusive but irredeemably contaminated by or reliant upon each other. After Saussure, this model is accessible and, on an abstract level, cogent. But what has happened after Derrida is that deconstruction is often cited as the theoretical underpinning of arguments for the incorporation of literary theory into critical practice, or literary studies within cultural studies, or the practice of reading philosophy as literature. This assumes an untenable transition from the ideal realm of metaphysics to the real world of social practice and represents an inappropriate conflation of different types of difference. This study is an attempt to redress some common misinterpretations of Derrida's work relating to the status of metaphysical oppositions and to block the equation that is often made between these metaphysical structures and the differences which operate within social institutions – not to reject deconstruction out of hand, then, but to point to its limitations in the face of disparate cultural differences.

From the moment deconstruction transgressed its national boundaries it encountered resistance from philosophers in the Anglo-American academy.

European philosophy does have its own tradition of positivism and Derrida is even regarded by some Continental philosophers as a charlatan, but Anglo-American philosophy in the twentieth century has been associated primarily with the analytical tradition, which rejected metaphysical inquiry in favour of positivistic investigations into language, logic, and sense-perception. One of the most notorious encounters between the two traditions took place in 1977 in the form of a published debate between Derrida and John Searle over the issue of intentionality in J.L. Austin's speech-act theory. This dialogue is remarkable for its antagonism – overt on Searle's part, explicitly denied by Derrida. Searle pulls no punches and opens by berating Derrida for what he sees as a misreading of Austin in 'Signature Event Context':

> It would be a mistake, I think, to regard Derrida's discussion of Austin as a confrontation between two prominent philosophical traditions. This is not so much because Derrida has failed to discuss the central theses in Austin's theory of language, but rather because he has misunderstood and misstated Austin's position . . . and thus the confrontation never quite takes place.[1]

Derrida counter-attacks by claiming to agree: 'if there is only one sentence of the *Reply* to which I can subscribe, it is the first'.[2] Against Searle, he acknowledges a debt to Austin and accuses Searle of being 'ultimately more continental and Parisian than I am'. Derrida substantiates this assertion by instancing the metaphysical structures and concepts that Searle has inherited, namely:

> The hierarchical axiology, the ethical-ontological distinctions which do not merely set up value-oppositions clustered around an ideal and unfindable limit, but moreover *subordinate* these values to each other (normal/abnormal, standard/parasite, fulfilled/void, serious/non-serious, literal/non-literal, briefly: positive/negative and ideal/non-ideal)[.][3]

'All metaphysicians', continues Derrida, 'from Plato to Rousseau, Descartes to Husserl, have proceeded in this way', that is, to structure their thought around hierarchical oppositions.[4] Although Derrida is keen to emphasise their shared metaphysical inheritance, the fact remains that he and Searle are profoundly at odds.[5] Derrida's aggression is evident in his repeated references to 'Sarl' instead

---

[1]   John R. Searle, 'Reiterating the Differences: A Reply to Derrida', *Glyph* I (1977), p. 198.
[2]   Jacques Derrida, 'Limited Inc abc . . .', trans. Samuel Weber, *Glyph* II (1977), p. 172.
[3]   Ibid., p. 236.
[4]   Ibid., p. 236.
[5]   For a discussion of this exchange and critical responses see Sandy Petrey, *Speech Acts and Literary Theory* (London: Routledge, 1990), pp. 131–47.

of Searle. This appellation is apparently warranted by the fact that 'Limited Inc' discusses issues of copyright, authority and signature, as well as intention, and the French 'SARL' is an acronym equivalent to the American 'Inc' (incorporated), or British 'Ltd' (limited company), the point being that Searle does not have some sort of copyright on Austin's work. Such lexical manoeuvres cannot fail to have been offensive to Searle (Gerald Bruns points out that the rhetorical form of catachresis or *abusio* is typical of Derrida) and therefore Derrida's claim that he is not in dispute with Searle is unconvincing.[6] 'Limited Inc' is just one example of Derrida's intellectual obsession with the conceptual oppositions and hierarchies which he asserts underpin Western philosophy and which he incidentally, though no doubt intentionally, suggests that opposition exists where it is emphatically denied.

It is not an overstatement to say that Derrida is obsessed with oppositions; throughout his career he has repeatedly turned deconstruction on these metaphysical structures. Derrida's thought is rooted in the philosophical tradition, but has also been deeply coloured by the terms and techniques of Saussure's linguistic theory, as well as the structuralist anthropology of Claude Lévi-Strauss. His obsession with oppositions may be in part a reaction against the structuralism which elevated the principle of negative or binary opposition to a fundamental principle. According to Saussure, binary opposition is the means by which the units of language have value or meaning; each unit is defined against what it is not (*A*/not-*A*). Saussure presented such distinctions as fundamental to all language: 'in language there are only differences. Even more important: a difference generally implies positive terms between which the difference is set up; but in language there are only differences *without positive terms*'.[7] While structuralist linguistics makes extensive use of the binary paradigm in its model of language (*langue* and *parole*; synchronic and diachronic; signifier and signified), it should be remembered that binary oppositions *within* language are themselves functional rather than essential or fixed oppositions. This is obvious at the level of the phoneme, where any particular pairing is arbitrary. For Saussure, the terms 'opposition' and 'difference' are therefore interchangeable: '*la langue* is a system of oppositions or differences, and the task of the analyst is to discover what are these functional differences'.[8] *Différance* represents the supplementation of Saussure's atemporal difference – the principle by which linguistic signs acquire their value not by reference to objects outside the linguistic system but by their difference from other signs within that system – with deferral. David Wood suggests that Derrida makes 'no attempt to evaluate

---

[6]   Gerald L. Bruns, 'Writing Literary Criticism', *The Iowa Review* 12, 4 (1981), 35.

[7]   Ferdinand de Saussure, *Course in General Linguistics*, trans. Wade Baskin, ed. Charles Bally and Albert Sechehaye (London: Owen, 1959), p. 120.

[8]   Jonathan Culler, *Saussure* (London: Fontana, 1986), p. 46.

Saussure's model of language. Instead he offers us a kind of deepening of the principle of difference on which it rests.'[9]

But from the beginning, on Derrida's own admission, it has been apparent that deconstruction has only very limited efficacy in undermining these metaphysical structures and there is an argument to be made that it positively reinforces them. One way to establish the destructive potential of deconstruction is to take a closer look at *différance*, a 'quasi-concept' the foundational status of which is always refuted by Derrida but which lies at the heart of his philosophical system. In compiling the attributes of this quasi-concept Derrida instructs at the outset that '*différance is not*, does not exist, is not a present-being (*on*) in any form; and we will be led to delineate also everything *that* it *is not*, that is, *everything*; and consequently that it has neither existence nor essence'.[10] This appears to first to subscribe to the law of identity formulated by Aristotle in the *Metaphysics*: 'it is impossible for anything at the same time to be and not to be' {1006a}.[11] Derrida wishes to claim of *différance* that it hovers between existence and non-existence (presence and absence), thereby evading this law:

> If the displaced presentation remains definitively and implacably postponed, it is not that a certain present remains absent or hidden. Rather, *différance* maintains our relationship with that which we necessarily misconstrue, and which exceeds the alternative of presence and absence.[12]

Différance is a metaphysical-linguistic concept; like one of Plato's forms, it occupies the realm of ideas rather than the world of things but its effects can be observed.

That *différance* represents some kind of threat to metaphysical oppositions is clear:

> At the point at which the concept of différance, and the chain attached to it, intervenes, all the conceptual oppositions of metaphysics (signifier/signified; sensible/intelligible; writing/speech; passivity/activity; etc.) – to the extent that they ultimately refer to the presence of something present . . . become nonpertinent.[13]

---

9   David Wood, 'Following Derrida' in *Deconstruction and Philosophy: The Texts of Jacques Derrida*, ed. John Sallis (London: University of Chicago Press, 1987), p. 147.
10   Derrida, *Margins of Philosophy*, p. 6. This is incidentally tautologous in the best tradition of philosophical logic: *différance* does not exist *therefore* it has no existence.
11   Derrida's description of the 'arche-trace' (another quasi-concept), indicates his lack of respect for Aristotelian laws: 'the value of the transcendental arche must make its necessity felt before letting itself be erased. The concept of arche-trace must comply with both that necessity and that erasure. It is in fact contradictory and not acceptable within the logic of identity.' *Of Grammatology*, trans. Gayatri Chakravorti Spivak (London: Johns Hopkins University Press, 1974), p. 61.
12   Derrida, *Margins of Philosophy*, p. 20.
13   Jacques Derrida, *Positions*, trans. Alan Bass (London: Athlone, 1987), p. 29.

The power of *différance* to 'intervene' in the matter of metaphysical oppositions depends upon Derrida's assertion that the difference of *différance* (the *a* which distinguishes it from Saussure's *différence*) is neither purely sensible nor purely intelligible. The argument proceeds as follows: the *a* of *différance* can only function within the system of so-called 'phonetic writing' (a term which underlines the privileged status of speech over writing).[14] However, this *a* is not itself audible since it cannot be distinguished from the *e* that it replaces. Derrida goes on to assert that 'It will be objected, for the same reasons that graphic difference itself vanishes into the night, can never be sensed as a full term'.[15] So while the meaning of *différance* does not inhere in the spoken word, neither is it contained in the graphic or written word. This message was reinforced in the context of the original lecture, where the graphic difference between the *e* and the *a* would have been literally invisible to the audience. For the listener, there is therefore an unobtrusive slide between the metaphorical 'vanishes' and this literal invisibility, although out of this original context it is possible to argue that the meaning of *différance* does inhere in the written word. For Derrida meaning is context-bound but never fixed and he therefore concludes that full presence inheres neither in the graphic nor the phonetic sign so that *différance* 'must be permitted to belong to an order which no longer belongs to sensibility'.[16] He then proceeds to argue that simply because we cannot sense (see/hear) the full presence of *différance*, this does not imply that the difference is merely conceptual. So *différance* occupies an indeterminate and intermediate position *between* binary terms:

> Here, therefore, we must let outselves [*sic*] refer to an order that resists the opposition, one of the founding oppositions of philosophy, between the sensible and the intelligible. The order which resists this opposition, and resists it because it transports it, is announced in a movement of *différance* (with an *a*) between two differences or two letters, a *différance* which belongs neither to the voice nor to writing in the usual sense, and which is located, as the strange space that will keep us together here for an hour, *between* speech and writing[.][17]

As Alan Bass points out in a translator's note, Derrida's argument is also context-bound; the words used to denote intelligibility connote sensibility; the Greek word *theorein* (knowledge) originally included the sense of seeing, while the French *entendement* (understanding) also signifies hearing. Derrida's argument, although citing etymology and grammar as 'evidence', is pre-eminently

---

[14]   Jacques Derrida, *Margins of Philosophy*, trans. Alan Bass (London: Harvester Wheatsheaf, 1982), p. 4.

[15]   Ibid., p. 5.

[16]   Ibid., p. 5.

[17]   Ibid., p. 5.

metaphysical. But what effective form can this 'resistance' take if *différance* remains trapped in the 'strange space' between opposites?

Différance's primary claim to undermine oppositions is to destabilize the conventional hierarchical relations between terms; however, deconstructing hierarchies tends to involve the construction of new hierarchies. The fundamental metaphysical opposition for Derrida is the presence/absence binary and his primary concern is with the logocentrism of metaphysics, that is its assumption and privileging of 'presence'. In Saussure's theory of language, binary oppositions are theoretically neutral and Derrida quotes Gilles Deleuze to demonstrate his aversion to this notion: "'The dream of two equal forces, even if they are granted an opposition of meaning, is an approximate and crude dream, a statistical dream, plunged into by the living but dispelled by chemistry.'" [18] Derrida points to the logocentrism of structuralist theory, asserting that 'The "formal essence" of the sign can only be determined in terms of presence.' [19] More specifically, 'The formal essence of the signified is *presence*, and the privilege of its proximity to the logos as phonē is the privilege of presence.' [20] A hierarchical relationship thus obtains between signifier and signified. The effect of temporal difference is that the meaning of the sign is never fully present but rather infinitely postponed, so that the value of the signified is no longer guaranteed. Theoretically, this revised model has implications both for quintessentially 'logocentric' discourses like the sciences and for the most mundane of communications. In the *Cours* Saussure also explicitly prioritizes speech by deprecating the invidious effects of the written word on pronunciation and excluding writing as the proper object of linguistic enquiry. (Saussure did not write the *Cours* but, like Socrates, 'dictated' it to his pupils through his lectures.) Derrida responds to this by asking 'Where is the evil? . . . And what has been invested in the "living word", that makes such "aggressions" of writing intolerable?' [21] Saussure is quite candid about his distaste for the written word. *Différance*'s incorporation of deferral means that deconstruction cannot be criticized as logocentric although it is obvious that Derrida's preoccupation with writing has inverted the speech/writing relationship thus creating an anti-logocentric hierarchy.

Différance has the potential to subvert metaphysics from within, but a corollary of this position is that the potential of the agent is immediately compromised:

> Our discourse irreducibly belongs to the system of metaphysical oppositions. The break with this structure of belonging can be announced

---

[18] Quoted in Derrida, *Margins of Philosophy*, p. 17.
[19] Jacques Derrida, *Of Grammatology*, trans. Gayatri Chakravorty Spivak (London: Johns Hopkins University Press, 1974), p. 18.
[20] Ibid., p. 18.
[21] Ibid., p. 41.

only through a certain organization, a certain strategic arrangement which,
within the field of metaphysical opposition, uses the strengths of the field
to turn its own stratagems against it[.][22]

The power of *différance* to break out of metaphysics is from the outset
curtailed by its philosophical provenance within metaphysics and linguistics.
Derrida calls this effect the 'double bind', a principle which states that one is
necessarily constrained by the terms of the discourse one critiques. One would
expect Derrida to set about deconstructing the sign and Saussure's metaphors
appear pre-eminently susceptible to deconstruction: 'Language can also be
compared with a sheet of paper: thought is the front and the sound the back; one
cannot cut the front without cutting the back at the same time'.[23] If Derrida were
so minded, this 'sheet of paper' could function to co-implicate the founding
opposition of Saussure's theory: signifier/signified. However, Derrida elsewhere
asserts the necessity of the sign as an essential component of both *différance* and
metaphysics: 'we cannot do without the concept of the sign, for we cannot give
up this metaphysical complicity without also giving up . . . the risk of erasing
difference in the self-identity'.[24] So from the outset it becomes clear that
différance remains indebted to the binary structures of Saussurean linguistics and
metaphysics.

Différance has 'intervened' in metaphysical oppositions in a wide range of
canonical texts in linguistics, literature and politics, as well as philosophy, and in
most cases it works to subvert hierarchies but to reinforce binarism. As one of the
founding fathers of Western metaphysics, Plato comes under particularly intense
scrutiny. In 'Plato's Pharmacy' deconstruction is unleashed on the *Phaedrus*, a
Dialogue in which Phaedrus has concealed under his cloak the transcription of a
speech by the sophist Lysias. Phaedrus is eventually persuaded by Socrates to
read out the speech, which in turn prompts Socrates to discourse on the nature of
the soul and divine love, rhetoric and knowledge and, in the penultimate section,
the superiority of speech over writing. Derrida typically focuses on what appears
to be a passage of minor importance, just as typically emphasizing the
'supplementarity' of this topic: 'All the subjects of the dialogue, both themes and
speakers, seem exhausted at the moment the supplement, writing, or the
pharmakon, are introduced'.[25] He justifies his concentration on the incidental by
pointing to the structural connection in Plato's text between this discussion of
writing and the preceding commentary on truth, beauty, love and knowledge.

Derrida maintains that the binary principle is essential to Plato's concept of
writing:

---

[22]   Derrida, *Writing and Difference*, p. 20.
[23]   Saussure, *Course in General Linguistics*, p. 113.
[24]   Derrida, *Writing and Difference*, p. 281.
[25]   Derrida, *Dissemination*, p. 73. For a discussion of writing as supplement see
Of Grammatology, pp. 141–64.

Plato thinks of writing, and tries to comprehend it, to dominate it, on the
basis of *opposition* as such. In order for these contrary values (good/evil,
true/false, essence/appearance, inside/outside, etc.) to be in opposition,
each of the terms must be simply *external* to the other, which means that
one of these oppositions (the opposition between inside and outside) must
already be accredited as the matrix of all possible opposition.[26]

He attempts to undermine this classic binarism by citing etymology and semantic
nuance as he does in 'Différance' and the deconstruction of the *Phaedrus* pivots
on one word, *pharmakon*. The *pharmakon* is structurally identical to *différance*
and is a term signally appealing to Derrida because of its inherent double
meaning: 'This *pharmakon*, this "medicine", this philter, which acts as both
remedy and poison, already introduces itself into the body of the discourse with
all its ambivalence. This charm, this spellbinding virtue, this power of
fascination, can be – alternately or simultaneously – beneficent or maleficent.'[27]
Derrida also foregrounds his exploitation of semantic ambiguity when he states:
'we hope to display in the most striking manner the regular, ordered polysemy
that has, through skewing, indetermination, or overdetermination, but without
mistranslation, permitted the rendering of the same word by "remedy", "recipe",
"poison", "drug", "philter", etc.'[28] He tests the limits of this strategy by citing
words which are etymologically related to the *pharmakon* but absent from Plato's
text. The implication is that if a term is dependent for its value on that which it is
not (Saussure's principle), then that which it is not is somehow present in the
sign, even by virtue of its absence:

there is another of these words that, to our knowledge, is never used by
Plato. If we line it up with the series *pharmakeia-pharmakon-pharmakeus*,
we will no longer be able to content ourselves with reconstituting a chain
that, for all its hiddenness, for all it might escape Plato's notice, is
nevertheless something that passes through certain discoverable points of
presence that can be seen in the text. The word . . . seems strikingly absent
from the 'Platonic text'.
But what does *absent* or *present* mean here?[29]

The 'absent/present' word Derrida is referring to is *pharmakos* (scapegoat).
However, Derrida rejects the logocentric idea that this term might provide a key
with which to decipher the unitary meaning of Plato's text; its invocation should
rather be seen rather as part of the perennial attempt to problematize the
presence/absence opposition upon which, as he proceeds to argue, the
speech/writing hierarchy is founded. R. Hackforth, translator of the *Phaedrus*,

---

26   Derrida, *Dissemination*, p. 103.
27   Ibid., p. 70.
28   Ibid., p. 71.
29   Ibid., p. 129.

notes that Plato himself was unconcerned with hidden meanings – since there was a diversity of potential meanings but no means to decide between them, he refused to expend much effort in arbitration. On the other hand, he was also in the habit of making 'etymological jests . . . sometimes rather pointlessly'.[30] Saussure undertook research into concealed anagrams in classical poetry, although he was doubtful of the validity of this study.[31] By contrast, Derrida's practice is to forcibly disinter contradictory, hidden and absent terms from Plato's text and to allow these etymological excavations to bear a significant weight in the argument.

The first explicit, if oblique, reference to the *pharmakon* in the *Phaedrus* itself occurs in the Boreas myth narrated by Socrates. According to this myth, a maiden is killed on the bank of the river Ilissus 'while at play with Pharmaceia' {229c}. The relevance of this myth to the rest of the *Phaedrus* is not clear.[32] But for Derrida, its significance lies in the paradoxical effects of Pharmaceia, who proves fatal, thereby neatly emphasizing the contradictory properties of the *pharmakon*: kill *and* cure: 'Through her games, Pharmaceia has dragged down to death a virginal purity and an unpenetrated interior.'[33] According to Derrida, nothing is so inviolate, as his discussion of the hymen (another analogue of *différance*) in 'The Double Session' makes clear:

> To repeat: the hymen, the confusion between the present and the nonpresent, along with all the indifferences it entails within the whole series of opposites (perception and nonperception, memory and image, memory and desire, etc.), produces the effect of a medium (a medium as element enveloping both terms at once; a medium located between the two terms). It is an operation that *both* sows confusion *between* opposites *and* stands *between* the opposites 'at once'.[34]

In spite of the reference to the dual meaning of 'medium', the stress is on the position of the hymen, a mediating entity, *between* opposites.

The *pharmakon* is next mentioned in Plato's text by Socrates; when Phaedrus teases him for a disinclination to walk outside the city walls, he replies, 'you seem to have discovered a recipe [*pharmakon*] for getting me out' {230d}. This 'recipe' is Lysias's (written) speech and its effects are described by Derrida (following Plato) as seductive: 'the *pharmakon* makes one stray from one's

---

[30]   Plato's *Phaedrus*, trans. R. Hackforth (Cambridge: Cambridge University Press, 1952), pp. 26, 36, n. 1. This is the version used by Johnson in her translation of *Dissemination*.

[31]   See Culler, *Saussure*, p. 107.

[32]   Pharmaceia is the goddess of medicine and according to the French translator, there was a fountain dedicated to Pharmaceia near the river. Derrida, *Dissemination*, p. 70. Hackforth suggests that the myth *may* have some 'organic significance', or might simply be a dig 'at the allegorical school of poetical interpretation'. Plato's *Phaedrus*, p. 26.

[33]   Derrida, *Dissemination*, p. 70.

[34]   Ibid., p. 212.

general, natural, habitual paths and laws'.[35] Just as the (absent) *pharmakos* served in the deconstruction of the presence/absence opposition, here the *pharmakon* causes Socrates to cross the city boundaries thus mediating, or undermining the inside/outside opposition. The 'unpenetrated interior' which Derrida associates with the Boreas myth is also ironized by this subsequent exchange between Socrates and Phaedrus and revealed precisely as mythical. Derrida states defensively that up to this point, the 'association between writing and the *pharmakon* still seems external; it could be judged artificial or purely coincidental.'[36] However, it is already clear that for Derrida it is rather the internal/external binary ('the matrix of all possible opposition'), that is artificial.

The explicit identification of writing with the *pharmakon* occurs with Socrates' relation of the myth of Theuth, or the origin of writing. In this myth, Theuth is the inventor of calculation, geometry, astronomy *and* writing. He presents this last invention to the king, Thamus, claiming that it is 'a recipe [*pharmakon*] for memory and wisdom' {274*e*} and here *pharmakon* is patently used in its positive or 'medicinal' sense. However, the king is unimpressed by his offering and declares that writing is in fact anti-mnemonic: 'If men learn this, it will implant forgetfulness in their souls: they will cease to exercise memory because they rely on that which is written, calling things to remembrance no longer from within themselves, but by means of external marks' {275*a*}. The king therefore castigates Theuth and disparages his invention: 'you, by reason of your tender regard for the writing that is your offspring, have declared the very opposite of its true effect' {275*a*}. The association of writing with the *pharmakon* is most fortuitous for Derrida since if the *pharmakon* itself is both good and bad, curative and fatal, it can be used to undermine the hierarchical opposition of speech and writing in Plato's philosophy. The fact that the king cannot write but dictates is cited by Derrida as evidence that writing is the secondary term in the speech/writing hierarchy:

> God the king does not know how to write, but that ignorance or incapacity only testifies to his sovereign independence. He has no need to write. He speaks, he says, he dictates, and his word suffices. Whether a scribe from his secretarial staff then adds the supplement of a transcription or not, that consignment is always in essence secondary.[37]

At this point the relation of speech and writing to the presence/absence hierarchy becomes clear. The king, both father figure and god, is the final arbiter of the value of writing. He represents the transcendental signified or guarantor of meaning (presence) in speech: 'The king or god . . . is thus the other name for

---

35   Ibid., p. 70.
36   Ibid., p. 72.
37   Ibid., p. 76.

the origin of value.'[38] There is some debate as to the provenance of the Theuth myth and Derrida disputes Plato's claim to originality by indicating its structural similarity with other ancient myths, such as the Egyptian myth of Thoth (not mentioned by Plato). Thoth is the son of the god-king, Ammon-Ra, and the vocal representative of Horus. In this myth, speech (Thoth) is secondary to a primary presence (Horus): 'The message itself is not, but only represents, the absolutely creative moment. It is a second and secondary word.'[39] As Derrida describes it, this myth has precisely the same structure:

> the figure of Thoth is opposed to its other (father, sun, life, speech, origin
> or orient, etc.), but as that which at once supplements and supplants it.
> Thoth extends or opposes by repeating or replacing. By the same token,
> the figure of Thoth takes shape and takes its shape from the very thing it
> resists and substitutes for. But it thereby opposes *itself*, passes into its
> other, and this messenger-god is truly a god of the absolute passage
> between opposites.[40]

The logocentric hierarchy is identified as a constant feature in philosophy: 'Even if we did not want to give in here to the easy passage uniting the figures of the king, the god, and the father, it would suffice to pay systematic attention . . . to the permanence of a Platonic schema that assigns the origin and power of speech, precisely of *logos*, to the paternal position.'[41] So in 'Plato's Pharmacy' the *pharmakon* functions like *différance*, demonstrating the relationship between conceptual opposites replacing independence (mutual exclusion) with interdependence.

The protocol of deconstruction in both 'Différance' and 'Plato's Pharmacy' seems quite clear and comprises three steps: (i) identification of the binary oppositions by which the text is structured; (ii) demonstration of the hierarchical organization of these binaries; (iii) investigation into the ways that the rhetoric of the text subverts the hierarchies its argument is predicated upon. But although, as Barbara Johnson suggests, deconstruction holds that binary oppositions are sustained at the cost of internal differences, the effect of deconstruction is to fortify these binaries.[42] This is because the term utilized in the third step of deconstructive analysis, whether imposed upon the text (*différance*) or borrowed from the text (*pharmakon*), always remains within and reinforces pre-existing metaphysical structures. Furthermore, the repeated application of this paradigm also tends to reinforce the structural equivalence of different binaries. The

---

[38]   Ibid., p. 76.
[39]   Ibid., p. 88.
[40]   Ibid., p. 93.
[41]   Ibid., p. 76.
[42]   Barbara Johnson, *The Critical Difference: Essays in the Contemporary Rhetoric of Reading* (Baltimore: Johns Hopkins University Press, 1980), pp. x–xi.

structural similarity between ancient myths as Derrida describes them seems uncontentious, but his analysis of the *Phaedrus* is itself formulaic and reductive. Jonathan Culler points out the pitfalls of blanket binarism:

> binary oppositions can be very misleading precisely because they present factitious organization. The moral is quite simple: one must resist the temptation to use binary oppositions to devise elegant structures. If A is opposed to B and X is opposed to Y then one could, in seeking further unification, set these oppositions together in a four-term homology and say that A is to B as X is to Y (in that the relation is one of opposition in both cases). But the formal symmetry of such homologies does not guarantee that they are in any way pertinent[.][43]

The use of schematic letters, pioneered by Aristotle in his development of abstract logic, is appropriate. In a letter written prior to the series of lectures, later transcribed as the *Cours de linguistique générale*, Saussure wrote: 'For a long time I have been above all preoccupied with the logical classification of linguistic facts.'[44] The application of the 'abstract' principle of binary opposition or *différance* onto the differences in literary or philosophical texts comprises a reductive process similar to that of syllogistic logic. Although difference and opposition are identical in structuralist theory, in a binary opposition and by extension in any structuralist analysis, differences are removed from context and thereby artificially polarized. As Culler admonishes, 'The advantage of binarism, but also its principal danger, lies in the fact that it permits one to classify anything. Given two items one can always find some respect in which they differ and hence place them in a relation of binary opposition.'[45] While the artificial polarization of differences is something one might expect Derrida to take exception to, the same thing seems to happen, although in a different way, through the agency of *différance* in linking together inside/outside, good/bad, speech/writing, Thamus/Theuth, and so on; Derrida artificially isolates differences and by foregrounding 'formal symmetry' reinforces it. The terms Derrida uses to describe the myths of writing: 'systematic', 'schema', which are often used disparagingly of structuralism, can justifiably be applied to deconstruction.

While poststructuralism is presented as a critique of structuralism's tendency to concentrate exclusively on the synchronic aspect of language and *différance* supplements Saussurean difference with deferral, in 'Plato's Pharmacy' Derrida cites particular myths (*parole*) to reveal the underlying structure (*langue*). At times his approach is deliberately ahistorical, 'bracketing off the problem of

---

[43]   Jonathan Culler, *Structuralist Poetics: Structuralism, Linguistics and the Study of Literature* (London: Routledge & Kegan Paul, 1975), p. 16.
[44]   Quoted in Culler, *Saussure*, p. 14.
[45]   Culler, *Structuralist Poetics*, p. 15.

factual genealogy and of the empirical, effective communication among cultures and mythologies'.[46] Of course Derrida typically oppugns the mutual exclusivity of the synchronic/diachronic opposition: 'If one had faith in the organization of a classical reading, one would perhaps say that I had just proposed a double grid: historical and systematic. Let us pretend to believe in this opposition. Let us do it for the sake of convenience'.[47] This 'illusory' structure had already been deconstructed by Saussure in the *Cours*:

> Speech always implies both an established system and an evolution; at every moment it is an existing institution and a product of the past. To distinguish between the system and its history, between what it is and what it was, seems very simple at first glance; actually the two things are so closely related that we can scarcely keep them apart.[48]

Lévi-Strauss followed Saussure in describing myth as a 'double structure, altogether historical and ahistorical'.[49] The ahistorical tendency of Saussurean linguistics and subsequent structuralist criticism is in fact legitimated by this theory. The implication is that the synchronic study of *langue* is necessarily historical and therefore that historical questions can be ignored. Ironically, the co-implication of history and structure has had precisely the same consequence for deconstruction as Derrida tends to make token gestures to history in the form of perfunctory notes and asides but focuses overwhelmingly on structure.

Derrida cautions against reducing the *Phaedrus* to a structural analysis, but immediately qualifies this admonition: 'No absolute privilege allows us absolutely to master its textual system. This limitation can and should nevertheless be displaced to a certain extent.'[50] This is another evocation of the double bind, intended to excuse recourse to a position of scientific mastery outside the text and the confinement within its binary structures. That deconstruction as a method of analysis in any way surpasses structuralist analysis is highly debatable. But again, Derrida excuses himself with reference to the double bind. The links between structuralist and poststructuralist analysis are emphasized when Derrida asks, 'What then, are the pertinent traits for someone who is trying to reconstitute the structural resemblance between the Platonic and the other mythological figures of the origin of writing?'[51] He continues, 'What we wish to do here is simply to point to the internal structural necessity which alone has made possible such communication and any eventual contagion of mythemes.'[52] This echoes Lévi-Strauss's method of analysis in 'The Structural

---

[46]   Derrida, *Dissemination*, p. 85.
[47]   Derrida, *Of Grammatology*, p. 97.
[48]   Saussure, *Course in General Linguistics*, p. 8.
[49]   Lévi-Strauss, *Structural Anthropology*, p. 210.
[50]   Derrida, *Dissemination*, p. 96.
[51]   Ibid., p. 86.
[52]   Ibid., p. 85.

Study of Myth'. Lévi-Strauss had already identified a mythical figure who 'occupies a position halfway between two polar terms' and who 'must retain something of that duality – namely an ambiguous and equivocal character'.[53] In addition, he notes that a mythical figure may be 'endowed with contradictory attributes – for instance, he may be good and bad at the same time'.[54] In a different work, Derrida cites Lévi-Strauss as his methodological predecessor, quoting from *The Savage Mind*: '"The opposition between nature and culture to which I attached much importance at one time . . . now seems to be of primarily methodological importance."'[55] (Lévi-Strauss here employs the nature/culture opposition, at the same time doubting the mutual exclusivity of the terms.) Derrida notes that 'Lévi-Strauss will always remain faithful to this double intention: to preserve as an instrument something whose truth value he criticizes'.[56] He also tellingly vindicates Plato (and thus himself) as subject to certain 'structural laws':

> The most general of these, those that govern and articulate the oppositions speech/writing, life/death, father/son, master/servant, first/second, legitimate son/orphan-bastard, soul/body, inside/outside, good/evil, seriousness/play, day/night, sun/moon, etc., also govern and according to the same configurations, Egyptian, Babylonian, and Assyrian mythology.[57]

Derrida focuses on textual differences which then are artificially isolated *by* '*différance* (with an *a*) as the displaced and equivocal passage of one different thing to another, from one term of an opposition to the other'.[58] He is less concerned with the actual or real differences between speech and writing than with the formal structure of the text in terms of its metaphysical oppositions and hierarchies. It becomes obvious that the methodological tools which Derrida inherits from structuralism and metaphysics, and which he alludes to in *Writing and Difference*, have a similarly reductive effect – a criticism apparently forestalled in *Of Grammatology*:

> Operating necessarily from the inside, borrowing all the strategic and economic resources of subversion from the old structure, borrowing them structurally, that is to say without being able to isolate their elements and atoms, the enterprise of deconstruction always in a certain way falls prey to its own work.[59]

---

[53] Lévi-Strauss, Claude, *Structural Anthropology* I (Harmondsworth: Penguin, 1968), p. 226.
[54] Ibid., p. 227.
[55] Quoted in Derrida, *Writing and Difference*, pp. 284–5.
[56] Derrida, *Writing and Difference*, p. 284.
[57] Derrida, *Dissemination*, p. 85.
[58] Derrida, *Margins of Philosophy*, p. 17.
[59] Derrida, *Of Grammatology*, p. 24.

Derrida has therefore already excused the fact that he remains within the binary structures of Plato's text by reference to the double bind, but these disclaimers have little material effect on the textual analysis and what is presented as necessary subjection is in fact closer to voluntary subscription.

Derrida emphasizes Plato's dependence on mutually exclusive binaries in order to deconstruct them. He identifies an energy at work within the *Phaedrus*, undermining the hierarchical structures upon which the argument – and the rest of metaphysics – is founded. This force is apparently so subversive that it has been suppressed by the author and ignored by subsequent commentators. Rarely does Derrida attribute anything approximating the mobility of *différance* to authorial intention. Recourse to intention arrests the play of *différance* and informs Derrida's remark in 'Plato's Pharmacy': 'on the supposition that the categories of the voluntary and the involuntary still have some absolute pertinence in a reading – which we don't for a minute believe, at least not on the textual level on which we are now advancing'.[60] Derrida is more concerned with unintentional ambiguities and double meanings, and he has a considerable professional investment in textual 'psychoanalysis' – reading against the grain by reading between the lines. While many philosophical systems rely explicitly or implicitly upon binary oppositions, it is nevertheless often the obvious *intention* of their authors to co-implicate these binaries. With reference to 'Plato's Pharmacy', Arne Melberg suggests that 'The risk you take with thinking of Plato in terms of oppositions . . . is to become a Platonist which Plato is not.'[61] For Plato in the *Protagoras*, opposites were essential, that is, 'one thing can have only one opposite' {333*a–b*}. However, an examination of some of the Dialogues indicates a significant affinity between Plato's and Derrida's conceptual structures. Intimations of *différance* can already be identified in Plato's description of the soul, which moves *between* the sensible and intelligible realms, gaining knowledge of the eternal forms in heaven to be regained in the mortal world by the philosopher. Another example of Plato's relative flexibility in the treatment of oppositions occurs in the *Phaedo*, where Socrates claims that to establish the existence of the immortal soul it is necessary to prove that living people are born from the dead. In order to prove this assertion, the subject of the inquiry is widened to include 'all things subject to coming-to-be' {70*d*}. Of these, Socrates asserts that 'opposites come to be only from their opposites – in the case of all things that actually have an opposite' {70*e*}. There is continual movement between such opposites: 'between the members of every pair of opposites, since they are two, aren't there two processes of coming-to-be, from one to the other, and back again from the latter to the former?' {71*a–b*}. Although Plato assumes essential opposites, the stress on movement between those opposites is accentuated in the supplementary proof:

---

60 Derrida, *Dissemination*, p. 73.

61 Arne Melberg, *Theories of Mimesis* (Cambridge: Cambridge University Press, 1995), p. 42.

> If there were not perpetual reciprocity in coming to be, between one set of things and another, revolving in a circle, as it were – if, instead, coming-to-be were a linear process from one thing into its opposite only, without any bending back in the other direction, do you realize that all things would ultimately have the same form: the same fate would overtake them, and they would cease from coming to be? {72a–b}

This mobility and reciprocity between metaphysical oppositions prefigures *différance* which shuttles between binary oppositions. Plato clearly does rely on oppositions but it is possible that Derrida deliberately neglects those texts which explicitly account for contradiction, mobility or supplementarity. He ignores the mobility of the soul and the relation of life and death in the Dialogues.

Deconstruction foregrounds binary oppositions but continues to subscribe to the binary model as a mode of description. The co-implication of opposites undertaken by deconstruction is already in place in Saussurean linguistics where the value of each phoneme in a binary opposition depends on the other. *Différance* in the end is not a particularly dynamic force and represents a minor modification or even synthesis of the various forms of metaphysical and linguistic opposition and difference: Plato's mobility; Hegel's co-implication of opposites in the dialectic and Heidegger's adoption of a similar model. *Différance*'s subversion of conceptual or metaphysical oppositions is limited to co-implication and actually falls short of the Hegelian dialectic because it fails to break out of the safety of the binary structure. In fact Derrida explicitly states in 'Différance' that he is not out to negate oppositions: 'one could reconsider all the pairs of opposites on which philosophy is constructed and on which our discourse lives, not in order to see opposition erase itself but to see what indicates that each of the terms must appear as the *différance* of the other'.[62] It is obvious, then, that deconstruction does not radically undermine even conceptual oppositions and any faith in Derrida's desire to reduce these structures to a homogeneous mass in the Nietzschean sense is completely misplaced. Eve Tavor Bannet is simply wrong when she asserts: 'Derrida collapses all oppositions – and with them all the constructs of language, culture and rational thought – back into an originating unity which evokes that of the Jewish God: One, Sovereign, Incorporeal and wholly Other'.[63] Deconstruction cannot be recruited even in the collapse of metaphysical oppositions because Derrida is fundamentally unwilling to posit the destruction of any metaphysical concept. In spite of his attempts to problematize binarism, *différance* makes no 'quantum leap' in the metaphysical history of oppositions and deconstruction comprises as schematic and reductive a form of analysis as structuralism. Rodolphe Gasché suggests that the collapse of oppositions is irreconcilable with an argumentative rigour he wishes to claim for

---

[62] Derrida, *Margins of Philosophy*, p. 17.

[63] Eve Tavor Bannet, *Structuralism and the Logic of Dissent: Barthes, Derrida, Foucault, Lacan* (Basingstoke: Macmillan, 1989), p. 184.

deconstruction: 'As long as its goal is believed to promote the . . . licentious free play, nihilistic cancelling out of opposites, abolition of hierarchies, and demystification or de-ideologization of Western philosophemes, deconstruction's definite and logical procedure cannot be grasped in all its specificity.'[64] Derrida does retain a certain commitment to logic, but although Gasché's interpretation has some validity, an equally plausible, though less charitable, interpretation is that *différance* positively requires oppositions to show its 'mobility' off to the best advantage – the further apart (artificially isolated and therefore polarized) two differences are, the faster *différance* can be seen to move.

And if deconstruction fails to subvert metaphysical structures, it can hardly be expected to have much effect outside metaphysics. Metaphysics operates only on the theoretical or conceptual level; it has never been orientated towards any practical application and tends to ignore the phenomenal world, something Plato readily conceded. In the *Parmenides* Socrates asserts that the forms are known not through reference to the physical world but through knowledge of the other world {133c–4c}.[65] For Plato, the Forms existed prior to any physical manifestation whereas for Aristotle, substance or essence (*ousia*) *was* physical. Aristotle criticized Plato for his reliance on first principles and for ignoring the disjunction between theory and reality and argued in the *Movement of Animals* that 'we must grasp this [principle] not only in theory, but also by reference to individuals in the world of sense; for with these in view we seek general theories, and with these we believe that general theories ought to harmonize' {698a}.[66] The salient distinction between the methods of Plato and Aristotle, between metaphysics and empiricism, is that between deduction and induction; the former refers to a purely logical argument which requires no external reference; the latter denotes the inference of a general law from particular observed circumstances. Metaphysics is by no means a master discourse; it has a strictly limited field of inquiry, which is perfectly valid on its own terms but ignores the physical world, inquiring instead into the foundations of thought using deductive reasoning. One of the effects of the current dominance of poststructuralist thought in the humanities has been the attenuation and denigration of equally valid empirical methods, which use inductive reasoning to form principles from physical evidence. Although metaphysics may analyse the philosophical assumptions of empirical discourse, it is conversely susceptible to realist, positivist or empirical analyses of its own *a priori* truths.

Geoffrey Bennington contests the separation of empiricism and metaphysics,

---

[64] Rodolphe Gasché, 'Infrastructures and Systematicity' in *Deconstruction and Philosophy: The Texts of Jacques Derrida*, ed. John Sallis (London: The University of Chicago Press, 1987), p. 3.

[65] *The Collected Dialogues of Plato*, ed. Edith Hamilton and Huntington Cairns (Princeton: Princeton University Press, 1961).

[66] *The Complete Works of Aristotle*, ed. Jonathan Barnes (Oxford: Princeton University Press, 1984).

attacking Peter Dews for 'maintaining, through his stupefyingly banal dialectic, the distinction between the empirical and the transcendental which is shown in deconstruction both to have no ultimate transcendental validity and to resist over-hasty attempts to confuse the distinction'.[67] He continues: 'deconstruction is . . . eminently describable (with Gasché) as a "radical empiricism"'.[68] While in metaphysical terms ('transcendental validity' is a metaphysical concept) the conceptual distinction between empiricism and metaphysics can be deconstructed, metaphysics is confined to the conceptual and has no jurisdiction over empirical or historical inquiry which is concerned with verifiable fact, physical evidence and actual differences. The realms of physics and metaphysics are clearly delineated and there is an irreducible difference between the noumenal and the phenomenal, the ideal and the real. Foucault denounced Derrida for renouncing the world for the word and this is a reasonable objection to the extent that Derrida chooses to work within metaphysics.

Stephen Yarbrough asserts that Derrida is preoccupied with the misapplication of metaphysical concepts:

> One of Derrida's chief claims is that an entire class of concepts – 'metaphysical' concepts – are intrinsically improper whenever they are applied to reality. In other words, it is always improper to take a metaphysical concept literally. Western thought, Derrida claims, relies upon the force of proprieties of usage (*kurion*) masking improprieties of application.[69]

Yarbrough is correct in assuming that Derrida's concepts should not be taken literally; the hymen and the *pharmakon*, for example, are clearly convenient metaphors for metaphysical difference. In 'Plato's Pharmacy' Derrida betrays not the slightest anxiety regarding the disjunction between metaphysical structures and actual differences and is concerned only with the text as it provides a vehicle for a discussion of metaphysical oppositions.

It comprises a more effective a strategy in the destabilization of many conceptual oppositions to work outside metaphysics and to point out, for example, that speech and writing are not binary opposites, but are quite clearly related, though different, forms of representation and communication and that historically writing has often been prioritized over speech. The tendency of literary theory is to suggest that conceptual oppositions produce (construct) cultural difference; the alternative is that conceptual oppositions merely *describe* culturally significant differences which have independent existence. The truth lies

---

[67]   Geoffrey Bennington, *Legislations: The Politics of Deconstruction* (London: Verso, 1994), pp. 102–103.

[68]   Ibid., p. 103.

[69]   Stephen R. Yarbrough, *Deliberate Criticism: Toward a Postmodern Humanism* (London: University of Georgia Press, 1992), p. 83.

somewhere in between: conceptual oppositions both describe and reinforce sets of cultural differences but neither necessitate a mutually exclusive relationship between those differences nor preclude exchange and interrelation. The oppositions examined in the following chapters are neither permanent binary structures nor structural equivalents but comprise more or less arbitrary braces of differences. Historically, some of these differences have been harnessed together, like the winged horses of Plato's soul, as conceptual binaries and represented as diametrically opposed. Once it is established that there is no essential grounding for pairs of differences or necessary structural equation *between* pairs of differences, then they can be reconsidered as specific textual and material differences within particular cultural contexts without incurring charges of essentialism or reductiveness and inevitably provoking deconstructive critique.

Part I focuses on textual (formal) differences and looks at the ways that these differences may dissolve and reform in different contexts. Literary realism and metafiction are identified by distinct formal techniques but in the process of reading these differences may be neutralized, allowing a 'realist' reading of an anti-realist text and undermining the poststructuralist argument that metafiction compromises the reader's ontological categories. Literary and philosophical texts can also often be identified by formal means but whereas 'hybrid' texts are seized on by poststructuralists as indicating a radical generic instability, within a cultural context which includes academic discipline, authorial intention, and other kinds of institutional determinant, genre boundaries re-emerge. Part II examines the effect of deconstructing conceptual oppositions within the discipline of literary studies and addresses the practical issues of teaching literature and literary theory in the university. Chapter 4 investigates the attempt to incorporate literary theory within English literature degrees and argues that in the context of undergraduate teaching theory should not be assimilated within critical practice on both intellectual and practical grounds. Chapter 5 foregrounds the historical connections between literary studies and cultural studies and argues against the collapse of the two disciplines. Part III examines some of the sillier and more invidious claims of literary theorists, assessing the relationship between philosophical argument and literary rhetoric in postmodern theory and finally questioning the value of metaphysical analysis to political critique.

PART I

Chapter 2

Mimesis and Metafiction

What a duce, do you think I am writing a Romance? Don't you see that I am copying Nature . . .?[1]

The relation between mimesis or literary realism and metafiction, that is the flaunting of a text's fictional status, is theoretically antithetical; a novel cannot point to its own narrative construction and at the same time persuade the reader to suspend his disbelief. The classical hierarchy, established by Aristotle and dominant until the mid-twentieth century, privileged mimesis. But ever since Saussure wrenched apart signifier and signified, this hierarchy has been reversed so that, after centuries of the mimetic ideal, the attempt to mirror the world in fiction is being presented by poststructuralists as naïve. In *Structuralist Poetics*, for example, Jonathan Culler insists that 'literature is something other than a statement about the world' and cautions the critic against making 'the unseemly rush from word to world'.[2] For Derrida, the prime offence of literary realism is its claim to hold up a mirror to reality, to make language itself transparent; he even appears sceptical of the extra-textual – *'il n'y a pas de hors texte'* – and is directly critical of Plato's logocentric ideal.[3] Although mimesis and metafiction are in some senses at odds, there is a tenuous argument to be made that postmodernist metafiction is itself a new sort of realism: if world is text and text is world, the text of the novel is neither a transparent nor opaque window on reality (realism), but *is* reality – more real than illusionist realism could ever be. Post-Marxists also have ideological objections to realism: Peter Widdowson maintains that realism is complicit with the bourgeois ideology which conceals the real relations of the individual and society.[4] In *Critical Practice*, Catherine Belsey claims that classic realism offers the reader 'the position of subject as the origin both of understanding and of action'.[5] It emphasises 'the individual as a free, unified, autonomous subjectivity', interpellating the reader and thus maintaining the capitalist machine and bourgeois ideology.[6] Belsey and

---

[1]   Samuel Richardson, Letter to Miss Mulso, in Miriam Allot, *Novelists on the Novel* (London: Routledge & Kegan Paul, 1965), p. 41.

[2]   Jonathan Culler, *Structuralist Poetics: Structuralism, Linguistics and the Study of Literature* (London: Routledge & Kegan Paul, 1975), p. 130.

[3]   See Jacques Derrida, *Of Grammatology*, trans. Gayatri Chakravorty Spivak (London: Johns Hopkins University Press, 1974), p. 158; *Dissemination*, trans. Barbara Johnson (London: Athlone, 1981), 1972, p. 190.

[4]   Peter Widdowson, 'The Anti-History Men: Malcolm Bradbury and David Lodge', *Critical Quarterly* 26, 4 (1984), 5–31.

[5]   Catherine Belsey, *Critical Practice* (London: Methuen, 1980), p. 67.

[6]   Belsey, *Critical Practice*, p. 67.

Widdowson fear that in reading mimetic literature the naïve reader will identify with the subject position delineated by the bourgeois text and blindly support the capitalist state. They duly expose the conventions of realism and its pretensions to 'transparency', to help the alienated reader discover the invidious workings of bourgeois ideology and select more enlightening reading matter.

The postmodern predilection for metafiction leads Linda Hutcheon to misrepresent Aristotle by broadening the reference of the term. Hutcheon attempts to collapse the mimesis/metafiction opposition by arguing that because metafiction dramatizes narrative it is mimetic of *process* where traditional realism is mimetic of *product*.[7] She states that Aristotle presents both drama (mimesis) and narration (diagesis) as forms of imitation and alludes to Homer's practice of characterizing the narrator in the *Odyssey*, suggesting that here 'The content has expanded to include diegesis or the process of narration itself'.[8] Hutcheon is correct in her assertion that Aristotle regards narrative as a mimetic *form*; however, he cannot be recruited to support the idea of narrative as imitative *of* the fictional process itself. In fact, Aristotle presents metafiction and mimesis as irreconcilable and lauds Homer for his refusal to intrude upon the narrative: 'The poet should say very little in his own character, as he is no imitator when doing that' {1460*a*}.[9] For Aristotle, both narrative and drama are the *means* of representation: 'one may either speak at one moment in narrative and at another in an assumed character, as Homer does', but 'The objects the imitator represents are actions' {1448*a*}, and these objects should be interpreted as the actions of the characters rather than those of the author or reader. Hutcheon promotes too wide a definition of metafiction, incorporating both 'auto-representation' (the linguistic self-consciousness of the *nouveau roman*, *Ada* or *Finnegan's Wake*), and fictive self-consciousness. This is to stretch the term too far; where *Finnegan's Wake* ignores the world in favour of the word, the modernist foregrounding of language cannot be equated with the postmodernist foregrounding of fiction since it has a different effect and is born of different intentions. Metafiction deliberately foregrounds and explicitly thematizes the text's fictional status and the reading experience; modernist or postmodernist word-play may defamiliarize, but is not generally designed to alienate in this pseudo-Brechtian manner.

The literary forms favoured by poststructuralist theorists include the linguistic self-consciousness of modernist texts and the literary self-consciousness of postmodernism, both of which apparently subvert the conventions of 'classic' realism. Derrida presents Mallarmé's metafictive text, *Mimique*, as an antidote to Platonic mimesis because it demonstrates a freedom from the nostalgia for

---

[7]   Linda Hutcheon, *Narcissistic Narrative: The Metafictional Paradox* (London: Methuen, 1984), ch. 2.

[8]   Ibid., pp. 40–41.

[9]   *The Complete Works of Aristotle*, ed. Jonathan Barnes (Oxford: Princeton University Press, 1984).

presence: 'this imitator having in the last instance no signified, this sign having in the last instance no referent'.[10] Belsey recommends the 'interrogative' text which 'invites the spectators to reflect on fiction as a discursive practice and the ways in which discourse allows them to grasp their relation to the real relations in which they live'.[11] In addition, the poststructuralists propose that metafiction confuses or collapses the ontological categories of word and world (signifier and signified), fact and fiction. It is true that postmodern metafiction often foregrounds both the narrative construction of the novel and the reader's role in creating meaning, thus (theoretically) inserting the reader into the text of the novel and puncturing the boundary or frame of the fictional world. However these theorists sometimes fail to take into account the historical diversity of literary realism and the related sophistication and flexibility of the 'recreational' reader (a term more appropriate than 'naïve') and are themselves overly credulous of the deconstruction of ontological boundaries. If the contextual determinant of the real reading process is brought into the equation then both the opposition of mimesis and metafiction and the collapse of the reader's ontological categories are no longer tenable; they become irrelevant when the reader's familiarization with metafictive devices and will to suspend disbelief allow a 'realist' reading of an anti-realist novel.

The novel is a genre which is founded on realism. Orthodox accounts of the birth of the British novel in the eighteenth century, for example, stress its difference from the Romance, a difference which lay in its attempt to represent a recognizable secular world and it is clear that the novelists themselves were convinced that they were establishing a new literary form which was true to life.[12] Ian Watt in his seminal historicist account, *The Rise of the Novel*, asserts that the defining characteristic of the novel is its 'formal realism; formal, because the term realism does not here refer to any special literary doctrine or purpose, but only to a set of narrative procedures'.[13] These procedures comprise the presentation of details and particulars through 'a more largely referential use of language than is common in other literary forms'.[14] In a theory-driven but apparently coherent definition, Culler suggests that realism is achieved through the depiction of:

---

[10]   Derrida, *Dissemination*, p. 207. According to Richard Kuhns, Mallarmé 'sought a language of "dead" images whose certainty and specificity would overcome the vagaries and ambiguities of words taken from ordinary language'. *Literature and Philosophy: Structures of Experience* (London: Routledge & Kegan Paul, 1971), pp. 244–5. But unlike the self-enclosed system of formal logic poetic language cannot escape connotation and therefore referentiality.

[11]   Belsey, *Critical Practice*, p. 102.

[12]   See also Ian Watt, *The Rise of the Novel: Studies in Defoe, Richardson, and Fielding* (London: Penguin, 1963); *Arnold Kettle, An Introduction to the English Novel* I, 2nd edn (London: Hutchinson, 1967).

[13]   Watt, *The Rise of the Novel*, pp. 32–3.

[14]   Ibid., p. 33.

items whose only apparent role in the text is that of denoting a concrete reality (trivial gestures, insignificant objects, superfluous dialogue). In a description of a room items which are not picked up and integrated by symbolic or thematic codes . . . and which do not have a function in the plot produce what Barthes calls a 'reality effect' (*l'effet de réel*) . . .. The pure representation of reality thus becomes, as Barthes says, a resistance to meaning, an instance of the 'referential illusion', according to which the meaning of a sign is nothing other than its referent.[15]

Although it is difficult and sometimes inappropriate to separate the purely referential from the symbolic in a work of fiction, there is such an attention to detail in Richardson's *Pamela* where the heroine writes home with detailed itineraries of her clothes: 'he gave me two suits of fine Flanders laced head-clothes; three pair of fine silk shoes, two hardly the worse, and just fit for me (for my lady had a very little foot,) and the other with wrought silver buckles in them, and several ribbands and top-knots of all colours; four pair of white cotton stockings' etc.[16] Specificity and concrete detail help to create a realistic world. As well as this kind of material particularity, the early novel also prioritized the individual over the type, a tendency attributed by Watt to the rise of mercantilism and bourgeois ideology.[17]

That metafiction was not a feature of the early eighteenth-century novels can be ascribed to a desire on the part of authors and publishers to convince readers of the literal truth of the text. At this formative stage in the novel's history, realism sometimes masqueraded as reality; Defoe's *Robinson Crusoe* was originally presented and often accepted for a historical account of a real man's adventure, edited rather than authored by Defoe. Lennard Davis describes how the relatively primitive state of communications meant that 'News' was often neither particularly new nor easily authenticated, thus blurring the distinction between fact and fiction. Davis asserts that 'The readers of these novels, ballads, *newes*, and so on clearly valued the idea that a narrative *might* have been true, but they bought the narratives whether true or false'.[18] However, as communications improved and the news/novels distinction began to be more sharply delineated, the novelists had to modify their claims to literal truth. In the prefaces to *Roxana* and *Pamela*, Defoe and Richardson made only qualified assertions of historical

    15   Culler, *Structuralist Poetics*, p. 193.
    16   Samuel Richardson, *Pamela* I (London: Dent, 1962), p. 8. Although according to Margaret Ann Doody, Pamela owes a debt to the 'letter writer', an exemplary manual. The rustic (Pamela) was a stock character, characterized by a concern 'with the concrete; small possessions and small sums of money'. *A Natural Passion: A Study of the Novels of Samuel Richardson* (Oxford: Clarendon, 1974), p. 30.
    17   The dominant British philosophy of the eighteenth century was empiricism which, as Watt suggests, shares a preoccupation with the particular.
    18   Lennard J. Davis, *Factual Fictions: The Origins of the English Novel* (New York: Columbia University Press, 1983), p. 70.

veracity but in the body of the novels still eschewed self-conscious metafiction.

The tradition of metafiction in the novel is often traced back to Cervantes' *Don Quixote*. Offended both by what he saw as the moral hypocrisy of *Pamela* and its failure to observe classical proprieties, Henry Fielding published his parody *Joseph Andrews*. In the preface this work is distinguished 'from the productions of romance writers' and a debt to Cervantes is owned.[19] The text contains lengthy asides which foreground the mechanics of the reading process and the narrative techniques:

> It is an observation sometimes made, that to indicate our idea of a simple fellow, we say, *He is easily to be seen through*: Nor do I believe it a more improper denotation for a simple book. Instead of applying this to any particular performance, we chuse rather to remark the contrary in this history, where the scene opens itself by small degrees, and he is a sagacious reader who can see two chapters before him.[20]

Although called a 'history' in line with those earlier works which purported to be factual, these interjections function to foreground narrative design.

Metafiction reached new heights (or depths) of blatant self-reference in the eighteenth century with Lawrence Sterne's *Tristram Shandy*, which was also designed to mock the novel genre by flamboyantly foregrounding its fictional status and literary techniques. *Tristram Shandy* was later given Victor Shklovsky's stamp of approval when he called it 'the most typical novel in world literature'.[21] That the contemporary reading public were well able to digest such an extreme metafiction can be deduced from the fact that along with the opprobrium of Dr Johnson, the book achieved considerable popular success.[22]

A cursory survey of major nineteenth-century novelists indicates the long-established accommodation of metafiction *within* literary realism. Although for a significant number of authors the attempt at verisimilitude appeared to require a self-effacing narrator, this period also marked the convergence of previously oppositional literary modes as metafiction was assimilated within the dominant realism. The most common metafictional device used in nineteenth-century fiction is the intrusive narrator and Jane Austen's narrator can be extremely officious. In *Mansfield Park* realistic illusion is temporarily suspended when the narrator remarks: 'I purposely abstain from dates on this occasion, that every one

---

[19]   Henry Fielding, *Joseph Andrews*, ed. R.F. Brissenden (Harmondsworth: Penguin, 1977), p. 30.

[20]   Ibid., p. 65.

[21]   Victor Shklovsky, 'Sterne's *Tristram Shandy*: Stylistic Commentary' in *Russian Formalist Criticism: Four Essays*, ed. Lee T. Lemon and Marion J. Reis (London: University of Nebraska Press, 1965), p. 57.

[22]   See Christopher Ricks, introduction, *The Life and Opinions of Tristram Shandy, Gentleman* by Laurence Sterne, ed. Graham Petrie (Harmondsworth: Penguin, 1967), p. 8.

may be at liberty to fix their own, aware that the cure of unconquerable passions, and the transfer of unchanging attachments, must vary much as to time in different people.'[23] This brings to mind the 'description' of the desirable widow Wadman in *Tristram Shandy*: 'Sit down, sir, paint her to your own mind – as like your mistress as you can – as unlike your wife as your conscience will let you – 'tis all one to me – please but your own fancy in it.'[24] *Northanger Abbey*, in addition to digressions of this type, contains lengthy passages on the nature of the Romance. In *Middlemarch* George Eliot uses the introduction of the 'low' character Joshua Rigg as an occasion for a discussion of the craft of writing:

> And here I am naturally led to reflect on the means of elevating a low subject. Historical parallels are remarkably efficient in this way. The chief objection to them is, that the diligent narrator may lack space, or (what is often the same thing) may not be able to think of them with any degree of particularity, though he may have a philosophical confidence that if known they would be illustrative. It seems an easier and shorter way to dignity, to observe that – since there never was a true story which could not be told in parables where you might put a monkey for a margrave, and *vice versa* – whatever has been or is to be narrated by me about low people, may be ennobled by being considered a parable; so that if any bad habits and ugly consequences are brought into view, the reader may have the relief of regarding them as not more than figuratively ungenteel, and may feel himself virtually in company with persons of some style.[25]

Here one of the virtues of realism, 'particularity', is ironically promoted by means of a narrative aside. David Lodge asserts that Eliot's 'diegetic style' forces the reader to 'think for himself'.[26] But significant lapses of attention are also permitted when the omniscient narrator tactfully withdraws from the action. The difference between these nineteenth-century novels and *Tristram Shandy* is quantitative as well as qualitative. While Sterne's metafiction is both extravagant and sustained, the occasional digressions in *Middlemarch* or *Mansfield Park* pose no threat to readerly equanimity, especially in the case of readers already familiar with the convention of metafiction itself. That many theoretically unsophisticated twentieth-century readers are familiar with devices of metafiction, then, is not in dispute. The rôle of the reader was ignored by Watt in *The Rise of the Novel*, but in *The Rhetoric of Fiction* (1961), Wayne Booth attacks the equation of the novel with formal realism as narrow and inappropriate genre criticism.[27] He cites Jean-

[23]   Jane Austen, *Mansfield Park* (Harmondsworth: Penguin, 1966), p. 454.

[24]   Laurence Sterne, *The Life and Opinions of Tristram Shandy, Gentleman*, ed. Graham Petrie (Harmondsworth: Penguin, 1967), p. 450.

[25]   George Eliot, *Middlemarch* I (London: Dent, 1930), pp. 299–300.

[26]   David Lodge, *After Bakhtin: Essays on Fiction and Criticism* (London: Routledge, 1990), p. 53.

[27]   Wayne C. Booth, *The Rhetoric of Fiction*, 2nd edn (London: Penguin, 1987), p. 41.

Louis Curtis's argument that reading is based on a 'tacit contract with the novelist' and points out that if the use of the intrusive omniscient narrator is an established and widespread convention it is likely to be naturalized by the reader and hence will not detract from the reality effect, thus anticipating Culler's theory of literary competence.[28] There would, of course, have been 'incompetent' contemporary readers of eighteenth- and nineteenth-century novels, unable to naturalize metafictive devices, but there is certainly no reason to suppose that at this period such readers would have experienced a significant confusion of their ontological categories – apart from anything else, these categories were not under suspicion.

Modernist novelists and critics upheld the mimetic ideal, but excoriated the methods of classic realism. Erich Auerbach suggests that the modernists 'hesitate to impose upon life, which is their subject, an order which it does not possess in itself'.[29] Woolf criticized Mr Bennett and his ilk for writing 'of unimportant things ... making the trivial and the transitory appear the true and the enduring'.[30] She was clearly convinced that the significant matter of fiction lay beneath the trivial and mundane surface which for Culler and Barthes is the essence of realism:

> life is forever pleading that she is the proper end of fiction and that the more he sees of her the better his book will be. She does not add, however, that she is grossly impure; and that the side she flaunts uppermost is often, for the novelist, of no value whatever. Appearance and movement are the lures she trails to entice him after her, as if these were her essence, and by catching them he gained her goal.[31]

Modernism also marked a downturn for metafiction; notable in his absence is the intrusive narrator; the fragile structure of subjective realism could not be expected to sustain such rude interruptions. Modernist principles and practices profoundly affected the critical standing of classic realism generally and attitudes to metafiction in particular; E.M. Forster criticized Fielding's and Thackeray's tendency to narrative digression: 'it is devastating, it is bar-parlour chattiness, and nothing has been more harmful to novels of the past'.[32] It is clear that neither James nor Woolf rejects realism *per se* since, 'The only reason for the existence of a novel is that it does attempt to represent life.'[33] But whereas the odd narrative digression would have left the reality effect unscathed, the reader is not infinitely

---

[28]   Ibid., pp. 52, 42.
[29]   Erich Auerbach, *Mimesis* (New York: Doubleday, 1957), p. 485.
[30]   Quoted in Lyn Pykett, *Engendering Fictions: The English Novel in the Early Twentieth Century* (London: Edward Arnold, 1995), p. 92.
[31]   Virginia Woolf, *Collected Essays* II, ed. Leonard Woolf (London: Hogarth, 1966), p. 135.
[32]   E.M. Forster, *Aspects of the Novel* (London: Edward Arnold, 1927), pp. 111–12.
[33]   Henry James, *Partial Portraits* (London: Macmillan, 1888), p. 378.

accommodating and realism is not infinitely flexible. The fact that the modernists produced a heightened literary prose less like common discourse than that used in Victorian fiction and experimented with literary conventions meant that the reality effect would be proportionately diminished. The novel use of language would block straightforward reference by obtruding on the reading experience.

In Britain, the revival of 'classic' realism fronted by the 'Angry Young Men' of the 1950s and 1960s was short-lived and in the 1970s it once again lost ground to experimentalism. Randall Stevenson argues that the tensions of writing in a 'foreign' language inform the suspicion of referentiality evident in the work of Joyce and Nabokov.[34] These authors in fact operate on the cusp of modernism/postmodernism with *Finnegan's Wake* and *Ada* instigating the polyglottal obsession with language which has been inherited by Salman Rushdie and Umberto Eco. Postmodernist fiction tends to jettison the mimetic lyricism of modernism in favour of an even more self-conscious linguistic play which is designed to foreground the materiality of language. It follows modernism in certain thematic concerns: alienation and loss of faith, subjectivity, the relation between word and the world, time and space and there are certain continuities in literary form, such as the non-linear narrative. Insofar as postmodernism *has* mimetic aspirations they are to represent the chaos and confusion of human existence, but much postmodernist fiction appears to summarily reject the mimetic ideal of both 'objective' (nineteenth-century) and subjective (modernist) realism.

The British novel has always been identified with realism and is regarded by some commentators as a hostile environment for the more exotic postmodern forms. According to Stevenson (writing in 1991), Britain is now participating in the postmodern epoch to the extent that 'A certain self-reflexiveness even finds its way into otherwise realistic novels'.[35] Richard Todd, amongst others, asserts that British postmodernism comprises a self-conscious reworking of the British realist tradition.[36] To suggest that the defining characteristic of British postmodernism is its self-conscious reworking of realism itself betrays a certain insularity. Both Stevenson and Todd are over-zealous in their attempts to characterise the national literature: the kind of occasional self-reflexiveness identified by Stevenson is typical of the nineteenth-century novel while the fiction of Italo Calvino or Gabriel Garcia Marquez shows that experimentation with or within the realist tradition is characteristic of *mainstream* – moderately rather than radically experimental – postmodernism in Europe and the Americas as well as Britain.

---

[34] Randall Stevenson, 'Postmodernism and Contemporary Fiction in Britain' in *Postmodernism and Contemporary Fiction*, ed. Edmund J. Smyth (London: Batsford, 1991), pp. 32–3.

[35] Ibid., p. 27.

[36] Richard Todd, 'Confrontation Within Convention: On the Character of British Postmodernist Fiction' in *Postmodern Fiction in Europe and the Americas*, ed. Theo D'haen and Hans Bertens (Amsterdam: Rodopi, 1988), pp. 115–25.

There are nevertheless some British authors whose fiction embodies the sometimes awkward incorporation of postmodernism within British realism, but demonstrates the persistent presence of 'incidental' metafiction within literary realism. One such author is Iris Murdoch, whose realism depends in part on traditional, descriptive 'scene-setting' such as occurs at the opening of *A Fairly Honourable Defeat*:

> Hilda . . . reclined limply, exhibiting shiny burnished knees below a short shift dress of orangy yellow. Her feet were bare. Her undulating dark hair showed some needle-thin lines of grey. Her burly boyish-faced husband . . . sat open-shirted, cooking in the sun. He was red, hoping later to be brown. His shock of abundant fair hair had faded with the years . . ..[37]

Here we see the detailed and specific picture-painting and scene-setting characteristic of realism. This type of narrative is characteristic of Murdoch and is attacked by both Harold Bloom and A.S. Byatt, who apparently retain a modernist distaste for this mode of narration.[38] Bloom in particular evinces a marked disdain for what he describes as Murdoch's 'formulaic procedures', 'anachronistic style and outmoded narrative devices', criticisms which Elizabeth Dipple ascribes to a general tendency to belittle the British novelistic tradition for its provincialism.[39] Murdoch's novels of the 1970s and 1980s are confined to the intellectual, bourgeois or bohemian middle classes and are often set in the nicer parts of London or the country.[40] Such novelistic self-limitation brings to mind Austen's self-deprecating description of 'the little bit (two Inches wide) of Ivory on which I work with so fine a brush, as produces little effect after much labour'.[41] But even though Murdoch's novels are provincial in their self-imposed restrictions, at times the narrative betrays a certain postmodern irony and self-consciousness. In *The Black Prince*, the main narrative is preceded by two forewords, one by the 'editor' and one by the anti-hero, Bradley Pearson, and followed by six 'postscripts' by various characters. Patricia Waugh cites this novel as Murdoch's most explicitly metafictional because of its subject matter (two novelists who are sometimes read as two aspects of Murdoch herself),

---

[37]   Iris Murdoch, *A Fairly Honourable Defeat* (Harmondsworth: Penguin, 1972), p. 11.

[38]   Harold Bloom (ed.), *Iris Murdoch* (New York: Chelsea House, 1986); A.S. Byatt, *Degrees of Freedom: The Early Novels of Iris Murdoch*, 2nd edn (London: Vintage, 1994).

[39]   See Bloom, *Iris Murdoch*, pp. 1–7; Elizabeth Dipple, *The Unresolvable Plot: Reading Contemporary Fiction* (London: Routledge, 1988), p. 185.

[40]   Peter Conradi identifies the 'upper middle-class matron whose creative impulse is unsatisfied' as one of Murdoch's stock characters. 'The Metaphysical Hostess: The Cult of Personal Relations in the Modern English Novel', *ELH* 48 (1981), 428.

[41]   *Jane Austen's Letters*, 3rd edn, ed. Deirdre Le Faye (Oxford: Oxford University Press, 1995), p. 323.

intertext (*Hamlet*), and various prefaces and postscripts.[42] But although all the postscripts give different versions of the story, indicating a typically postmodern concern with the construction of narrative, and in spite of the novel-writing theme and intertext, the largely conventional treatment of narrative time and conventionally realistic narrative mode means that foreword and postscript function as a traditional framing device.

Hilda Spear points to the metafictive elements in *The Black Prince*, *The Sacred and Profane Love Machine*, *A Word Child* and *Henry and Cato*, suggesting that 'the most striking innovation in these novels is the consciously deliberate narration. The reader is made aware that a story is being told'.[43] This is nowhere more apparent than in *The Green Knight* which opens:

> 'Once upon a time there were three little girls – '
> 'Oh look what he's doing now!'
> 'And their names were – '
> 'Come here, come *here*.'
> 'And they lived at the bottom of a well.'[44]

As in Joyce's *Portrait of the Artist of a Young Man*, this parodies the 'classic' fairy-tale beginning. But where Joyce continues with the defamiliarizing device of the child's consciousness, Murdoch immediately summons the classic realist omniscient narrator to explain: 'The first speaker was Joan Blacket, the second was Louise Anderson, the one so urgently summoned was a dog, the little girls mentioned were Louise's children, the place was Kensington Gardens, the month was October.'[45] The thumping pedantry of the delivery serves to parody the technique, but the reader's desire to enter into the fictional world can neutralize most kinds of irony.

The Philosopher's Pupil makes use of various metafictive devices, including that of the intrusive narrator, 'N'. N introduces himself on page 23: 'I am the narrator: a discreet and self-effacing narrator. This book is not about me.'[46] He signs off in a truly postmodernist vein, remarking that 'The end of any tale is arbitrarily determined', and alluding coyly to 'the assistance of a certain lady' (that is, Murdoch herself).[47] Dipple makes the point that the reader forgets about the narrator for long stretches of the text and argues that this attests to Murdoch's commitment to realism.[48] The reader is indeed likely to forget the narrator for the

---

[42]   See Patricia Waugh, *Metafiction: The Theory and Practice of Self-Conscious Fiction* (London: Methuen, 1984), pp. 118–19.

[43]   Hilda Spear, *Iris Murdoch* (London: Macmillan, 1995), p. 73.

[44]   Iris Murdoch, *The Green Knight* (London: Penguin, 1994), p. 1.

[45]   Ibid., p. 1.

[46]   Iris Murdoch, *The Philosopher's Pupil* (Harmondsworth: Penguin, 1984), p. 23.

[47]   Ibid., p. 558.

[48]   Dipple, *The Unresolvable Plot*, p. 188.

simple reason that he intrudes only rarely in the narrative, being given the second short prefatory and concluding chapters, and very seldom lapsing into the first person in between. Although passages such as these are clearly metafictive, in terms of quantifiable effect they do not greatly surpass those narratorial interjections in Austen and Eliot.

The desire to claim Murdoch's fiction as a worthy object of academic study in an anti-realist climate leads some commentators to over-emphasize its postmodern elements. Steven Kellman reads Murdoch's first novel, *Under the Net*, as metafictional or 'self-begetting' (a tendency he characterizes as un-British) because of its hero, Jake, another unproductive novelist.[49] However, novels about novels or artist figures are not necessarily structurally metafictive or locally self-reflexive. In *Iris Murdoch: The Saint and the Artist*, Conradi attempts to recoup Murdoch by arguing that her interest in the idea of an infinite regress is 'of its time', as is 'her insistence that "truth" cannot be secured'.[50] Although Murdoch willingly adopted certain obviously postmodernist techniques, she was probably the novelist least of her time with her unfashionable ethical Platonism and self-confessed debt to realism. Her eccentric adherence to the ethical and literary theories discussed here and in the next chapter explains the fact that any postmodern devices are occasional and incidental rather than sustained and structural, and that the reality effect predominates in formal terms.

David Lodge is another British novelist who experiments with metafiction. His early work is unambiguously realist but his novels increasingly manifest postmodern self-consciousness as structuralism took an imaginative hold on the academy. *How Far Can You Go?* is the most obviously metafictive of his novels. The action follows the fortunes of a group of Catholics and their struggles with Church doctrine and Lodge avails himself of the intrusive narrator, who cosily discusses narrative technique with the 'gentle reader' in the traditional manner: 'Each character . . . has already been associated with some selected detail of dress or appearance which should help you to distinguish one from another.'[51] Lodge, apparently in *propria persona*, also makes an appearance: 'I teach English literature at a redbrick university and write novels in my spare time' and some of the novels are alluded to elsewhere in the text.[52] In a critical essay Lodge asserts that such a 'drastic' device 'invariably reveals some anxiety about the ethical and epistemological nature of fictional discourse and its relationship to the world'.[53] Daniel Ammann imagines that 'this blend of fact and fiction may be even more

---

[49]   Steven G. Kellman, 'Under the Net: The Self-Begetting Novel' in *Iris Murdoch*, ed. Harold Bloom (New York: Chelsea House, 1986), pp. 95–103.

[50]   Peter J. Conradi, *Iris Murdoch: The Saint and the Artist*, 2nd edn (London: Macmillan, 1989), p. 262.

[51]   David Lodge, *How Far Can You Go?* (Harmondsworth: Penguin, 1981), p. 14.

[52]   Ibid., p. 243.

[53]   David Lodge, 'The Novelist Today: Still at the Crossroads?' in *New Writing*, ed. Malcolm Bradbury and Judy Cooke (London: Minerva, 1992), p. 207.

confusing and disturbing to some readers than the simple metafictional comments'.[54] Considering they were here both writing in the 1990s, Lodge and Ammann retain a surprising faith in the continued defamiliarizing power of this device. Narratorial intrusions parody the nineteenth-century convention but their incidence is similarly low. If the reader is schooled in the eighteenth- and nineteenth-century tradition, he will be able to face the metafictive devices of Murdoch and Lodge with perfect equanimity.

To a degree, though, metafiction is formally quantifiable: the greater the number of metafictive devices, the greater obstruction the text will provide for the realist reader. Such a reader is faced with a greater challenge to accommodate metafictive devices within a realist reading with Italo Calvino's *If on a Winter's Night a Traveller*, an exemplary European postmodern metafiction which opens: 'You are about to begin reading Italo Calvino's new novel, *If on a winter's night a traveler* [*sic*].'[55] The 'story' is enclosed within a full frame and ends in the same manner: 'And you say, "Just a moment, I've almost finished *If on a winter's night a traveler* by Italo Calvino."'[56] But unlike the traditional frame, which hermetically seals a narrative, Calvino's is closer to Derrida's *parergon* or chiasmus, a deconstructed or collapsed frame that is both inside and outside the body proper of the text.[57] Calvino intersperses 'classically' metafictive (numbered) chapters, with named chapters which are parodies of various fictional genres. The numbered chapters, which form a continuous narrative, are addressed to 'you', the Reader, and in this metafictional story 'you' read the first (named) chapter, 'If on a Winter's Night a Traveller', but find that the book has been wrongly bound and 'you' have in fact been reading the first chapter of a different novel. 'You' then return to the publisher for a copy of this book and are issued with a similarly deceptively bound novel, and so it goes on. The metafictional chapters also parody the classic realist love-story as 'you', the Reader, and Ludmilla, the 'Other Reader', meet, overcome various obstacles, and finally get married. The narrator asks, 'Do you believe that every story must have a beginning and an end?'; *If on a Winter's Night a Traveller* deconstructs the classic (Aristotelian) plot structure.[58] The classic realist expectations of the reader are thematized while they are parodied; 'you' remark that 'this is a novel where, once you have got into it, you want to go forward, without stopping', but the structure of *If* prevents this as each false fictional start is arrested, suspended, and then

[54]   Daniel Ammann, *David Lodge and the Art-and-Reality Novel* (Heidelberg: Carl Winter, 1991), p. 44.
[55]   Italo Calvino, *If on a Winter's Night a Traveller*, trans. William Weaver (London: Picador, 1982), p. 1.
[56]   Ibid., p. 205.
[57]   See Jacques Derrida, *The Truth in Painting*, trans. Geoff Bennington and Ian McLeod (London: University of Chicago Press, 1987), p. 61; *Acts of Literature*, ed. Derek Attridge (London: Routledge, 1992), p. 238.
[58]   Calvino, *If on a Winter's Night a Traveller*, p. 204.

succeeded by another.[59] 'You' and Ludmilla are postmodern readers, nostalgic for the lost 'condition of natural reading, innocent, primitive'. Barthes's 'Text' is metafictive – 'it asks of the reader a practical collaboration'.[60] Ludmilla, belligerently anti-Barthesian, at one point asserts, 'There's a boundary line: on one side are those who make books, on the other those who read them. I want to remain one of those who read them, so I take care always to remain on my side of the line.'[61]

For many theorists, the function of metafiction is to cross the line, to blur the boundaries between fact and fiction, the word and the world, by reminding the reader of his role in the production of meaning.[62] Elizabeth Ermarth maintains that postmodern novels, unlike conventional linear narratives, foreground the experience of reading as a continual present.[63] Waugh states that metafictional novels 'show not only that the "author" is a concept produced through previous and existing literary and social texts but that what is generally taken to be "reality" is also constructed and mediated in a similar fashion. "Reality" is to this extent "fictional" and can be understood through an appropriate "reading" process'.[64] For Welch Everman,

> On the one hand, the tale is only a tale, only fiction, only words. On the other hand, however, the work goes beyond itself, beyond its printed text and into the text of the Reader's (real) world. This novel is purposely literary, and yet it wants to push against the limits of the literary and break through to a place beyond language.[65]

Peter Lamarque and Stein Olsen read the opening frame of If in a similar dualistic way: 'The first sentence is both true and fictional in intent.'[66] By reminding the reader of his role in the production of meaning and the fictional status of the text itself, metafiction inserts the real author and reader into the narrative. But to imply that metafiction causes the reader to be continually conscious of his reading or the mechanics of writing is to underestimate the ability of the

---

[59]   Ibid., p. 64.

[60]   Roland Barthes, *Image-Music-Text*, trans. Stephen Heath (London: Fontana, 1977), p. 163.

[61]   Calvino, *If on a Winter's Night a Traveller*, p. 75.

[62]   See Welch D. Everman, *Who Says This?: The Authority of the Author, the Discourse, and the Reader* (Carbondale and Edwardsville: Southern Illinois University Press, 1988), p. 122.

[63]   Elizabeth Deeds Ermarth, 'The Crisis of Realism in Postmodern Time' in *Realism and Representation: Essays on the Problem of Realism in Relation to Science, Literature, and Culture*, ed. George Levine (Madison: University of Wisconsin Press, 1993), pp. 214–24.

[64]   Waugh, *Metafiction*, p. 16.

[65]   Everman, *Who Says This?*, p. 122.

[66]   Peter Lamarque and Stein Haugom Olsen, *Truth, Fiction, and Literature: A Philosophical Perspective* (Oxford: Clarendon, 1994), p. 66.

'competent' reader to neutralize, naturalize, or simply ignore foregrounded literary devices. The reader of *If*, though addressed as 'you', can be read as a fictional character and this is encouraged by 'your' progressive fictionalization in the text. Hutcheon concedes that 'The reader is . . . a function implicit in the text, an element of the narrative situation. No specific real person is meant.'[67] Dipple more pertinently points out the fact that the reader of *If* is a *particular* fictional character.[68] Barthes properly retains the distinction between fleshly and paper author: 'It is not that the Author may not "come back" in the Text, in his text, but he then does so as a "guest". If he is a novelist, he is inscribed in the novel like one of his characters.'[69] Calvino himself appears to retain a clear distinction between the word and the world asking, in the essay 'The Written and the Unwritten Word', 'But is mimesis the right way? My starting point was the irreconcilable contrast between the written and unwritten world; if their two languages merge, my argument goes to pieces.'[70] Although Calvino's novel proved popular, it has a degree of experimentalism and structural metafictionality which is likely to provide difficulties for the non-academic reader. Umberto Eco's commentary on a text by Alphonse Allais seems apt: 'The naive reader will be unable to enjoy the story (he will suffer a final uneasiness), but the critical reader will succeed only by enjoying the defeat of the former.'[71] Calvino appears to have a certain sympathy for the naïve reader even while teasing him mercilessly. 'You' and Ludmilla compare favourably with Ludmilla's humourless academic sister, Lotaria, and her colleagues who value literature only as the object of various modish theories. In spite of this unsympathetic characterization of academics, *If* would be likely to irritate a recreational reader because much of the pleasure to be gained from it is academic – the ideal reader is a Lotaria rather than a Ludmilla.

Formal accounts of metafiction are always somewhat inadequate because of the importance of context in interpretation and the active contribution of the reader.[72] While Lamarque and Olsen sometimes make philosophical heavy weather of analysing the truth status of fiction, they rightly maintain that fact is largely irrelevant to literature because factual inference is blocked by what they call the 'fictive stance':

> in presenting a story, or reporting it, a speaker blocks inferences from the
> fictional content to how things are in the world. There will of course be

---

[67]   Hutcheon, *Narcissistic Narrative*, p. 139.

[68]   Dipple, *The Unresolvable Plot*, p. 107.

[69]   Barthes, *Image-Music-Text*, p. 161.

[70]   Quoted in Dipple, *The Unresolvable Plot*, p. 103.

[71]   Umberto Eco, *The Role of the Reader: Explorations in the Semiotics of Texts* (Bloomington: Indiana University Press, 1984)

[72]   See Gregory Currie, *The Nature of Fiction* (Cambridge: Cambridge University Press, 1990).

connections between fictional content and the world . . . but the barrier of
the non-extensional context limits inferential access to these connections.[73]

This is something akin to literary competence or naturalization and accounts for
the fact that apparently unrealistic presentation, technically innovative form, or
fantastic content can be naturalized by the competent reader.[74] Both formal and
metaphysical accounts of metafiction will tend to overlook the flexibility of
literary competence or the fictive stance, that is the willing suspension of belief.[75]
The fictive stance can undergo a power failure and may be unbalanced by
unconventional literary devices; the reader's lack of familiarity with language,
descriptive detail or literary technique can frustrate authorial intent to create
naturalistic illusion.[76] It is impossible to predict a reality effect from any
particular literary form without knowing the competence of the reader, but it is
clear that radically experimental texts are most likely to frustrate a realistic
reading.

A novel which very deliberately flouts the realist tradition is Christine
Brooke-Rose's *Thru* (1975). Informed and endorsed by the structuralist and
poststructuralist theories of Greimas, Lacan, Barthes, and Derrida, Brooke-Rose
produced, in her own words, 'a novel about the theory of the novel, . . . a text
about textuality and intertextuality, ... a fiction about the fictionality of fiction'.[77]
She experiments with typography:

Through the driving-mirror four eyes stare back
two of them in their proper   place
Now right on
Q   ask us
to de   V   elop   foot on gas
how m(any   how)   eyes?[78]

Brooke-Rose has asserted that this typography is visually mimetic (in the manner
of concrete poetry), but the text is certainly not realistic. *Thru* is even less
accessible to the ordinary reader and can be interpreted only by the academic who
is conversant with poststructuralist theory and therefore more likely endorse the
idea of the narrative construction of experience. Brooke-Rose has stated her
intention that the book was written for academics but it is not always accessible

---

[73]   Lamarque and Olsen, *Truth, Fiction, and Literature*, p. 88.
[74]   For an account of literary competence see Culler, *Structuralist Poetics*, ch. 6.
[75]   Lamarque and Olsen, *Truth, Fiction, and Literature*, pp. 43–6.
[76]   See Lodge's account of the dating of John Braine's *Room at the Top* in
Language of Fiction, pp. 245–9.
[77]   'A Conversation with Christine Brooke-Rose', interview by Maria del Sapio
Garbero in *British Postmodern Fiction*, ed. Theo D'haen and Hans Bertens (Amsterdam:
Rodopi, 1993), p. 105.
[78]   Christine Brooke-Rose, *Thru* (London: Hamish Hamilton, 1975), p. 1.

even for these professionals; as McHale candidly admits 'it certainly is not very clear, and never gets any clearer either'.[79] As Waugh suggests, *Thru* is peripheral to the novel tradition because of its rejection of traditional narrative form.[80] Brooke-Rose has admitted that *Thru* harmed her reputation because of its reputed incomprehensibility and pretentiousness; the non-academic reader is likely to be left in blissful ignorance with his ontological categories intact because he simply will not be able to read the book.

There are two further related literary devices (not exclusively postmodern) which may theoretically create ontological disruption: intertextuality and 'faction' – the inclusion of real-life or historical characters within fictions. Both these strategies involve the inclusion of figures from outside the text: the first from another fictional world; the second from the real world. *Thru* includes characters from other fictions which are not naturalized in the text and according to McHale this practice 'violate[s] the norm of textual-ontological unity (one text/one world), in effect producing an ontologically composite or heterogeneous text . . . that mingles or straddles worlds'.[81] However, although this kind of literary experiment may prevent the suspension of disbelief, that is entrance into the fictional world, it will still not produce any real confusion of the reader's own ontological categories. A postmodern fiction which includes real people is Umberto Eco's *The Name of the Rose*, which includes references not only to historical figures contemporaneous with the time of the fictional world, but also allusions to twentieth-century theorists. McHale suggests that this creates a confrontation rather than a confusion 'between the novel's fictional world and real-world historical "fact"' (note postmodern scare quotes).[82] He asserts that the resulting 'queasiness of ours is precisely an ontological queasiness, a sympton of our uncertainty about the exact boundaries between historical fact and fiction in this text'.[83] However, it is doubtful whether McHale, a sophisticated academic reader, felt even slightly sick when reading *The Name of the Rose*, and the popularity of the novel suggests that neither did the non-academic reader.

Hutcheon notes the paradoxical popularity of postmodern fictions, but the phenomenon is easily explained. Eco explains that Allais's text has two themes, one obvious for the naïve reader [his use] and one concealed for the critic.[84] McHale notes, though only to discard, Charles Jencks' definition of postmodernism as a double-coding which addresses the elite through high-art codes and a mass public through popular codes, but many postmodern novels,

[79] Brian McHale, *Postmodernist Fiction* (London: Routledge, 1987), p. 121.
[80] Quoted in Waugh, *Metafiction*, pp. 147–8.
[81] Brian McHale, *Constructing Postmodernism* (London: Routledge, 1992), pp. 216–17.
[82] Ibid., p. 152.
[83] Ibid., p. 152.
[84] Umberto Eco, *The Role of the Reader: Explorations in the Semiotics of Texts* (Bloomington: Indiana University Press, 1984), p. 26.

Eco's included, perform in exactly this way, concealing metafictional allegories within fictions which also contain enough of conventional plot and characterization to satisfy the non-academic reader, who prefers, in Barthes's terminology, the *lisible* to the *scriptible* and *plaisir* to *jouissance*.[85] The balance between tradition and experiment is dramatized and rather better realized in Salman Rushdie's *Midnight's Children*. In this novel the narrator-protagonist Saleem Sinai relates his life story to his consort Padma, a reader even more naïve than Calvino's Ludmilla. Padma believes Saleem's narrative to be factual and her credulity is unpredictable: 'what others will swallow as effortlessly as a laddoo, Padma may just as easily reject. No audience is without its idiosyncrasies of belief.'[86] Saleem notes Padma's reactions to the metafictive elements of his narrative: 'Padma has started getting irritated whenever my narration becomes self-conscious.'[87] He modifies his narrative mode accordingly: 'I must return (Padma is frowning) to the banal chain of cause-and-effect.'[88] Although this narrator is sometimes frustrated: 'I wish, at times, for a more discerning audience', he acknowledges the necessity of realist convention; Padma's 'ignorance and superstition [are] necessary counterweights to my miracle-laden omniscience'.[89] In fact the metafictive elements of *Midnight's Children* are incorporated quite smoothly within the dominant magical realism and although Rushdie treats novelistic conventions with a certain postmodern irony, he makes large concessions to conventional narrative forms.

Poststructuralist theory plays with the idea of collapsing word and world, time and space, with reference to the narrative construction of reality, the chaotic and alienating experience of living in the postmodern city, global communications, the postmodern economy, and so on. Postmodern fiction may endorse or be informed by this theory by deconstructing classical artistic conventions of coherence (the linear narrative) and referring to the same contemporary conditions. The majority of the population, however, continues to prefer coherent linear narratives and it is significant that the majority of postmodern novelists concede this point and temper technical innovation with traditional story-telling. James Kirwan argues that the Aristotelian 'concern with "resemblance" is one that has hardly ever been out of favour, and today "convincing", "unconvincing", "realistic", and "unrealistic" are perhaps the most common evaluative terms used of art, particularly outside its academic study.'[90] In fact realism tends more often to be a criterion of literary merit in the sphere of literary journalism rather than literary criticism. Lorna Sage, reviewing *Jackson's Dilemma* in the *TLS*,

---

[85] Quoted in Waugh, *Metafiction*, pp. 147–8.

[86] Salman Rushdie, *Midnight's Children* (London: Pan, 1982), p. 55.

[87] Ibid., p. 65.

[88] Ibid., p. 295.

[89] Ibid., pp. 102, 150.

[90] James Kirwan, *Literature, Rhetoric, Metaphysics: Literary Theory and Literary Aesthetics* (London: Routledge, 1990), p. 63.

upbraided Murdoch for failing to 'describe the day-to-day ordinary world with conviction'.[91] Within academia it is only the irascible Raymond Tallis who has been prepared to tackle the anti-realists on their own territory.[92] Those theorists who regard the predominance of realism in the novel as unfortunate tend to underplay a constitutive aspect of the genre and to promote academic novelties, such as *Thru*, because they dramatize and engage particular academic interests. Postmodern metafiction is misrepresented by poststructuralist theorists who are over-impressed by the metaphysical transgression of ontological boundaries. And in any case, poststructuralist theory cannot tell us with any authority that our lives are narrative fictions or our experience linguistically constructed without reference to neuroscience and psychology. Both formal and philosophical accounts of metafiction tend to underestimate the recreational reader's willing or wilful suspension of disbelief, his or her desire to enter into the fictional other world, and such readers are not naïve but highly competent. The only audience whose ontological categories will be deconstructed by metafiction will be those academics who have already suspended their belief in the very significant difference between word and world.

---

[91] Lorna Sage, review of *Jackson's Dilemma* by Iris Murdoch, *TLS* (29 September 1995), p. 25.

[92] For pro-realist and anti-postmodernist reviews see J.F., review of *Margery Kempe* by Robert Glück, *TLS* (17 November 1995), p. 28; Katy Emck, 'Fear of Floating', review of *The Skull of Charlotte Corday and other Stories* by Leslie Dick, *TLS* (17 November 1995), p. 26; Hal Jensen, 'In Quotation Marks', review of *Marked for Life* by Paul Magrs, *TLS* (3 November 1995), 23.

Chapter 3

Literature and Philosophy

The relationship between literature and philosophy is of particular interest to Derrida, a philosopher by training who has turned his attention to both the concept of literature and to literary texts. He has deconstructed the conceptual opposition between literature and philosophy and philosophy's historical claims to superiority by foregrounding their common ground – writing or textuality. Although many texts contain formal features which indicate their belonging to one or other conceptual category, formal analysis can also expose stylistic and structural similarities, the existence of 'hybrid' or crossover texts, and the irrefutable fact that philosophical texts make use of figurative or literary language. Deconstruction here does have a relevance and application outside metaphysics, although its textual analysis is directed towards metaphysical issues and its invariable conclusion, that genre is a fundamentally unstable category, disparages contextual determinants. A historical study of literary and philosophical texts endorses the idea of a permeable and mobile boundary between the two, but contextual determinants also include institution, discipline, intention and reception. An analysis which addresses these diverse factors endorses the idea that genre is dependent on context but can better account for the fact of its contingent fixity.

The distinction between literature and philosophy is as old as philosophy itself which from the beginning declaimed its superior status. An often-cited example of the hierarchy in action is the expulsion of the poet from the commonwealth in Plato's *Republic* where the philosopher is king. The reason Socrates gives for this ostracism is that dramatic art involves identification with multiple fictional personae and is therefore potentially morally injurious. In spite of a grudging admiration for Homer, Socrates maintains that the tragedian, like all imitators, is 'in his nature three removes from the king and the truth' {597e}.[1] Taking a couch as an example, he explains that God creates the ideal (real) couch and the cabinet maker makes the particular couch, but the painter of the couch produces only an imitation of the *appearance*, or phantasm of the particular. In addition, poetry, with its adornments of rhythm, metre, and harmony {601a}, appeals to the faculty 'that is remote from intelligence' {603b} and encourages womanly emotion rather than rational stoicism. In all parts poetry is the inferior of philosophy, which is concerned with truth and reality (knowledge of the Forms). The citizens of the ideal state will therefore expel the poet, 'crown him with fillets of wool, anoint his head with myrrh, and conduct him to the borders

---

[1] *The Collected Dialogues of Plato*, ed. Edith Hamilton and Huntington Cairns (Princeton: Princeton University Press, 1961).

of some other country'.[2] In the *Phaedrus*, the true philosopher Socrates is teased
for 'never leaving town to cross the frontier nor even . . . so much as setting foot
outside the walls' (although he is tempted outside by the seductive pharmakon)
{230*d*}. Iris Murdoch suggests that Plato's antagonism towards literature may
have been a defensive mechanism designed to obscure the fact that philosophy
was a relatively new discipline and to eclipse 'The poets . . . [who] were the
traditional purveyors of theological and cosmological information'.[3] Although
Plato always maintained the superiority of philosophy over literature, he did
suggest a certain common ground in divine inspiration, the 'third form of
possession or madness, of which the Muses are the source' {245*a*}. This madness
is a prerequisite for both poetry and philosophy and 'if any man come to the gates
of poetry without the madness of the Muses, persuaded that skill alone will make
him a good poet, then shall he and his works of sanity with him be brought to
nought by the poetry of madness' {245*a*}. The philosopher is also likened to a
mad visionary and is taken by 'the best of all forms of divine possession' {249*d*}.
However, it is the philosopher who has unique access to the ideal realm while 'Of
that place beyond the heavens none of our earthly poets has yet sung' {247*c*}.
Aristotle agreed with Plato to the extent that poetry was primarily mimetic, but
he denied its moral depravity. In the *Poetics*, he questions the separation of
literature and philosophy, attributing the delight which men take in 'mimetic
objects' to the faculty of reason: 'to be learning something is the greatest of
pleasures not only to the philosopher but also to the rest of mankind' {1448*b*}.[4]
For Aristotle, literature is philosophical in the sense that it speaks of universals
rather than the particulars which are the provenance of history {1451*b*}. But in
spite of this conciliatory attitude, the hierarchy is still at work in Aristotle's
account since art is presented as the poor man's philosophy. This line was
perpetuated by the neo-classicists but it is the Enlightenment which is commonly
credited with strengthening the division and sustaining the hierarchy by confining
literature to the subjective realm and affirming philosophy's scientific status.

Before postmodernism, the relative values of literature and philosophy were
gauged by their respective abilities to access truth. In Plato's philosophy, truth is
literally a metaphysical concept because it rests in the eternal Forms, accessible
to the soul outside the physical world, and recoverable only by the philosopher.
The survival of Plato's hierarchy is apparent in Keats's judgement that poetry 'is
not so fine a thing as philosophy – for the same reason that an eagle is not so fine
a thing as truth'.[5] However, since Aristotle's association of literature with

---

[2]   *The* Republic *of Plato*, trans. F.M. Cornford (Oxford: Clarendon, 1941), p. 83.
[3]   Iris Murdoch, *The Fire and the Sun: Why Plato Banished the Artists* (Oxford:
Clarendon, 1977), p. 1.
[4]   *The Complete Works of Aristotle*, ed. Jonathan Barnes (Oxford: Princeton
University Press, 1984).
[5]   Quoted in James Seaton, *Cultural Conservatism, Political Liberalism: From
Criticism to Cultural Studies* (Ann Arbor: University of Michigan Press, 1996), p. 30.

literature with universals, the ideal of truth has been common to both discourses. For postmodernist philosophers (metaphysicians to a man), however, the status of any kind of truth is at an all-time low. Lyotard passes over the scientific requirement that objects of knowledge 'must be available for repeated access, in other words, they must be accessible in explicit conditions of observation' and points instead to the dependence of science on narrative legitimation and the economic criterion of performativity.[6] Such postmodern theories present all discourses as 'narratives', and suggest that none has privileged access to truth or fact. Richard Rorty asserts that philosophical truth-seekers, whom he labels 'metaphysical prigs', are a dying breed in this relativistic era.[7] However the postmodernists do clearly indulge in their own brand of metaphysical truth-seeking, even if it is to decry the concept of truth.

The truth of literature has always been metaphorical rather than metaphysical, but shares with metaphysics a disinterest in scientific or empirically verifiable fact; as Muriel Spark puts it, 'Fiction . . . is a kind of parable. You have to make up your mind it's not true. Some kind of truth emerges from it, but it's not fact.'[8] The distinction between metaphysical truth and scientific fact is made by the narrator in *Midnight's Children*: '"What's real and what's true aren't necessarily the same." True, for me, was from my earliest days something hidden inside the stories Mary Pereira told me . . .. *True* was a thing concealed just over the horizon.'[9] The deconstruction of logocentrism means that philosophy loses its claim of superiority in 'truth-getting' over literature while literature's metaphoricity and indirectness are seen as somehow more honest. But Robyn Ferrell, who follows Derrida in the deconstruction of generic and disciplinary boundaries, suggests that literature is still unable to assert its superiority over philosophy because

> The opposition of philosophy and literature is a philosophical one, and not the work of the literary. The literary, in living with the sovereign power of philosophy to designate the order of things, may make a virtue of necessity and celebrate its rich and unpredictable effects.[10]

The opposition of literature and philosophy is highly susceptible to

---

[6]   Jean-François Lyotard, *The Postmodern Condition: A Report on Knowledge*, trans. Geoff Bennington and Brian Massumi (Manchester: Manchester University Press, 1984), p. 18.

[7]   Richard Rorty, 'Deconstruction and Circumvention', *Critical Inquiry* 11 (1984), pp. 2–3.

[8]   Quoted in Patricia Waugh, *Harvest of the Sixties: English Literature and its Background 1960 to 1990* (Oxford: Oxford University Press, 1995), p. 115.

[9]   Salman Rushdie, *Midnight's Children* (London: Pan, 1982), p. 79.

[10]   Robyn Ferrell, 'Xenophobia: At the Border of Philosophy and Literature' in *On Literary Theory and Philosophy: A Cross-Disciplinary Encounter*, ed. Richard Freadman and Lloyd Reinhardt (London: Macmillan, 1991), p. 144.

deconstruction, which foregoes crude one-upmanship in favour of a two-pronged campaign (philosophical and literary-critical) against the Platonic hierarchy. This involves the metaphysical critique of philosophy's logocentrism and a rhetorical analysis which foregrounds its literary figures. In 'Tympan', Derrida deconstructs the metaphysical claims by which philosophy has claimed superiority over all other discourses and promotes 'writing' as the ground of philosophy: 'beyond the philosophical text there is not a blank, virgin, empty margin, but another text . . . the *written* text of philosophy . . . overflows and cracks its meaning'.[11] The piece plays on various puns: the French *tympaniser* is an archaic verb meaning to criticize or ridicule publicly, suggesting Plato's treatment of the poet in the *Republic*. 'Tympan' is a deconstruction of Aristotle in *De Anima*, for whom 'The air inside the ears has been walled up inside so as to be immovable' {420a}. 'Tympanum' denotes the eardrum, a membrane which separates the outer and inner ear, but which *mediates* the sound which passes through it and, by analogy questions the traditional separation between discourse and metadiscourse. That which separates the internal from the external, and which traditionally underpins the claim of any metadiscourse, is presented as permeable, illustrating the point that discourse and metadiscourse, literature and philosophy, occupy the same metaphysical space.

Derrida's strategies include the typographic as well as the rhetorical. 'Tympan' is typeset in two columns: one comprises Derrida's critique of the metaphysical assumption of neutrality and exteriority; the other a quotation from the autobiography of Michel Leiris. There are also three epigraphs from Hegel and substantial footnoting. This is another device aimed at dispelling the philosophical myth by which criticism 'has believed that it controls the margin of volume and that it thinks its other', because what would normally be a blank margin is physically occupied by other texts.[12] The typographic interventions of 'other' texts represent another type of deconstructive 'enactment', designed to illustrate the point that philosophy does not include and control literature, but that literature invades philosophy without its prior consent. However, it is significant that a narrow white margin remains between the two columns of discourse, thus indicating the continuing stand-off between the discourses. The increasing awareness of the written constitution of philosophy promoted by deconstruction has encouraged the relatively uncontentious view that philosophy (or literary criticism for that matter) can have aesthetic qualities and uses rhetoric to command assent. Donald Henze remarks that 'Traditionally, philosophical writing has been part of literature . . . and good philosophical writing . . . has been rightly regarded as good literature.'[13] But traditionally philosophers have

---

[11]   Jacques Derrida, *Margins of Philosophy*, trans. Alan Bass (Brighton: Harvester, 1982), p. xxiii.

[12]   Ibid., p. x.

[13]   Donald Henze, 'The Style of Philosophy', *The Monist* 63, 4 (1980), 420.

regarded literary style as incidental while for literary artists and critics the medium was the message. The New Critics, for example, regarded the form and content of a literary work as inseparable, hence their indictment of the heresy of paraphrase. Poststructuralists undermine the distinction between the idea of form as ornament and form as essence. The concept of enactment suggests that philosophical meaning is also expressed via its form (an idea akin to the New Critical heresy of paraphrase) and this undermines the literature/philosophy distinction which is traditionally reinforced by the form/content opposition.

Although much philosophy relies upon imagination, literary figures and fictional analogies, there are formal or textual differences which can determine category. Derrida, however, in 'The Law of Genre', is highly suspicious of both the metaphysical assumptions and ideological implications of formal genre theories which presume that 'There should be a trait upon which one could rely in order to decide that a given textual event, a given "work", corresponds to a given class (genre, type, mode, form etc.). And there should be a code enabling one to decide questions of class-membership on the basis of this trait.'[14] Such a trait 'is absolutely necessary for and constitutive of what we call art, poetry or literature.'[15] Derrida identifies the formal 'trait' as the entity which transgresses the conceptual boundary between text and context:

> In the code of set theories, if I may use it at least figuratively, I would speak of a sort of participation without belonging . . . . The trait that marks membership inevitably divides, the boundary of the set comes to form, by invagination, an internal pocket larger than the whole; and the consequences of this division and of this overflowing remain as singular as they are limitless.[16]

The trait is therefore a somewhat slippery entity, which, contra formalism, does not belong inside the text but rather occupies an indeterminate position, like the *parergon*, both inside and outside: 'this supplementary and distinctive trait . . . does not properly pertain to any genre or class. The re-mark of belonging does not belong.'[17] Derrida also examines a particular text, Blanchot's *La folie du jour*, chosen for its genre-transgressive (metafictional) virtues. But because genre is a metaphysical concept the double bind operates: 'Even though I have launched an appeal against this law, it was she who turned my appeal into a confirmation of her own glory.'[18] Derrida's point in this essay is always that genre is a metaphysical category.

---

[14] Jacques Derrida, *Acts of Literature*, ed. Derek Attridge (London: Routledge, 1992), pp. 228–9.

[15] Ibid., p. 229.

[16] Ibid., pp. 227–8.

[17] Ibid., p. 230.

[18] Ibid., p. 250.

Although differentiation appears to be a natural function, the perception of particular similarities or differences is conditioned by the viewer's own perspective and the learnt conventions of classification. Nevertheless, however much the criteria for divisions may be arbitrary, empirically verifiable differences exist. In deconstructing essentialist genre categories, what poststructuralist metaphysicians tend to underplay is the fact that these categories are not simply imposed from without but are formulated in response to actual differences. Genre is often decried as a reification, and it is true that although literature and philosophy perform perfectly well as concepts there exist no concrete entities which correspond to these terms. However, there do exist collections of texts which share certain formal traits and many individual texts can unproblematically be assigned a particular category because of those formal properties: *Hamlet*, for example, is a tragic drama; *Lucky Jim* a comic novel; *Paradise Lost* an epic poem. In such cases the existence of those features which determine classification is a verifiable fact. Even Raymond Williams, who advises that the job of Marxist theory is to analyse genre theory as social practice, admits the existence of 'particular literary forms'.[19] Genre distinction also operates in philosophy in the categories of metaphysics, phenomenology, logical positivism and so on in terms of subject matter, method of approach and mode of expression. Derrida of course deconstructs such distinctions in 'Limited Inc', but it nevertheless seems reasonable to suggest that there are certain styles associated with certain types of philosophy, not least his own. That Hegel's *Logic* is a work of philosophy and *War and Peace* a work of literature can be determined with reference to text alone. While formal genre theories may be inadequate to deal with maverick authors and their transgeneric texts, it should be remembered that such texts are the exception rather than the norm, and that the majority of literary and philosophical texts are written within formal generic conventions, albeit ones which change over time.

Although formal genre theory is not spurious, neither is it wholly adequate to the analysis of literature and philosophy because, as the Marxists stress, these categories operate within a specific cultural and historical context. But it in no way undermines the validity of generic distinctions to admit that they are supported and in part constructed by institutional determinants such as discipline. The formal establishment of English as a discipline required, for practical and professional purposes, a relatively discrete canon. Again, it does not undermine the practical distinctions made between literary and philosophical texts to admit that there has been exchange between their respective disciplines. This is something F.R. Leavis tried to forestall; in a debate with René Wellek, he emphatically demanded the separation of philosophy (theory) and criticism to prevent the 'consequences of queering one discipline with the habits of

---

[19] Raymond Williams, *Marxism and Literature* (Oxford: Oxford University Press, 1977), p. 182.

another'.[20] Christopher Norris decries 'the idea that philosophical arguments can migrate across disciplines (in this case from philosophy to literary criticism) without suffering a consequent loss of cogency and rigour', and his own professional trajectory through poststructuralist theory has carried him from the department of English to the department of Philosophy at the University of Cardiff.[21] Geoffrey Hartman, impatient with disciplinary separatism, appears to be responding directly to Leavis's point when he states, 'Without the pressure of philosophy on literary texts, or the reciprocal pressure of literary analysis on philosophical writing, each discipline becomes impoverished. If there is the danger of a confusion of realms, it is a danger worth experiencing.'[22] But Yale school deconstruction, as practised by Hartman, becomes literary criticism in spite of itself, hence Derrida's public distaste, and Derrida, as Norris notes, remains primarily interested in the philosophical questions of literature.

A poststructuralist strategy designed to break down the barriers between literature and philosophy is to read 'against the grain'. This practice is defined by Culler as a situation 'where the work is read against the conventions of discourse'.[23] It is a form of anti-intentionalism, which examines the way the language of a text may undermine its ostensible meaning. Reading against the disciplinary grain involves focusing on the way that philosophical argument is undermined by literary devices, in other words, it is a form of deconstruction. Clearly certain philosophical texts prove more rewarding than others for the deconstructionist and since formal logic contains no literary devices it is summarily dismissed by Derrida. On the other hand, deconstructive texts are already self-consciously literary and do not require a concerted rooting out of concealed metaphor. Derrida's 'literary' readings of philosophy therefore tend to focus on those philosophers, such as Plato, for whom the literary medium appears to subvert the message. Rorty puts the delayed birth of this practice down to disciplinary history, suggesting that formerly it simply did not occur to students of either literature or philosophy to read texts from the other discipline.[24] While both poststructuralists and New Critics castigate reference to intention, the author usually writes for a specific purpose and within a set of generic conventions which are highly significant in determining the way a text is read, particularly on initial publication. The reader is of course at liberty to work against the original intention and reception, but the very act of reading against the grain recognizes this original context and an oppositional discipline is a prerequisite. Culler

---

[20]   F.R. Leavis, *The Common Pursuit* (Harmondsworth: Penguin, 1963), p. 213.

[21]   Christopher Norris, *What's Wrong with Postmodernism: Critical Theory and the Ends of Philosophy* (London: Harvester Wheatsheaf, 1990), p. 141.

[22]   Harold Bloom et al., *Deconstruction and Criticism* (London: Routledge & Kegan Paul, 1979), p. ix.

[23]   Jonathan Culler, *Structuralist Poetics: Structuralism, Linguistics and the Study of Literature* (London: Routledge & Kegan Paul, 1975), p. 130.

[24]   Rorty, 'Deconstruction and Circumvention', p. 21, n. 4.

suggests that deconstruction in fact needs the conceptual opposition of philosophy and literature as 'a distinction between literature and philosophy is essential to deconstruction's power of intervention: to the demonstration, for example, that the most truly philosophical reading of a philosophical work – a reading that puts in question its concepts and the foundations of its discourse – is one that treats the work as literature'.[25] As argued in Chapter 1, this dependence on oppositions is generally true of deconstruction.

An example of a philosophical reading of a literary text is Paul de Man's deconstruction of Yeats's 'Among School Children'. De Man asserts that when we read the line, 'How can we tell the dancer from the dance?', we cannot decide between the literal-grammatical (that is, straightforward question) and the poetic (rhetorical) question. De Man asserts that, 'The couple grammar/rhetoric, certainly not a binary opposition since they in no way exclude each other, disrupts and confuses the neat antithesis of the inside/outside pattern.'[26] He also asserts that, 'Rhetoric radically suspends logic and opens up vertiginous possibilities of referential aberration.'[27] Christopher Norris argues that 'Logic, grammar and rhetoric are not simply different aspects of language but disjunct dimensions which can enter into conflict and radically undermine each other's authority.'[28] James Kirwan asserts that 'we read as literature when the truth of what is literally asserted does not matter to us'.[29] But this statement is misleading; we read as literature when text and/or context suggest this is the appropriate way to read. De Man's logical-grammatical reading of 'Among School Children' is certainly not a conventional piece of literary criticism although it is undertaken in a department of English and has as its object a canonical work of literature. This work of literature itself, however, cannot be made into a work of philosophy by being read differently. Stanley Fish makes an important point in *Professional Correctness* when he argues that just because genre or disciplinary boundaries are culturally constructed this doesn't mean they don't exist.[30] Literature and philosophy are metaphysical categories which are susceptible to deconstruction; literary and philosophical texts may share formal traits, but cultural convention means that the deconstruction of these categories and texts does not result in a generic 'free-for-all'.

---

[25]   Jonathan Culler, *On Deconstruction: Theory and Criticism after Structuralism* (London: Routledge & Kegan Paul, 1983), pp. 149–50.

[26]   Paul de Man, 'Semiology and Rhetoric' in *Textual Strategies: Perspectives in Post-Structuralist Criticism*, ed. Josué V. Harari (Ithaca: Cornell University Press, 1979), p. 132.

[27]   Ibid., p. 129.

[28]   Christopher Norris, *The Deconstructive Turn: Essays in the Rhetoric of Philosophy* (London: Methuen, 1983), p. 19.

[29]   James Kirwan, *Literature, Rhetoric, Metaphysics: Literary Theory and Literary Aesthetics* (London: Routledge, 1990), p. 74.

[30]   Stanley Fish, *Professional Correctness: Literary Studies and Political Change* (Oxford: Clarendon, 1995), p. x.

Gerald Bruns supports the collapse of 'Enlightenment' categories, defending Geoffrey Hartman both as philosopher and creative critic; he compares Derrida's writing to the work of modernist artist Marcel Duchamp, who called a pickaxe 'art', remarking that 'No universally reigning distinction . . . between one genre and another . . . can obtain.'[31] This is true on the metaphysical level and such 'conceptual' art is a prime example of authorial intention working against genre conventions. However, although certain factors clearly militated against the reception of the pickaxe as art object (its original construction, intended function and provenance), other contextual factors prevailed. Bruns refers to the significance of 'the local and historical situation', that is Duchamp's identity and authority as an artist, the placing of the pickaxe in his studio, and the reception of this as a work of art.[32] By the same token, Derrida's professional identity and expertise as a philosopher and Hartman's as a literary critic work to contain their discourses.[33]

There is no shortage of hybrid or genre-transgressive texts but a 'comprehensive' genre theory, that is one which examines both text and context, is able to account for the fact that the generic identity of such texts is usually relatively stable. A case in point is Plato, whose Dialogues explicitly privilege philosophy over literature (and speech over writing), but are written in a literary (dramatic) form, and make extensive use of myth, allegory and metaphor. This was an irony not lost on Sidney:

> now Plato's name is laid upon me, whom, I must confess, of all philosophers I have ever esteemed most worthy of reverence, and with great reason: since of all philosophers he is the most poetical. Yet if he will defile the fountain out of which his flowing streams have proceeded, let us boldly examine with what reasons he did it.[34]

[31]   Gerald L. Bruns, 'Writing Literary Criticism', *The Iowa Review* 12, 4 (1981), p. 32.

[32]   Ibid., p. 31.

[33]   As Bruns also notes, Duchamp's flouting of convention is typical of modern art. Media coverage of the 1995 Turner prize supports this remark. Short listed for this prize were Mona Hatoum, whose video installation, 'Foreign Body', was created by inserting cameras in her bodily orifices, Damien Hirst, the fêted creator of works comprising dead animals in formaldehyde, and Mark Wallinger, celebrated for buying a race horse and naming it 'A Real Work of Art'. At the same time an installation by Tony Kaye at the British Design and Art Festival of Excellence at the Saatchi Gallery comprised a homeless person, Roger Powell (price £1,000). But the very fact that these gestures still provoke media attention and public outrage suggests that the more traditional genre conventions that he decries continue to operate. See Mike Ellison, 'No butts as Hirst is tipped for top art prize', *The Guardian* (13 July 1995), p. 3 and John Mullin, 'Homeless man becomes £1,000 work of art and joins fellow exhibits at top design festival', *The Guardian* (13 July 1995), p. 6.

[34]   Sir Philip Sidney, *An Apology for Poetry or The Defence of Poetry*, 2nd edn, ed. Geoffrey Shepherd (Manchester: Manchester University Press, 1973), p. 128.

But Martin Warner argues that applying the modern literature/philosophy dichotomy to the Dialogues is inappropriate since classical philosophers made no such distinction. He substantiates this by reference to the *Phaedo* where philosophical argument and myth are 'brought together under the figure of music' (Apollo).[35] But this is a highly tendentious line to take when one considers the pronouncements against the poet and promotion of the philosopher in the *Republic*, which are not usually read as deliberately ironic, even by poststructuralists. Norris notes that 'Sir Philip Sidney scored a palpable hit when he remarked that Plato himself was not above using 'poetic' means – metaphor, allegory and myth – in the service of his philosophic arguments.'[36] What Sidney actually says is that 'though the inside and strength were Philosophy, the skin as it were and beauty depended most of Poetry', thus endorsing the form/content–literature/philosophy distinction.[37] The niceties of intention are not easy to establish but whether the literary devices are regarded as ornamental or indispensable to the argument, the Dialogues present no real problem of classification because of their disciplinary position and history. That they are written in dramatic form and use literary devices in no way compromises their status as seminal philosophical texts.

Warner rightly argues that the dramatic form, characterization and mythical 'digressions' are not merely peripheral to, but constitutive of, the philosophical import of the *Phaedo* (and the *Phaedrus*). Charles Griswold argues that 'use of a dialogue form could inhibit the author from simply expounding a doctrine in a dogmatic way, accompanied by impressive declarations and polemics meant to establish the truth of the doctrine' – a rhetorical device *par excellence*.[38] Warner suggests that, 'For the defence to be convincing it must not be a walk-over; thus neither Simmias nor Cebes are mere "yes-men".'[39] It could be argued, however, that the Dialogues are as dogmatic as any philosophical treatise and command assent in no less peremptory a fashion. While Socrates' interlocutors put up a token resistance they always accede pretty quickly. In the *Phaedo*, Simmias's responses to Socrates run as follows: 'Certainly'; 'Quite so'; 'Yes'; 'That is so'; 'It seems so'; 'Indeed we do'; 'Of course'; 'Certainly not' [in agreement with Socrates]; 'Certainly'; 'What you say is absolutely true, Socrates' {65b–66a}, and so on.

Arthur Danto suggests 'That plain prose has a better chance of being received

[35] Martin Warner, *Philosophical Finesse: Studies in the Art of Rational Persuasion* (Oxford: Clarendon, 1989), p. 86.
[36] Christopher Norris, *The Contest of Faculties: Philosophy and Theory After Deconstruction* (London: Methuen, 1985), p. 99.
[37] Sidney, *An Apology for Poetry*, p. 97.
[38] Charles Griswold, 'Style and Philosophy: Plato's Dialogues', *The Monist* 63, 4 (1980), 543.
[39] Warner, *Philosophical Finesse*, p. 87.

as true is a stylistic maxim not unknown in adopting a philosophical diction'.[40] Speculating, like Sidney, on Plato's motives for choosing an apparently unconvincing medium, Warner asserts that the Phaedo was designed as an example of good 'or "noble" rhetoric, guided by dialectic but going beyond it in order to persuade the reader of the nature and value of the philosophic enterprise'.[41] But in Plato's scheme, rhetoric, however good, is the inferior of philosophy and Warner therefore suggests since the Dialogues are written, not living, speech, they are not meant to be wholly persuasive.[42] Arne Melberg subscribes to this theory, arguing for a deliberate (literary) irony: 'All these discreetly ironic reminders of the different levels and possibilities of the text, and of the tensions between the story told and the telling of the story' are there because 'Plato cannot resist making us suspicious'.[43] These analyses posit a disjunction between the overt argument in the Dialogues and Plato's use of rhetorical and literary devices, and also make the (literary) assumption that Socrates does not represent Plato's unmediated voice. But again, a 'literary' reading does not make a literary text; Derrida's reading of the *Phaedrus* reinforces rather than subverts its generic identity. The literary devices in the text should be acknowledged, but so should the historical and disciplinary context of the text.

While Plato's literariness is conventionally regarded as something of an embarrassment, Derrida's philosophical style is deliberately flamboyant and literary, representing part of his strategy to confuse metaphysical categories. Kirwan compares Derrida with Heidegger as the sort of writer who manages to confuse genres: 'the question of denotational sense is even more confused, and in this confusion often lies the problem of whether they are philosophy or literature'.[44] But, as with Plato, the difficulty of establishing genre is in reality negligible. Although Derrida's objects of inquiry are diverse (literature, art, politics), like Plato he remains within the metaphysical tradition. As Kirwan suggests, Derrida is only the latest in a line of self-consciously 'poetic' philosophers from whom he draws inspiration. Hegel, subject of Derrida's most conventional philosophical work, had a predilection for the pun, while for Heidegger, the 'aesthetic turn' was consequent on the insight that art accesses truth in the way that philosophy cannot. Nietzsche saw all language as metaphor and truth or Being as both metaphor and illusion. He consequently lauded the artist over the philosopher and turned to a metaphorical style of philosophy.

---

[40] Arthur C. Danto, 'Philosophy as/and/of Literature' in *Literature and the Question of Philosophy*, ed. Anthony J. Cascardi (London: Johns Hopkins University Press, 1987), p. 5.

[41] Warner, *Philosophical Finesse*, p. 102.

[42] Ibid., p. 89.

[43] Arne Melberg, *Theories of Mimesis* (Cambridge: Cambridge University Press, 1995), p. 28.

[44] Kirwan, *Literature, Rhetoric, Metaphysics*, p. 100.

According to James Winchester, Nietzsche believed that 'The world itself admits of no ordering principles, not even principles of process. It is purely contingent. Human existence however requires order and therefore, to survive, humans create artificial orders'.[45] These artificial orders included philosophy which was consequently described as a fiction: 'Whereas necessary fictions are constraints imposed by life, style is a self-imposed constraint.'[46] Nietzsche turned to 'fiction' with *Thus Spake Zarathustra*. This work certainly cannot be classified as a novel; it is rather one of those 'liminal' texts, whose form transgresses traditional genre categories. Its literary qualities are primarily poetic – metaphor, exalted language – but the narrative structure follows the form of the dialectic and the style evokes Biblical parable. A recent book on Nietzsche was advertised as rendering 'the question "Is it philosophy or is it literature" no longer relevant'.[47] Its authors describe *Thus Spake Zarathustra* as a 'peerless fiction', but in spite of the radical anti-genre claims, admit that 'like other poets and critics before him – and not withstanding his revolutionary protestations – Nietzsche is a captive of generic limitations as much as he is of history.'[48] In this case context is more significant than form since in spite of its hybrid nature *Thus Spake Zarathustra* was written by a philosopher and continues to be read as philosophy, that is by philosophers in philosophy departments.

In spite of Derrida's acceptance of disciplinary constraints, he attempts to reach for a form which defies categorization. Of *Glas* he affirms: 'It is neither philosophy nor poetry. It is in fact a reciprocal contamination of one by the other, from which neither can emerge intact. This notion of contamination is, however, inadequate . . .. One is trying to reach an additional or alternative dimension beyond philosophy and literature.'[49] This attempt is marked by a typography similar to that in 'Tympan'; Derrida analyses Hegel's philosophy in the left-hand column and the work of Jean Genet in the right. Quotations are inset but no references given. According to Kamuf, this 'demonstrates the borderless condition of texts', and *Glas* tortuously co-implicates the work of Hegel and Genet.[50] The analysis of Hegel is conventional in Derridean terms, but the analysis of Genet is something different:

> The phallic flower is cuttable-culpable. It is cut, castrated, guillotined,
> decollated, unglued. Sooner: it appears only on the scaffold is what is

[45]   James J. Winchester, *Nietzsche's Aesthetic Turn: Reading Nietzsche after Heidegger, Deleuze, Derrida* (Albany: State University of New York Press, 1994), p. 121.

[46]   Winchester, *Nietzsche's Aesthetic Turn*, p. 121.

[47]   Bernd Magnus, Stanley Stewart and Jean-Pierre Mileur, *Nietzsche's Case: Philosophy as/and Literature* (London: Routledge, 1993), back cover.

[48]   Magnus et al., *Nietzsche's Case*, p. 95.

[49]   Jacques Derrida, 'Deconstruction and the Other', interview by Richard Kearney in *Dialogues with Contemporary Continental Thinkers*, ed. Richard Kearney (Manchester: Manchester University Press, 1984), p. 122.

[50]   *A Derrida Reader*, p. 314.

defalcated there, what is removed and left to fall. This appearing, this
luminous phenomenon decorporated – of the flower, was glory.[51]

This is a kind of writing which surpasses conventional philosophical style; it
similar to the creative criticism of Hartman and the poetic literary appreciation of
Hélène Cixous. However, as in 'Tympan', the margins which physically separate
the various discourses (primary text/quotation; literature/philosophy) remain to
evoke generic and disciplinary boundaries

In *The Post Card* Derrida tries an alternative strategy, that of writing in a
distinctly literary mode, the epistolary. *The Post Card* has a first-person narrator
and Kamuf warns against identifying the narrator with Derrida, one of the first
principles of literary criticism:

> Although the principal correspondent seems identifiable in almost every
> way with Jacques Derrida, the signatory of 'Envois', at the same time
> nothing could be less certain than this sort of identification. In accordance
> with the postal principle . . . 'identity' is but the spacing of a self-address,
> analogous therefore to the distance between addressor and addressee.
> There is no telling where that gap widens sufficiently to accommodate the
> conventions of a fictional first-person narrator.[52]

This echoes Gallop's advice that we should not necessarily identify Plato with
Socrates in the Dialogues. However the 'narrative voice' is nevertheless typically
Derridean and there is no reason *not* to identify narrator with author. Rorty asserts
that at this point in his career Derrida 'is no longer warning us that the "discourse
of philosophy" will get us if we don't watch out'.[53] It appears, however, that
Derrida is warning us of precisely this:

> Do people (I am not speaking of 'philosophers' or of those who read Plato)
> realize to what extent this old couple has invaded our most private
> domesticity, mixing themselves up in everything, and making us attend for
> centuries their colossal and indefatigable anaparalyses?[54]

The Post Card addresses the peregrinations of meaning: 'Once intercepted . . . the
message no longer has any chance of reaching any determinable person, in any
(*determinable*) place whatever. This has to be accepted, and *j'accepte*. But I

---

[51] Jacques Derrida, *Glas*, trans. John P. Leavey, Jr and Richard Rand (London:
University of Nebraska Press, 1986), p. 20.

[32] *A Derrida Reader*, p. 485.

[53] Richard Rorty, 'Two Meanings of "Logocentrism": A Reply to Norris' in
Redrawing the Lines, ed. Reed Way Dasenbrock (Minneapolis: University of Minnesota
Press, 1989), p. 214.

[54] Jacques Derrida, *The Post Card: From Socrates to Freud and Beyond*, trans.
Alan Bass (London: University of Chicago Press, 1987), p. 18.

recognize that such a certainty is unbearable, for anyone'.[55] *The Post Card* is neither marketed nor read as a work of fiction, but rather as a reworking of Derrida's perennial philosophical preoccupations with the logocentric assumptions of metaphysical discourse.

Danto suggests that 'philosophers with really new thoughts have simply had to invent new forms with which to convey them' and Derrida can be categorized as such a philosopher although his ideas and techniques are not entirely novel.[56] However, such techniques fail to reach the 'alternative dimension beyond literature and philosophy' because of the weight of disciplinary and generic convention. While the novelty of deconstruction meant that it did confuse traditional Anglo-American philosophers and literary critics, on one hand the flexibility of generic boundaries and on another their institutional reinforcement explains the fact that deconstruction has now been incorporated into both disciplines rather than floating free of either in some inter- or post-disciplinary void. In fact there is very little of literature in Derrida's writing; at times it approaches the 'creative criticism' diligently practised by Hartman but in the main it must be classified as pure metaphysics.

Iris Murdoch, like Derrida, trained in philosophy and was the author of several philosophical monographs, but unlike Derrida, she was also a commercially successful and well-received novelist. She took a diametrically opposed view to that of Derrida in her desire to keep separate literature and philosophy: 'As soon as philosophy gets into a novel, a work of literature, it ceases to be philosophy. It becomes something else. . . . The harder the writer works to present his ideas in abstract form, the less good his work of art is likely to become.'[57] She does concede the creative nature of philosophy: 'Of course, philosophy is an imaginative activity, and if one thinks of the great philosophers, they are very often picture-makers – people who produce enormous metaphors and pictures to explain things'.[58] This is particularly true of metaphysics which requires great powers of imagination since it is limited neither by formal language nor by empirical reference. Murdoch, however, emphatically proclaims the desirability of keeping philosophy out of literature, asserting that the two genres have different functions: 'Philosophy aims to clarify: it is essential to philosophy that it should, in some sense, be clarification. Literature is, very often, mystification – and, besides, literature is for fun, literature entertains.'[59] Her novels have often been categorized as 'philosophical', a term she rejects, and as a novelist she declares that she 'would rather know about sailing ships and

---

[55]   Derrida, *The Post Card*, p. 51.

[56]   Danto, 'Philosophy as/and/of Literature', p. 9.

[57]   Iris Murdoch, 'Iris Murdoch on Natural Novelists and Unnatural Philosophers', interview by Bryan Magee, *The Listener* (27 April 1978), p. 535.

[58]   Ibid., p. 534.

[59]   Ibid., p. 533.

hospitals than about philosophy'.[60] Ironically, Murdoch's separatist sentiments are sometimes voiced by her fictional characters. In *Jackson's Dilemma*, Benet, an amateur philosopher researching Heidegger, is described as feeling a similar sentiment: 'Later Heidegger he detested . . . his poeticisation of philosophy, discarding truth, goodness, freedom, love, the individual, anything the philosopher ought to explain and defend.'[61] In spite of her avowed separatist principles, there are clearly connections between Murdoch's philosophy and fiction but they just as clearly do not work to collapse the literature/philosophy distinction.

Early in her career Murdoch was influenced by the existentialist philosophy of Sartre, whose works include the novel *La Nausée*. However, in her preface to *Sartre: Romantic Rationalist*, she distinguishes between 'the novel proper', 'the novel of ideas' and the 'modern metaphysical tale', placing the 'novelist proper' above the philosopher for the reason that:

> He has always implicitly understood, what the philosopher has grasped less clearly, that human reason is not a single unitary gadget the nature of which could be discovered once for all. [. . .] He has always been, what the very latest philosophers claim to be, a describer rather than an explainer; and in consequence he has often anticipated the philosophers' discoveries.[62]

The novel proper is 'about people's treatment of each other, and so it is about human values'.[63] She concludes that Sartre, symptomatically, is unable to write a great novel because metaphysical abstraction gets in the way: *La Nausée* succeeds primarily in presenting Sartre's metaphysical outlook, but fails to clothe this with 'any form of normal human project, sexual, political, or religious'.[64] Elsewhere, however, she states that *La Nausée* 'is the one really good philosophical novel . . . which might be said to be a novel demonstrating something about contingency'.[65] This may be, she thinks, because existentialism is already 'a rather literary philosophy. It emphasises all sorts of things to do with the human predicament'.[66]

Murdoch's philosophy is moral and highly unfashionable; she quickly became disenchanted with existentialism and subsequently drew most heavily on Plato. She refers approvingly to 'Plato's Pharmacy' in *The Fire and the Sun* but remains much closer to Plato's ideals in her pursuit of the true and the good. In *The*

---

[60] Ibid., p. 535.
[61] Iris Murdoch, *Jackson's Dilemma* (London: Chatto & Windus, 1995), p. 13.
[62] Iris Murdoch, *Sartre: Romantic Rationalist* (London: Bowes & Bowes, 1953), p. 8.
[63] Ibid., p. 70.
[64] Ibid., p. 18.
[65] Murdoch, interview by Bryan Magee, p. 535.
[66] Ibid., p. 535.

Sovereignty of Good Murdoch critiques existentialist, deterministic and analytic philosophies, formulating an idea of the good as the unattainable, unknowable but ultimate goal. She also plunders Platonic philosophy for an ethical literary theory. In the *Republic* Socrates remarks that 'all this procedure of the arts and sciences that we have described indicates their power to lead the best part of our soul up to the contemplation of what is best among realities' {532c}. For Murdoch, 'This well describes the role of great art as educator and revealer.'[67] She privileges art over philosophy, asserting that 'Art is far and away the most educational thing we have, far more so than its rivals, philosophy and theology and science.'[68] She subscribes to the postmodernist reversal of the Platonic hierarchy, but retains Platonic ideals; the common ground between philosophy and literature, for Murdoch, is their pursuit of truth: 'They are both truth-seeking, truth-revealing activities in some sense'.[69]

Critics have often judged Murdoch's novels by her own criteria and a common criticism of her early work is that philosophical ideas occlude literary realism and produce a theory-ridden fiction. *Under the Net* certainly makes a rather heavy-handed use of a metaphor from Wittgenstein's *Tractatus*. Wittgenstein here describes language as a net which is cast over a formless and disordered reality and in *Under the Net*, the hero Jake writes in a neo-Platonic dialogue:

> the movement away from theory and generality is the movement toward truth. All theorizing is flight. We must be ruled by the situation itself and this is unutterably particular. Indeed it is something to which we can never get close enough, however hard we may try as it were to crawl under the net.[70]

Elizabeth Dipple respects Murdoch's wishes by refusing to call her a 'philosophical novelist', arguing that what saves *Under the Net* as a novel 'is that it is absolutely unnecessary to know the philosophical reference'.[71] A. S. Byatt concludes that 'the novel could be described as a philosophical novel very precisely, since there is clearly a very conscious attempt to pattern the events in Jake's story in terms of ideas of freedom, of philosophical approaches to reality. . . . But it is nevertheless a novel, and not simply a philosophical game.'[72] Peter Conradi argues that 'There is always more event, story, incident than the idea-

---

67 Iris Murdoch, *The Sovereignty of Good* (London: Routledge & Kegan Paul, 1970), p. 65.

68 Murdoch, *The Fire and the Sun*, p. 86.

69 Murdoch, interview by Bryan Magee, p. 535.

70 Iris Murdoch, *Under the Net*, p. 91.

71 Dipple, *Iris Murdoch*, p. 135.

72 A.S. Byatt, *Degrees of Freedom: The Early Novels of Iris Murdoch*, 2nd edn (London: Vintage, 1994), p. 13.

play can use up, here as everywhere in her work'.[73] Although Dipple describes Murdoch's early novels as contrived, Murdoch's champions often refuse to admit that the first novel appears mannered and dated, partly due to its reliance on a démodé philosophy, and partly due to the fact that the philosophical 'dialogue' is awkward and incidental.[74]

Another philosophical influence on Murdoch's literary theory and practice was the 'mystic' Simone Weil. Murdoch recounts Weil as having 'said that morality was a matter of attention not of will' and concludes that 'We need a new vocabulary of attention'. Murdoch asserts that 'there is a moral challenge involved in art: in the self-discipline of the artist, expelling fantasy and really looking at things other than himself'.[75] This preoccupation with things other than oneself is already apparent in *Under the Net*; at the opening of the novel, Jake has little sense of the independent existence of his lackey, Finn: 'I count Finn as an inhabitant of my universe, and cannot conceive that he has one containing me'.[76] By the close of the novel, however, he begins to perceive Finn as a separate entity: 'I felt ashamed of being parted from Finn, of having known so little about Finn, of having conceived things as I pleased and not as they were.'[77] This awareness of another is indicative of authenticity in existentialist philosophy and of a related moral growth in the novel.

The concept of attention influences Murdoch's chosen *mode* of fictional representation, that is realism, the bourgeois literary form which is currently regarded with great suspicion by postmodern theorists. In *The Sovereignty of Good*, she asserts that 'morality, goodness, is a form of realism'.[78] As Murdoch moves from the stylized existentialism of her first novel to a more conventional realism, the symbolic awareness of other people and things is combined with realistic description. In the later novels there is also a distinction between different types of attention. The epiphanic vision is symptomatic of self-delusion and fantasy, while attention to the mundane is the mark of ethical awareness and maturity. An example of the latter type of attention occurs in *Bruno's Dream* (1969) where Diana, whose husband has left her for her sister, is caring for the dying Bruno:

> And she saw the ivy leaves and the puckered door knob, and the tear in the pocket of Bruno's old dressing-gown with a clarity and a closeness which she had never experienced before. The familiar roads between Kempsford Gardens and Stadium Street seemed like those of an unknown city, so many were the new things which she now began to notice in them: potted

---

73 Peter J. Conradi, *Iris Murdoch: The Saint and the Artist*, 2nd edn (London: Macmillan, 1989), p. 31.
74 See Dipple, *Iris Murdoch*, ch. 5.
75 Murdoch, interview by Bryan Magee, p. 535.
76 Murdoch, *Under the Net* (London: The Reprint Society, 1955), p. 9.
77 Ibid., p. 279.
78 Murdoch, *The Sovereignty of Good*, p. 59.

plants in windows, irregular stains upon walls, moist green moss between
paving stones. Even little piles of dust and screwed-up paper seemed to
claim and deserve her attention.[79]

In *The Sovereignty of Good*, Murdoch remarks on the human 'tendency to
conceal death and chance by the invention of forms' and asserts that the function
of tragedy, comedy, and painting is 'to show us suffering without a thrill and
death without a consolation'.[80]

Diana's contemplative attention to both people and things in *Bruno's Dream*
can be compared with Morgan's vision in *A Fairly Honourable Defeat* (1970)
which begins with the heightened perception of the natural world ('The flowers
were beginning to quiver in front of her eyes. How extraordinary flowers are, she
thought. Out of these dry cardboardy rods these complex fragile heads come out,
skin-thin and moist . . . .'[81]), and develops into a sort of existentialist sick fit:
'Was it giddiness she was feeling now, a dazzled sensation of spinning
drunkenness, or was it something else, disgust, fear, horror as at some
unspeakable filth of the universe?'[82] Throughout the novel Morgan, Hilda's
bohemian sister, spouts morally vacuous, quasi-philosophical rubbish. Speaking
to her husband, Tallis, from whom she is separated, she remarks: 'I'm going to
love people. That's what I mean by living differently. That'll be my new way of
life. I'm going to be free and love people.'[83] Tallis, a rather pathetic but perceptive
character, correctly identifies this self-expression as 'sickening rot', calling
Morgan 'hopelessly theory-ridden' (a serious crime in Murdoch's book). In this
novel Murdoch is still influenced by existentialist concepts; Morgan is unable to
recognize and communicate with other individuals and is therefore 'inauthentic'.

Murdoch often uses stones as a means of expressing her concerns with
individuality and attention and also to indicate the moral stature and emotional
health of her characters. In *The Nice and the Good* (1968), pebbles on a beach are
first described by the narrator:

> The pebbles gave a general impression of being either white or mauve, but
> looked at closely they exhibited almost every intermediate colour and also
> varied considerably in size and shape. All were rounded, but some were
> flattish, some oblong, some spherical; some were almost transparent,
> others more or less copiously speckled, others close-textured and nearly
> black, a few of a brownish-red, some of a pale grey, others of a purple
> which was almost blue.[84]

---

[79]   Iris Murdoch, *Bruno's Dream* (St Albans: Triad, 1977), p. 268.
[80]   Murdoch, *The Sovereignty of Good*, p. 87.
[81]   Iris Murdoch, *A Fairly Honourable Defeat* (Harmondsworth: Penguin, 1972),
p. 186.
[82]   Ibid., p. 187.
[83]   Ibid., p. 213.
[84]   Iris Murdoch, *The Nice and the Good* (St Albans: Triad/Panther, 1977), p. 153.

These pebbles are collected by the twins, Henrietta and Edward Biranne, who are enlightened beings and therefore delight in the particularity of each stone. Uncle Theo, a deeply troubled homosexual, is rather appalled by the 'multiplicity and randomness' of the stones:

> The intention of God could reach only a little way through the opacity of matter, and where it failed to penetrate there was just jumble and desolation. So Theo saw it, and what was for the twins a treasury of lovable individuals (it grieved the twins that they could not distinguish *every* stone with their attentions and carry it into the house) was for Theo an expanse of abomination where the spirit had never come.[85]

Murdoch has proclaimed it her intention to render the opacity of life in her fiction; Theo's desire to reach beneath this surface is doomed to failure.

Philosophy does not merely inform the ideas in Murdoch's novels, but also the imagery. The texts of Plato and Sartre are of course pre-eminently suitable for such literary borrowings. The most well-worn philosophical image in the later novels is lifted from Plato's parable of the cave in the *Republic*, an allegory in which Socrates describes how prisoners in a cave would take shadows from the fire to be real objects and if released would be dazzled by the sun and regard real objects as chimerical {514a–515e}. In *A Fairly Honourable Defeat* Platonic imagery and existentialist philosophy combine. Preceding Morgan's vision, 'there was a great deal too much light. Light was vibrating inside her eyes and she could see nothing but dazzling and pale shadows as if the whole scene had been bleached and then half blotted out by a deluge of light.'[86] Afterwards, 'She felt the sun burning into the back of her neck as if it was directed thorough a prism.' In *The Sea, The Sea* the unenlightened hero, Charles Arrowby, keeps a diary:

> Since I started writing this 'book' or whatever it is I have felt as if I were walking about in a dark cavern where there are various 'lights', made perhaps by shafts or apertures which reach the outside world. (What a gloomy image of my mind, but I do not mean it in a gloomy sense.) There is among those lights one great light towards which I have been half consciously wending my way. It may be a great 'mouth' opening to the daylight, or it may be a hole through which fires emerge from the centre of the earth. And am I still unsure which it is, and must I now approach in order to find out?

Charles is dedicated to winning back his childhood sweetheart, now an emotionally unstable middle-aged woman: 'now I find that, wandering in my

---

85   Ibid., pp. 153–4.
86   Murdoch, *A Fairly Honourable Defeat*, p. 186.

cavern, I have in fact come near to the great light-source and am ready to speak about my first love'.[87] He muses: 'This image has come to me so suddenly, I am not sure what to make of it.'[88] The informed reader is not left in the dark, however, and can turn to Murdoch's discussion of the Platonic myth in *The Fire and the Sun* (first published one year before *The Sea, The Sea*), or to Plato's original text.[89] However, while the parable of the cave provides a hermeneutic key – Morgan and Charles Arrowby cannot bear to look at the sun therefore they are deluded – it is possible to reach this conclusion through internal evidence alone. Both are self-regarding unsympathetic characters whose self-obsessions and misperceptions lead to a great deal of destruction and pain: Charles Arrowby steadfastly refuses to admit the fact that his first love is no longer available and indirectly causes the death of her adopted son; Morgan, also indirectly, causes the death of Hilda's husband, Rupert.

Any literary text will contain a philosophy in the general sense of the word as connected system of ideas, world-view or moral outlook. And significantly the general philosophical stance which can be extrapolated from Murdoch's novels is quite different from that articulated in *The Sovereignty of Good*. In *Nuns and Soldiers* the morally scrupulous characters are Anne Cavidge, ex-nun, and Peter, 'the Count', a Polish exile. Anne is in love with the Count, the Count with Gertrude, another selfish petty-bourgeoise, who seeks to hold both the Count and Anne in a retinue of admirers following her husband's death. Because Anne and the Count are unwilling to compromise their personal integrity they both lose their chance of happiness while Gertrude triumphs, finally pairing off with another morally flimsy character. Anne perceives the situation correctly:

> It was, for Gertrude, easy. She had fielded him casually, as if in passing. She had only to stretch out her hand, she had only to whistle ever so softly.... And Anne could guess that this was not just a benevolent act. Gertrude needed his esteem to support her. She had always valued his love and saw no reason why she should not go on enjoying it forever.[90]

Gertrude and her second husband are equally selfish but neither appears to be condemned by the narrative tone. Murdoch refuses to arbitrate between the ascetic and the bourgeois, because to present a clear-cut moral would go contrary to her intention to produce realistic (complex and 'muddy') fiction.

Pearl Bell criticizes Murdoch for the failure to either philosophize or fictionalize successfully, attacking in particular Murdoch's representation of the Anglo-Jewish family in *Nuns and Soldiers*. Not enough, she says, is explained and 'Though she is called a philosophical novelist, it is difficult to get any idea

---

87   Iris Murdoch, *The Sea, The Sea* (London: Triad/Panther, 1980), p. 77.
88   Ibid., p. 77.
89   Murdoch, *The Fire and the Sun*, p. 4.
90   Iris Murdoch, *Nuns and Soldiers* (Harmondsworth: Penguin, 1981), p. 467.

from her novels of what she thinks about contemporary culture, society, politics, what judgments she has arrived at about the issues that confront us all.'[91] Bell states that Murdoch makes no 'effort to dramatize abstract ideas in her fiction' and that 'what is particularly ironic about Iris Murdoch the "philosophical novelist" is that her novels seem so wilfully unreflective and devoid of ethical and metaphysical scrupulousness.'[92] Peter Conradi considers it inappropriate to apply Murdoch's own literary theory to her novels, but it seems reasonable to refer to Murdoch's statement that she does not wish to 'dramatize abstract ideas' and asserted that it is not the business of literature to clarify but to mystify. As shown above, Murdoch very obviously does dramatize her philosophical ideas in fiction; but what Bell calls 'ethical and metaphysical scrupulousness' is the sort of philosophical 'dryness' which Murdoch considers does not translate well into fiction.

Richard Rorty clearly disparages the idea of distinguishing between literature and philosophy: 'Only if one takes this genre to be more than an intriguing historical artefact will the contrast between philosophical closure and literary openness seem important.'[93] He is dismissive of any formal distinction between literature and philosophy, suggesting that 'The only form of the philosophy-literature distinction which we need is one drawn in terms of the (transitory and relative) contrast between the familiar and the unfamiliar'.[94] In an interview, Norris gets Derrida on his side against Rorty: 'philosophy is not *simply* a "kind of writing"; philosophy has a very rigorous specificity which has to be respected, and it is a very hard discipline with its own requirements, its own autonomy, so that you cannot simply mix philosophy with literature'.[95] Rorty's thesis that philosophy is just a 'kind of writing' is not necessarily radical in implication, although hotly contested by Norris; philosophy *is* a kind of writing but it is usually a *different* kind of writing from literature with distinct conventions and disciplinary history. In *Memoires for Paul de Man* Derrida remarks 'I have never known how to tell a story. And since I love nothing better than remembering . . . I have always felt this inability to be a sad infirmity.'[96] Although it would be unwise to take Derrida's remarks at face value, *The Post Card* confirms the validity of this self-criticism. It is precisely the separation of the techniques of philosophy from those of fiction and the submersion of philosophical concepts within the fictional world that enables Murdoch to tell stories. Writers of fiction use literary devices to persuade the reader to suspend disbelief and enter a

---

[91] Pearl K. Bell, 'Games Writers Play', *Commentary* 71, 2 (1981), p. 71
[92] Ibid., p. 70.
[93] Rorty, 'Deconstruction and Circumvention', p. 20.
[94] Ibid., p. 3.
[95] Jacques Derrida, 'In Discussion with Christopher Norris', *Deconstruction* II, ed. Andreas C. Papadakis (London: Academy Editions, 1989), p. 11.
[96] Jacques Derrida, *Memoires for Paul de Man*, trans. Cecile Lindsay et al., revised edn (Oxford: Columbia University Press, 1989), p. 3.

fictional world. Assent to the particular philosophical or ethical position therein depends not on argumentation but imagination and identification, so while a literary text may convey a moral or imply a philosophical stance, it must entertain before it can instruct. Philosophy, even performative deconstruction, is required to make, or even 'enact' a particular philosophical point; something which Derrida never fails to do, though not always clearly. The terms 'literature' and 'philosophy' are without easily definable referents but are not particularly problematic categories, they are simply convenient labels for a culturally significant nexus of historical and textual differences.

PART II

Chapter 4

Literary Theory and Critical Practice

The hierarchical relationship between theory and practice is indicated by theory's definition as 'a systematic statement of rules or principles to be followed'.[1] Although, historically, theory – particularly formalist theory – has enjoyed this status in literary studies by providing models and methods for critical practice, deconstruction seeks to co-implicate the theory/practice opposition and thereby subvert the hierarchy. The relation between theory and practice has been giving the discipline of literary studies very real practical problems, which have been most pressing in the classroom at first degree level. Since Continental theory has become part of the undergraduate syllabus in Britain, the academic institution has been searching for ways to get students to put theory into practice, that is apply it to the literary text and this desire has manifested itself in the publication of a rash of undergraduate 'theory-in-practice' Readers. Deconstruction is often associated with the idea of integrating theory and practice but, as Derrida has suggested, deconstruction loses something in its translation into Yale School formalism. In spite of its association with deconstruction, the trend for applied theory conforms to the stereotypical British predilection for practical action over abstract thought and may represent a carefully concealed attempt to domesticate, by practically orienting, 'foreign' theory. Whatever the underlying motivation for collapsing theory and practice, complex abstract notions cannot be dealt with properly through literary criticism and deconstruction is an inappropriate critical model on which to base an English degree.

Horace Fairlamb notes that 'For some practitioners of deconstruction, its putative significance is the final end of the traditional foundational hegemony of theory over practice.'[2] Although the inconsistency of philosophical faith in the effectiveness of theory from Aristotle onwards belies the very existence of Fairlamb's 'foundational hegemony', it is clear that Derrida does wish to destabilize the hierarchy. Although not exact equivalents, there is a significant connection between the theory/practice, intelligibility/sensibility, and ideal/real binaries and Derrida of course seeks to deconstruct all of these oppositions. In 'Spectres of Marx' he endorses 'a thinking of the event that necessarily exceeds a binary or dialectical logic, the logic that distinguishes or opposes *effectivity or actuality* (either present, empirical, living – or not) and *ideality* (regulating or

---

[1]   *The Compact Oxford English Dictionary*, 2nd edn (Oxford: Clarendon, 1991).

[2]   Horace L. Fairlamb, *Critical Conditions: Postmodernity and the Question of Foundations* (Cambridge: Cambridge University Press, 1994), p. 81.

absolute non-presence)'.[3] The deconstruction of the intelligibility/sensibility binary in 'Différance' centres on the etymology of 'theory', foregrounding the connection between these binaries. The word has its roots in the Greek *theoria* (*theoros* spectator, *theoreo* look at). Derrida therefore notes that the term '*theorein*', which denotes the intelligible, also connotes seeing (sensibility). This etymology informs the assertion in 'The Principle of Reason' that 'Metaphysics associates sight with knowledge'.[4] It is also cited by Adena Rosmarin as the foundation of the modern distinction between theory and practice, the separation between 'knowledge and its object, between the passivity of viewing and the activity of knowing'.[5] Etymology is hardly proof positive of either connection or disjunction between seeing and knowing, or theory and practice. The conflation of sight and knowledge by reference to the Greek etymology is further undermined by Socrates' refusal to equate knowledge with sight in the *Phaedo*:

> I was afraid that by observing objects with my eyes and trying to comprehend them with each of my other senses I might blind my soul altogether. So I decided that I must have recourse to theories, and use them in trying to discover the truth about things. Perhaps my illustration is not quite apt, because I do not at all admit that an inquiry by means of theory employs 'images' any more than one which confines itself to facts. {99e–100a}

Derrida states that 'Shutting off sight in order to learn is of course only a figurative manner of speaking. No one will take it literally.'[6] Of course thought does not operate in a physical vacuum, but sense-perception is not particularly relevant to certain metaphysical abstractions.

In *The Truth in Painting* Derrida deconstructs the theory/practice binary in Kant's *Critique of Judgement*. Typically, he concentrates on the preface which contains a summary of the findings of the first and second *Critiques* and maintains the disjunction between theory and practice:

> A Critique of pure reason, i.e. of our faculty of judging on a priori principles, would be incomplete if the critical examination of judgement, which is a faculty of knowledge, and, as such, lays claim to independent principles, were not dealt with separately. Still, however, its principles cannot, in a system of pure philosophy, form a separate constituent part

---

   3   Jacques Derrida, 'Spectres of Marx', *New Left Review* 205 (May/June 1994), pp. 45–6.
   4   Jacques Derrida, 'The Principle of Reason: The University in the Eyes of Its Pupils', trans. Catherine Porter and Edward P. Morris, *Diacritics* 19 (1983), p. 4.
   5   Adena Rosmarin, 'Theory and Practice: From Ideally Separate to Pragmatically Joined', *The Journal of Aesthetics and Art Criticism* 43, 1 (1984), p. 31.
   6   Derrida, 'The Principle of Reason', p. 5.

intermediate between the theoretical and practical divisions, but may when needful be annexed to one or other as occasion requires {168}.[7]

Derrida latches on to Kant's 'annexing' of judgement to both theory and practice, arguing that here 'we are plunging into a place that is *neither* theoretical *nor* practical or else *both* theoretical *and* practical. Art (in general), or rather the beautiful, if it takes place, is inscribed here.'[8] Kant contested the power of reason over action and the non-effectiveness of theoretical principles is explicitly asserted when he denies any practical consequences of establishing the *a priori* conditions of aesthetic judgement: 'The present investigation of taste [is] . . . not being undertaken with a view to the formation or culture of taste, (which will pursue its course in the future, as in the past, independently of such inquiries,) but being merely directed to its transcendental aspects'.[9] Following this notification of the transcendental nature of the inquiry, Kant confidently asserts: 'I feel assured of its indulgent criticism in respect of any shortcomings on that score' {170}, to which Derrida responds: 'With this transcendental aim, Kant demands to be read without indulgence.'[10] To aid him in his unmerciful task, Derrida requisitions Kant's *parergon*, a ready-made deconstructive tool which functions like the *pharmakon*. It is defined by Kant as an ornamentation or adjunct to the aesthetic object, such as the frame around a painting, which augments 'the delight of taste . . . only by means of its form' {226}. For Derrida the *parergon* is significant not because it marks the edge of 'the body proper of the *ergon*' (as it does for Kant) but because it connects this body to 'the whole field of historical, economic, political inscription in which the drive to signature is produced . . . . No "theory", no "practice", no "theoretical practice" can intervene effectively in this field if it does not weigh up and bear on the frame.'[11] This interpretation initially seems to imply that it is possible for a deconstructive or 'parergonal' theory to 'intervene effectively' in the real world. However, the significance of the *parergon*, like that of the *pharmakon*, is that it mediates and includes two polarities, in this case the inside and outside, the theoretical and the actual or practical. Like Nietzsche, Derrida co-implicates theory and practice under a third principle (parergonality) thus subverting the effective power of theory – if two terms are subsumed by a third, then neither can claim any power over the other.

[7] Immanuel Kant, *The Critique of Judgement*, trans. James Creed Meredith (Oxford: Oxford University Press, 1980), pp. 4–5.
[8] Jacques Derrida, *The Truth in Painting*, trans. Geoff Bennington and Ian McLeod (London: University of Chicago Press, 1987), p. 38.
[9] Kant, *The Critique of Judgement*, p. 6. In the *Critique of Practical Reason*, which seeks to establish the *a priori* grounds for moral action, Kant formulates the famous categorical imperative: act only so that your actions could form the basis for a universal moral law. However, this rule does not constitute the source of moral principles, but provides only the means of testing such principles.
[10] Derrida, *The Truth in Painting*, p. 42.
[11] Ibid., p. 61.

However, although Derrida also wishes to exceed the binary, he is characteristically more equivocal than Nietzsche. In 'The Principle of Reason' he gestures 'beyond the conceptual opposition between "conception" and "act", between "conception" and "application", theoretical view and praxis, theory and technique', but this 'beyond' marks the step outside metaphysics which he is, as always, unwilling to take.[12]

Derrida is suspicious of theory on its own account because of its pretensions to objectivity and scientism. In *Of Grammatology*, 'grammatology' is defined as the science (theory) of writing, although Derrida typically undermines the possibility of ever formulating such a theory: 'such a science of writing runs the risk of never being established as such and with that name. Of never being able to define the unity of its project or its object. Of not being able either to write its discourse on method or to describe the limits of its field.'[13] This is because, according to Derrida's 'theory', it is impossible to stand outside writing and to achieve an objective scientific viewpoint. The fundamental inadequacy of theory to the deconstructive project of subverting logocentrism is made clear:

> the necessary decentering cannot be a philosophic or scientific act as such, since it is a question of dislocating . . . the founding categories of language and the grammar of the *epistémè*. The natural tendency of *theory* – of what unites philosophy and science in the *epistémè* – will push rather toward filling in the breach than toward forcing the closure.[14]

But theories, even scientific ones, are not necessarily the totalizing entities that Derrida takes them for and may without contradiction be presented as provisional or context-dependent, even by scientists.

Derrida attempts to extricate deconstruction itself from the theory/practice binary by denying the existence of any deconstructive principles which could be identified as a theory and taken to govern a practice. In the preface to *Of Grammatology* Derrida questions the demonstration of theoretical precepts through application:

> The first part of this book, 'Writing before the Letter', sketches in broad outlines a theoretical matrix. It indicates certain significant historical moments, and proposes certain critical concepts. These critical concepts are put to the test in the second part, 'Nature, Culture, Writing'. This is the moment, as it were, of the example, although strictly speaking, that notion is not acceptable within my argument.[15]

---

¹² Derrida, 'The Principle of Reason', p. 9.
¹³ Derrida, *Of Grammatology*, trans. Gayatri Chakravorty Spivak (London: Johns Hopkins University Press, 1974), p. 4.
¹⁴ Ibid., p. 92.
¹⁵ Ibid., p. lxxxix.

The ability of deconstruction to undermine the theory/practice binary is itself undermined by a kind of practical double bind. Derrida's attempt to evade theory fails and in spite of his frequent injunctions and best efforts the 'rules' of deconstruction are formulated. Early works such as *Of Grammatology* explicate broadly coherent theories of writing or textuality which continue to inform or govern deconstructive practice. There are several studies which quite rightly refuse to take Derrida at his word. Fairlamb questions deconstruction's potential to subvert or evade theory, referring disparagingly to 'some practitioners of deconstruction' who maintain without imagining any inconsistency that 'grammatology and deconstruction depend on what Derrida refers to as "the general system of economy" of which deconstruction is the practice'.[16] Fairlamb is describing an implicit faith in the effective power of grammatology over a practice which attempts to subvert theory and concludes that while deconstruction comprises a critique of foundationalist theory, it is itself theoretical.[17] Christopher Johnson proposes 'one possible response to those who claim the irreducibility of Derrida's work would be that his disseminatory style is itself a theory'.[18] A more common plea for exempting deconstruction from the binary is that it manages to avoid theory by enacting its principles. However, Derrida is so anxious to dissociate deconstruction from either term of the theory/practice binary that he also denies that deconstruction is either 'an *act* or an *operation*'.[19] In the end there is no justification for the collapse of the binary or the subversion of the hierarchy with reference to deconstruction; the deconstructive style is informed and governed by the principles of multiple signification, anti-logocentrism, and so on, and those principles are formulated as theories.

Thomas McCarthy argues on a more general level that 'if knowledge itself is understood to be a social product, the traditional oppositions between theory and practice . . . break down, for there are practical dimensions to any social activity, theorizing included'.[20] This is certainly true, but only works on the general, or theoretical, level by subsuming theory and practice beneath an overarching concept, social activity. Theory is certainly practice when it signifies the *activity of theorizing*. But it is still possible, at this level, to distinguish between general theoretical statements and the *application* of these principles or models to actual texts or examples. As McCarthy also notes, 'Not all critical work need be or can be done . . . at the same level of specificity or generality.'[21]

---

[16]   Fairlamb, *Critical Conditions*, pp. 81–2.
[17]   Ibid., p. 103.
[18]   Christopher Johnson, *System and Writing in the Philosophy of Jacques Derrida* (Cambridge: Cambridge University Press, 1993), System and Writing, pp. 8–9.
[19]   Derrida, 'Letter to a Japanese Friend', trans. David Wood and Andrew Benjamin in *Derrida and Différance*, ed. David Wood and Robert Bernasconi (Evanston: Northwestern University Press, 1988), p. 3.
[20]   David Couzens Hoy and Thomas McCarthy, *Critical Theory* (Oxford: Blackwell, 1994), pp. 17–18.
[21]   Ibid., p. 18.

Derrida concedes a certain disjunction between theory and practice which could be interpreted as admitting the validity of the binary. When pointing out the limitations of Saussurean theory in 'Différance', Derrida summons the binary: 'that particular model which is phonetic writing *does not exist*; no practice is ever totally faithful to its principle' and 'Structuralism lives within and on the difference between its promise and its practice.'[22] However, he also acknowledges a similar disparity between theory and practice in his own work: 'I should have liked . . . to have been able to shape both my discourse and my practice, as one says, to fit the premises of my earlier undertakings. In fact, if not in principle, this was not always easy, not always possible, at times indeed very burdensome.'[23] Samuel Weber suggests that

> Having established a certain structural instability in the most powerful attempts to provide models of structuration, it was probably inevitable that Derrida should then begin to explore the other side of the coin, the fact that, *undecidability notwithstanding*, decisions are *in fact* taken, power *in fact* exercised, traces *in fact* instituted.[24]

The failure to put deconstructive principle into practice is related directly to the disjunction between the metaphysical/linguistic theory of radical indeterminacy and polysemy and the practical experience of 'closure'. Arguably, it is not merely difficult but impossible to realize deconstructive principles; the infinite regression of meaning simply does not impinge on most discourse, even that of deconstruction. According to Arkady Plotnitsky, 'deconstruction points toward "the necessity of interminable analysis." But one must also account for the necessity of termination, for any analysis or interpretation is necessarily terminated at some point. At the very least, death of one kind or another . . . will terminate an analysis.'[25] Plotnitsky undertakes to thread his way between the dream of infinity and the fact of closure in Derrida's theory and identifies a pragmatic component which allows for this mediation. This element is the '*programmatological*, at the intersection of a pragmatics and a grammatology'.[26] But Derrida, particularly in his early (theoretical) work, prioritizes the 'grammatological' over the pragmatic by stressing indeterminacy. The salient

[22] Derrida, *Of Grammatology*, p. 39; *Writing and Difference*, trans. Alan Bass (London: Routledge, 1978), 1967, p. 26.
[23] Jacques Derrida, 'The Time of a Thesis: Punctuations', trans. Kathleen McLaughlin in *Philosophy in France Today*, ed. Alan Montefiore (Cambridge: Cambridge University Press, 1993), p. 49.
[24] Samuel Weber (ed.), *Demarcating the Disciplines: Philosophy Literature Art* (Minneapolis: University of Minnesota Press, 1986), p. x.
[25] Arkady Plotnitsky, 'Interpretation, Interminability, Evaluation: From Nietzsche Toward a General Economy' in *Life After Postmodernism: Essays in Value and Culture*, ed. John Fekete (London: Macmillan, 1988), p. 126.
[26] Plotnitsky, 'Interpretation, Interminability, Evaluation', p. 127.

disjunction however, is not between theory and practice, but between metaphysical theory and reality; as Lorna Sage puts it, 'theory is the region where common sense dies'.[27] Interpretation is not usually terminated by death but by a full stop.

As one would expect Derrida (like, but unlike Leavis), also denies formulating a *literary* theory. In 'The Time of a Thesis' he describes how his initial proposal for a thesis on 'The Ideality of the Literary Object' was abandoned and three sentences clearly indicate the steps he has attempted to take away from the 'literary-theoretical' question: 'What is literature? And first of all what is it "to write"? How is it that the fact of writing can disturb the very question "what is?"'[28] Although this appears to indicate a primary concern with the ontological, Derrida assures the panel that 'my most constant interest, coming even before my philosophical interest I should say, if this is possible, has been directed towards literature, towards that writing which is called literary'.[29] He sums up his attempt at non-theory thus: 'I tried to work out – in particular in the three works published in 1967 – what was in no way meant to be a system but rather a sort of strategic device, opening onto its own abyss, an unclosed, unenclosable, not wholly formalizable ensemble of rules for reading, interpretation and writing.'[30] But just as *Of Grammatology* explicates a metaphysical theory, Derrida's work on 'that writing which is called literary' incorporates a theory of the literary text. The precepts of this literary theory are coherent with and consequent on those principles developed in the more obviously philosophical texts and include the notion that the boundary between the literary text and the critical or commentary text is 'permeable', that literary theory is not external to its object of enquiry, and that the critic can therefore no longer claim mastery over the literary text.

The notion that deconstruction is a *method* of literary criticism is also predictably inimical to Derrida. He notes in *Of Grammatology* that 'No exercise is more widespread today and one should be able to formalize its rules.'[31] However, he is typically unwilling to formulate these rules and asserts elsewhere that:

> Deconstruction is not a method and cannot be transformed into one. Especially if the technical and procedural significations of the words are stressed. It is true that in certain circles (university or cultural, especially in the United States) the technical and methodological 'metaphor' that seems necessarily attached to the very word 'deconstruction' has been able

---

[27]   Lorna Sage, 'The Women's Camp', *TLS* (15 July 1994), p. 11.
[28]   Derrida, 'The Time of a Thesis', p. 37.
[29]   Ibid., p. 37.
[30]   Ibid., p. 40. The other texts referred to here are *Speech and Phenomena* and *Writing and Difference*. The 'defense' or viva was itself not standard since the doctorate was being awarded for published works.
[31]   Derrida, *Of Grammatology*, p. 24.

to seduce or lead astray. Hence the debate that has developed in these circles: Can deconstruction become a methodology for reading and for interpretation?[32]

However, in 'Living On: Border Lines', his essay in *Deconstruction and Criticism*, Derrida does formulate something like a critical methodology, albeit a negative one. He issues direct instructions in the correct way of reading: 'We should neither comment, nor underscore a single word, nor extract anything, nor draw a lesson from it. One should not, one should refrain from.'[33] Geoffrey Hartman, a New Critic turned poststructuralist who contributed to this book, later provided his own summary of deconstructive critical precepts: 'contemporary criticism', he states, 'aims at a hermeneutics of indeterminacy. It proposes a type of analysis that has renounced the ambition to master or demystify its subject (text, psyche) by technocratic, predictive, or authoritarian formulas.'[34] Deconstruction attempts to live out its principles in its practice by rejecting or parodying the techniques and apparatus of conventional criticism; in short, the traditional form of the literary essay. Derrida's 'Living On: Border Lines' is another 'graphic' text, which demonstrates its irreverence for academic conventions by inserting a continuous commentary, apparently addressed to the translator or co-author, in the space normally occupied by footnotes.

The transformation of metaphysical deconstruction into a literary-critical practice in the English academy has been faced with a double resistance. Deconstruction itself explicitly resists the concept of such transformation and the discipline of English has a long-standing and well-documented prejudice against 'abstract' thought generally and French theory in particular. Long before Colin MacCabe was encouraged to leave Cambridge and take poststructuralism with him, F.R. Leavis maintained that

> The business of the literary critic is to attain a peculiar completeness of response and to observe a peculiarly strict relevance in developing his response into commentary; he must be on his guard against abstracting improperly from what is in front of him and against any premature or irrelevant generalizing – of it or from it.[35]

For Leavis, the critic's 'first concern is to enter into position of the given poem . . . . In making value-judgments . . . he does so out of that completeness of possession and with that fulness of response.'[36] Martin Turnell wrote scornfully that

---

[32] Derrida, 'Letter to a Japanese Friend', p. 3.

[33] Jacques Derrida, 'Living On: Border Lines', in *Deconstruction and Criticism*, by Harold Bloom et al. (London: Routledge & Kegan Paul, 1979), p. 152.

[34] Geoffrey H. Hartman, *Criticism in the Wilderness: The Study of Literature Today* (London: Yale University Press, 1980), p. 41.

[35] F.R. Leavis, *The Common Pursuit* (Harmondsworth: Penguin, 1963), p. 213.

[36] Ibid., p. 213.

It is a notable fact that the French critic attaches more importance to the external order and coherence of his system than to its flexibility or its completeness. The result is that his work often turns out to be inferior to that of English writers whose philosophical equipment appears at first to be less impressive.[37]

Turnell appears perversely proud of the less than impressive British 'equipment'. He and Leavis were of the same mind; abstraction indicated a lack of sensibility and had the effect of repressing the response to the literary object which was necessary for that criticism which dealt first with particulars and only then with the larger 'sphere of morality'.[38] This demotion of theory was the product of a Platonic hierarchy; criticism is at one remove from the primary subjective response to the text and theory at an even further remove.

Deconstruction struck at the heart of English, whose concepts and methods had been developed by Richards, Empson and Leavis in England and the New Critics in America. One of the most obvious points of contention lay in a sharply divergent conception of the literary text. For Cleanth Brooks, 'the elements of a poem are related to each other . . .. The beauty of the poem is the flowering of the whole plant, and needs the stalk, the leaf, and the hidden roots.'[39] This notion of the poem as an organic and self-contained form is at direct odds with deconstructive notions of permeable boundaries. Christopher Norris posits Derrida's belief in 'the total dissolution of those boundaries that mark off one text from another, or that try to interpose between poem and commentary'.[40] However, in 'Living On: Border Lines' in *Deconstruction and Criticism*, a collaborative effort with the Yale School literary critics, Derrida maintains the necessity of boundaries: 'If we are to approach a text, it must have an edge.'[41] He also states that

it was never our wish to extend the reassuring notion of the text to a whole extra-textual realm and to transform the world into a library by doing away with all boundaries, all framework, all sharp edges (all *arêtes*: this is the word that I am speaking of tonight), but that we sought rather to work out the theoretical and practical system of these margins, these borders, once more, from the ground up.[42]

---

[37]   Martin Turnell, 'Literary Criticism in France (II)', *Scrutiny* 8 (1939), p. 298.

[38]   Martin Turnell, 'Literary Criticism in France (I), *Scrutiny* 8 (1939), p. 175.

[39]   Cleanth Brooks, 'Irony as a Principle of Structure' in *Debating Texts: A Reader in Twentieth-Century Theory and Method*, ed. Rick Rylance (Milton Keynes: Open University Press, 1987), p. 37.

[40]   Christopher Norris, *Deconstruction: Theory and Practice* (London: Methuen, 1982), p. 114.

[41]   Derrida, 'Living On: Border Lines', p. 83.

[42]   Ibid., p. 84.

In the 'footnote' text Derrida exhibits the pragmatic streak alluded to by
Plotnitsky, acknowledging that 'It is always an *external* constraint that arrests a
text in general, i.e., *anything*, for example life death.'[43]

Another area of disagreement between poststructuralism and New Criticism
is the latter's logocentrism. In 'The Dead End of Formalist Criticism', Paul de
Man points to the logocentrism of Richards's theory, which presupposes 'a
perfect continuity between the sign and the thing signified'.[44] Leavis asserts that
the critic's 'first concern is to enter into possession of the given poem (let us say)
in its concrete fulness, and his constant concern is never to lose his completeness
of possession, but rather to increase it'.[45] This statement, suggestive of the much-
derided evaluative criterion of 'felt life' and logocentric in essence, is inimical to
deconstruction which denies the possibility of gaining access to the full presence
of the literary work and promotes instead the elusive 'trace'.

There are, however, some areas of theoretical congruence between New
Criticism and poststructuralism and these have been discussed in Gary Day's
collection, *The British Critical Tradition*. This volume aims to demonstrate how
New Criticism 'anticipates and to some extent parallels the concerns of postmodern critical theory'.[46] Norris here characterizes William Empson in terms he
uses elsewhere to describe American deconstruction, stating that his 'method is
to multiply meanings to the point where methodical distinctions collapse in a
seemingly endless proliferation of sense'.[47] In addition to deconstruction's
multiplication of Empson's seven types of ambiguity, the heresy of paraphrase
could also be seen as a less radical version of poststructuralist semantic
indeterminacy, and the New Critical paradox as a forerunner of the deconstructive
aporia. In *Criticism in the Wilderness*, Hartman exhibits a Leavisite mysticism:
'If theory presupposes a scientific language, there may be an untheorizable
element in literature.'[48] However, while Norris compares some of Empson's
concerns with those of de Man (who refers approvingly to Empson in 'The Dead
End of Formalist Criticism'), he also points to less assimilable traits such as
Empson's stalwart rationalism and common-sense view of language. Although
radical indeterminacy represents an exaggeration of New Critical ambiguity, the
view of the literary text as an organic unity cannot be reconciled with
poststructuralist theories of textuality.

---

[43]   Ibid., p. 171.
[44]   Paul de Man, *Blindness and Insight: Essays in the Rhetoric of Contemporary
Criticism*, 2nd edn (London: Routledge, 1983), p. 232.
[45]   Leavis, *The Common Pursuit*, p. 213.
[46]   Gary Day (ed.), *The British Critical Tradition: A Re-evaluation* (London:
Macmillan, 1993), back cover.
[47]   Christopher Norris, 'Reason, Rhetoric, Theory: Empson and de Man' in *The
British Critical Tradition: A Re-evaluation*, ed. Gary Day (London: Macmillan, 1993), p.
153.
[48]   Hartman, *Criticism in the Wilderness*, p. 8.

Inspired by deconstruction, Hartman has devoted much of his career to healing the breach between theory, criticism and literature. In the preface to *Deconstruction and Criticism* he endorses a more 'philosophical' criticism and consistently attempts to invert the academic deference to the literary text by asserting the creative aspect of criticism, betraying a certain Romantic nostalgia, the literary specialism of many of the Yale critics. Hartman asserts that *because* the essays in *Deconstruction and Criticism* 'retain the form of commentary they also move toward a theory of commentary'.[49] Hartman here mistakenly conflates discourse and metadiscourse, exemplifying the deconstructionist tendency to elide any distinction between the critical and theoretical, thereby concealing a bias towards the latter. Literary theory – that is general statements about literature – and close textual commentary may coexist, but this does not mean that they are identical. In *Criticism in the Wilderness* Hartman asks, 'How did this divide between theory and practice come about? Is there hope for an unservile, an enlarged and mature, criticism, neither afraid of theory nor overestimating it?'[50] His book is designed, of course, to provide us with the rudiments of this criticism. Ironically, the non-effectivity of poststructuralist theory on critical practice is explicitly asserted by Hartman. Speaking of the aim of *Criticism in the Wilderness* he asserts, 'I began quite involuntarily to expand my notion of close reading into a theory of practice; that is, I had always wanted to plough back theory into practice. I saw that the practice was being misunderstood because there wasn't an explanatory theory.'[51] He cites Derrida as providing the means to formulate this theory but at the same time inconsistently asserts the disjunction of theory and practice: 'I was at an impasse (in terms of philosophy) for a theory of practice, and he found a way of doing it. That was functionally important . . . but I never changed my criticism because of him.'[52] Hartman advocates a critical technique which will 'allow a formal idea within critical theory to elicit the analysis of a poem, and vice-versa', but the assertion that he didn't change his criticism because of Derrida highlights a compatibility between deconstruction and New Criticism in practice.[53] In the preface to *Deconstruction and Criticism* he makes the modest claim that deconstructive criticism supplies 'a new rigor when it comes to the discipline of close reading'.[54] His essay in this collection comprises a deconstructive close reading of Yeats's 'Leda and the Swan' which is striking precisely for its marriage of New Critical and deconstructive formalisms. He first demonstrates his New Critical close reading skills: 'The mimetic faculty is stirred by rhythmic effects (the additional beat in "great wings

---

[49]   Geoffrey Hartman, *Deconstruction and Criticism*, preface, p. viii.

[50]   Hartman, *Criticism in the Wilderness*, pp. 3–4.

[51]   Geoffrey Hartman, 'Critical Practice and Literary Theory: An Interview with Geoffrey Hartman', by Vijay Mishra, *Southern Review* 18, 2 (1985), p. 189.

[52]   Ibid., p. 199.

[53]   Hartman, *Criticism in the Wilderness*, p. 5.

[54]   Geoffrey Hartman, *Deconstruction and Criticism*, preface, p. viii.

beating still," the caesural pause between "terrified" and "vague"), while inner
bonding through repetition and alliteration ("beating . . . beating", "*He holds her
helpless* . . .") tightens Yeats's verse as if to prevent *its* rupture.'[55] New Criticism
shares deconstruction's preoccupation with oppositions and Hartman's formal
analysis is followed by a typical deconstructive co-implication of the opposites:
mimesis/poesis, presence/absence, visible/invisible. While this type of close
reading is certainly more accessible to the reader than Derrida's more
performative work, it makes not the slightest progress towards Hartman's
declared intent to 'get beyond Formalism'. Rather than demonstrating a 'new
rigor', the coupling of deconstruction and New Criticism simply extends the old
techniques. New Criticism looks for the resolution of tension and closure while
deconstruction delights in radical indeterminacy and open-endedness, but the fact
that they can both produce broadly compatible formalisms illustrates the
disjunction between theory and practice.

The poststructuralist critic of course explains the coherence of New Criticism
and deconstruction as an example of the double bind. This strategy is followed by
both Hartman and de Man:

> what I insist on is that the kind of New Criticism (closer than close
> reading) which gradually evolved had effectively the result of what is now
> called Deconstruction. This was done through a technique, but not a cold
> technique, because my concern was always to get beyond Formalism while
> realising that you had to go through it.[56]

> The structural moment of concentration on the code for its own sake
> cannot be avoided, and literature necessarily breeds its own formalism....
> On the other hand – and this is the real mystery – no literary formalism,
> no matter how accurate and enriching in its analytic powers, is ever
> allowed to come into being without seeming reductive[.][57]

De Man compares the critical practice of Richards and Barthes: 'Richards's
form-object resulted from the postulate of a perfect continuity of consciousness
with its linguistic correlates; Barthes, on the other hand, proceeds from a historical situation. But, from the point of view of criticism, the result is the same since,
in both instances, criticism begins and ends with the study of form.'[58] But where
deconstruction is distinctly different from New Criticism is in the way it often
prioritizes its theoretical interests over and above the form of the literary text.

Deconstruction and Criticism ostensibly takes Romantic poetry as its literary
focus, but Derrida's interest in literary texts is kindled only insofar as they relate

---

    55   Hartman, *Criticism in the Wilderness*, pp. 22–3.
    56   Hartman, 'Critical Practice and Literary Theory', p. 194.
    57   Paul de Man, *Allegories of Reading: Figural Language in Rousseau,
Nietzsche, Rilke, and Proust* (New Haven: Yale University Press, 1979), p. 4.
    58   de Man, *Blindness and Insight*, p. 234.

to the metaphysical questions of boundaries, edges, 'invagination', translation, quotation and so on. Derrida glances at rather than (logocentrically) engages with the literary text and within the boundaries of his essay the licentious free-play identified by many critics of deconstruction appears to hold sway. Derrida refers to Shelley's poem, *The Triumph of Life* ('which it is not my intention to discuss here'),[59] and then passes on to Blanchot's *La folie du jour*. He notes a textual variant in the subtitle of Blanchot's text: *Un récit/Un récit? Récit* denotes both fictional narration and factual account and the variant question mark signifies the interrogation of fictionality – in other words, metafiction. He discourses at some length on madness, light and blindness, admittedly linking these themes with Shelley's *The Triumph of Life*:

> In a dissemination as glorious as it is fleeting, the *sema jour*, the 'same' *jour*, the other, is both *ajouré* and *ajourné* – in itself, so to speak, in the precarious instability of its title. The madness of the day, of this moment, is momentary. The abyss that carries it away is expressed (for example) when a voice says, 'Oh, I see the daylight, oh God.'[60]

Oh God! This is certainly not a form of close reading because rather than paying close attention to the words on the page it takes them as a starting point for an exposition on a tangential theme. Stuart Sim classifies Derrida's practice as 'off-criticism' and maintains that his performative tactics are designed to render the deconstructor invulnerable to further criticism.[61] Such writing certainly has creative aspects, and therefore transgresses the boundaries of conventional criticism, but whether it contributes anything to the literary or the critical corpus is doubtful. Norris describes 'Living On: Border Lines' as 'a virtuoso exercise of writing which assumes all the textual freedoms granted by an underdetermined or radically ambiguous context'.[62] It is a virtuoso deconstructive performance, but because it anti-logocentrically occludes rather than illuminates the text, attempting to enact deconstructive principles of intertextuality, it is of more value for those interested in deconstruction, or Derrida, than for those interested in learning something about the work of Shelley or Blanchot.

In spite, or perhaps because of, Derrida's proclaimed lack of expertise in matters Joycean, the essay, 'Ulysses Gramophone: Hear Say Yes in Joyce', marks a return to a more conventional use of scholarly apparatus: quotation, referencing, and notes. The essay opens with a discussion of the philosophical and linguistic character of affirmation, with reference to Molly Bloom's monologue at the close of *Ulysses*. Derrida considers topics coherent with those in 'Living On: Border

---

[59]   Derrida, 'Living On: Border Lines', p. 85.
[60]   Ibid., pp. 89–90.
[61]   Stuart Sim, *Beyond Aesthetics: Confrontations with Poststructuralism and Postmodernism* (London: Harvester Wheatsheaf, 1992), p. 60.
[62]   Norris, *Deconstruction: Theory and Practice*, p. 115.

Lines', such as translation and quotation: 'What right do we have to select or interrupt a quotation from *Ulysses*?'[63] He brings the principle of the double bind to bear on literary criticism, citing the institutional requirement for mastery over Joyce's ineffable text: 'Everything we can say about *Ulysses*, for example, has already been anticipated, including, as we have seen, the scene about academic competence and the ingenuity of metadiscourse. We are caught in this net.'[64] Derrida also muses on his own journeyings in conjunction with those of Leopold Bloom and his mythical forbear, Odysseus. It is at this point that deconstructive meandering again threatens to overrun the literary text. Derrida exploits those aleatory connections typical of deconstruction by describing various personal experiences which are tangentially connected with *Ulysses* (an incident in a Tokyo book shop, a yoghurt called 'YES'). This self-referentiality is of course self-conscious: 'But I am continuing the chronicle of *my experiences.*'[65] Although, as Steven Connor points out, the structure of Derrida's peregrinations follows that of Joyce's text, the essay's close falls far short of Molly Bloom's poetic affirmation ('yes I said yes I will Yes') as Derrida writes prosaically: 'I decided to stop here because I almost had an accident just as I was jotting down this last sentence, when, on leaving the airport, I was driving home after the trip to Tokyo.'[66]

The idea of 'mastery' over the literary text is something poststructuralists associate with conventional criticism and find discomfiting. Gayatri Spivak cites the double bind in defence of this position stating that 'as she deconstructs, all protestations to the contrary, the critic necessarily assumes that she at least, and for the time being, means what she says. Even the declaration of her vulnerability, must come, after all, in the controlling language of demonstration and reference.'[67] In many texts Derrida abandons conventional textual apparatus and 'the controlling language of demonstration and reference', a practice dictated by the theory of intertextuality. The dazzling surface of deconstruction conceals not only the machinery of metaphysical logic but blinds some enthusiasts to the exploitation of the literary text. Not Sim, however, who remarks that Hartman's criticism 'positively radiates knowledge and authority'.[68] Leavis, although he tends towards the dogmatic, at least foregrounds his manipulation of the text by the conventional use of textual apparatus.[69]

---

[63] Jacques Derrida, *Acts of Literature*, ed. Derek Attridge (London: Routledge, 1992), p. 277.

[64] Ibid., p. 281.

[65] Ibid.. p. 265.

[66] Ibid., p. 309.

[67] Gayatri Chakravorty Spivak, *Of Grammatology*, introduction, p. lxxvii.

[68] Sim, *Beyond Aesthetics*, p. 78.

[69] Raman Selden attributes the resulting dogmatism to an inherited Romantic tradition producing a 'confidence in a consensus of sensibility' (*Criticism and Objectivity* [London: Allen & Unwin, 1984], p. 22). However, confidence in objective value judgement was equally firmly grounded in the possibility of a universal system, the

In a review of Denis Donoghue's *The Practice of Reading*, Terry Eagleton argues 'There is no need . . . for theory and this kind of critical practice [close reading] to be at odds. As long as critics like Donoghue suggest, foolishly, that all literary theorists dislike literature, or that they all deny the existence of self, the battle lines will continue to be too rigidly drawn.'[70] He also, rightly, points to the fact that close reading can result in poor criticism. But there is something wrong with criticism which glances at (or off) the literary text in order to discourse obliquely on the metaphysical conditions of reading, and that is that the particular literary text becomes irrelevant. There is a fundamental conflict in deconstructive criticism between a receptivity to the 'otherness' of literature and the repudiation of logocentrism and mastery. While the former appears to encourage both close attention and sensitive responsiveness to the literary text – Leavisite principles – the latter rejects the possibility of a direct encounter. This results in a style which is intended to correct the illusion of critical distance, but produces an effect of unadulterated egotism. Morris Dickstein criticises deconstructive self-seeking and formalism, referring to 'the use of texts as opportunities for self-display' and 'as interchangeable occasions for a theoretical trajectory which always returns to the same points of origin'.[71] Jonathan Culler states that 'Rumors that deconstructive criticism denigrates literature, celebrates the free associations of readers, and eliminates meaning and referentiality, seem comically aberrant'.[72] They do not. Furthermore, everything blameworthy in deconstructive criticism arises from an attempt to put principle into practice: the deconstruction of metaphysical oppositions and metaphorical boundaries results in the wildly elliptical off-criticism attacked by Sim, or in a prevalence of theory over textual commentary, while the denial of critical objectivity and neutrality results in

---

exposition of which was an Enlightenment project. Kant attempted to resolve the problem of the dual (objective/subjective) nature of judgement in the *Critique of Judgement* (1790). In the 'Analytic of the Beautiful', he presents subjective experience as the proper source of aesthetic judgement: beauty is not appreciable by means of concepts and is therefore not deducible from aesthetic principles or laws. However, the form of aesthetic judgement ('it is beautiful') indicates that beauty is an objective property. The unique claim to the *universality*, and hence objectivity, of aesthetic judgement resides in the notion of 'common sense', which for Kant is the universally consistent working of *healthy* sense faculties. The individual with these healthy sense faculties can assume that his aesthetic judgement will be shared by others and is therefore universal. Deviant judgements will result only from defective sense faculties. The synthetic *a priori* ground (transcendental signified) of Kant's system is God: the perception of perfection in the aesthetic object allows the perceiving subject to apprehend the perfection of God.

[70] Terry Eagleton, 'Is Theory what other people think?', review of *The Practice of Reading* by Denis Donoghue, *TLS* (29 January 1999), p. 27.

[71] Morris Dickstein et al., 'The State of Criticism: The Effects of Critical Theories on Practical Criticism, Cultural Journalism, and Reviewing', *Partisan Review* 48, 1 (1981), 22.

[72] Jonathan Culler, *On Deconstruction: Theory and Criticism After Structuralism* (London: Routledge & Kegan Paul, 1983), p. 280.

solipsism. Literary criticism should at least *attempt* to convey more of the text
than of the critic, but the reader of 'Ulysses Gramophone' in the end hears more
of Derrida than of Molly Bloom or of Joyce. Of course students and academics
are interested in learning about deconstruction and the values of traditional
scholarship and literary criticism are open to analysis, but in this debate cannot
be conducted in the classroom before students are competent in the conventions
which are being deconstructed.

It is not necessary to redeem New Criticism by stressing its affinity with
poststructuralism; there is a case to be made for New Critical methods and
practice on other grounds. As K.M. Newton puts it, 'One of its major advantages
was that it was made accessible to students at virtually all levels'.[73] Christopher
Cordner is impatient with deconstruction's critique of presence and argues
against a radical overhaul of critical practice:

> If the proposal is . . . that we *ought* to read only in a way which banishes
> 'presence', then much that is deeply embedded in our practices of reading,
> as well as in our modes of engagement with other people, would have to
> be excised. Such a proposal would seem to me to have the tail of theory
> wagging the dog of praxis much too vigorously.[74]

Cordner is arguing, after Leavis, against the rule of theory and for the Leavisite
assumption of presence. Although he relies upon an oversimplification of the
poststructuralist position (Derrida et al. do not seek to banish presence entirely,
but concentrate on the elusive trace), it is worth re-examining Leavis's critical
methodology as Cordner suggests to see if it could be reconditioned for current
usage.

Unfortunately Leavis's criticism cannot be recruited in support of his
methodology – the peremptory and eccentric valuations in *Revaluation* bear
witness to this. Leavis justifies the exclusion of Tennyson and the Pre-Raphaelites
because 'their verse doesn't offer . . . any very interesting local life for inspection'
and demonstrates a curious literal-mindedness when vilifying Shelley's poetic
metaphors: 'In what respects are the "loose clouds" like decaying leaves? The
correspondence is certainly not in shape, colour, or way of moving.'[75] However,
the limitations of an individual critic do not necessarily invalidate his critical
method. In *Revaluation* Leavis proclaims it the proper 'business of the critic to
perceive for himself, to make the finest and sharpest relevant discriminations, and

[73]   Newton, *Theory into Practice*, p. 6.
[74]   Christopher Cordner, 'F.R. Leavis and the Moral in Literature' in *On Literary
Theory and Philosophy: A Cross-Disciplinary Encounter*, ed. Richard Freadman and
Lloyd Reinhardt (London: Macmillan, 1991), p. 80.
[75]   F.R. Leavis, *Revaluation: Tradition and Development in English Poetry*
(Harmondsworth: Penguin, 1972), pp. 13, 192.

to state his findings as responsibly, clearly, and forcibly as possible.'[76] Although the idea of a subjective response to a poem was fundamental to Leavis's theory, his method was empirical and objective: 'In dealing with individual poets the rule of the critic is . . . to work as much as possible in terms of particular analysis . . . and to say nothing that cannot be related immediately to judgements about producible texts.'[77] Although 'objectifying' the literary text, Leavisite criticism seeks to engage directly with it and is therefore responsive in a way that deconstruction often fails to be, in spite of its assertion of the irreducible 'otherness' of the literary. As Leavis puts it, 'even if he [the critic] is wrong he has forwarded the business of criticism – he has exposed himself as openly as possible to correction; for what criticism undertakes is the profitable discussion of literature.'[78] The post-Marxist might leap upon the idea of the critic reaping a profit from his critical practice and a feminist cavil at the patriarchal critic exposing himself thus, but such an approach provides the antidote to anti-logocentric 'off-criticism'.

In a forum in the *TLS* which asked whether literature and criticism have 'benefited, or suffered, from the rise of critical theory', Derrida declared himself unable to answer such a complex question in the space provided.[79] However, in a more expansive mood he explains the function of deconstruction:

> Nor do I feel that the principal function of deconstruction is to contribute something to literature. It does, of course, contribute to our epistemological appreciation of texts by exposing the philosophical and theoretical presuppositions that are at work in every critical methodology . . . . Deconstruction asks *why* we read a literary text in this particular manner rather than another.[80]

Although deconstruction is a valid, if limited, literary theory, which addresses the metaphysical questions of literature and language, it is jumping the gun to ask this of a first-year undergraduate who is still learning basic critical methods. The principal claim of New Criticism to superiority in the classroom is that it actively discourages the sort of introspective approach which tends to bypass the literary text. Although the American New Critics may have been cultural conservatives, New Criticism with its critical vocabulary and close attention to the text (still

---

[76]   Ibid., p. 15.

[77]   Ibid., p. 10.

[78]   Ibid., pp. 15–16.

[79]   'The Rise of Theory – a Symposium', *TLS* (15 July 1994), p. 13. Although 'critical' and 'literary' theory are used interchangeably here, critical theory is a distinct, socially-orientated branch of philosophy. For a recent account see Hoy and McCarthy, *Critical Theory*.

[80]   Jacques Derrida, 'Deconstruction and the Other', interview by Richard Kearney in *Dialogues with Contemporary Continental Thinkers*, ed. Richard Kearney (Manchester: Manchester University Press, 1984), p. 124.

apparent in Hartman's reading of 'Leda') provides a better basic training in the close reading of literary texts than deconstruction and, in practice, is not incompatible with a contextual or historical reading.

The problem of how to teach literary theory remains. Although the introduction of Continental theory to the Anglo-American academy provided a boost for professional criticism, it caused pedagogical problems when it was introduced into English courses in the 1980s and to undergraduates schooled in the relatively unselfconscious method of close reading or practical criticism. Publishers responded to the new developments in literary studies and to the difficulties experienced by teachers and students by producing the theory Readers which anthologized and introduced representative structuralist, poststructuralist, Marxist and Russian Formalist theories.[81] However, the fact that the majority of English students had been reared almost exclusively on 'A' level English, that is close reading, meant that metaphysical abstraction was wholly alien.[82] Anyone who has taught theory to undergraduates, particularly first-year students of English literature, will be familiar with the majority response of puzzlement, boredom, frustration and resentment while the few pick up the baton and run.[83] Since the 1980s, strategies have been developed to counter student resistance, including the introduction of theory via its application to the literary text – 'theory-in-practice'. K.M. Newton alludes to student demand, noting that 'anyone who takes part in a theory course with students will know that one is constantly being asked to direct them to where they can find theory being applied to practice'.[84] The theory-in-practice Readers have claimed an increasing share of a market now saturated with 'straight' theory Readers.[85] In 1993 a series edited by

---

[81]   These include Rick Rylance (ed.), *Debating Texts: A Reader in Twentieth-Century Theory and Method* (Milton Keynes: Open University Press, 1987); David Lodge (ed.), *Modern Criticism and Theory: A Reader* (London: Longman, 1988); K.M. Newton (ed.), *Twentieth-Century Literary Theory: A Reader* (London: Macmillan, 1988); Raman Selden, *A Theory of Criticism From Plato to the Present: A Reader* (London: Longman, 1988); Philip Rice and Patricia Waugh (eds), *Modern Literary Theory: A Reader* (London: Edward Arnold, 1989).

[82]   In France, the humanities strand of the *baccalauréat* (the 'A' level equivalent) traditionally included literature, linguistics and philosophy. See W.R. Fraser, *Reforms and Restraints in Modern French Education* (London: Routledge & Kegan Paul, 1971), p. 19.

[83]   See Lawrence I. Lipking, 'The Practice of Theory', *ADE Bulletin* 76 (Winter 1983), 22–9.

[84]   Newton, *Theory into Practice*, p. 1.

[85]   Douglas Tallack (ed.), *Literary Theory at Work: Three Texts* (London: Batsford, 1987); Raman Selden, *Practising Theory and Reading Literature: An Introduction* (Hemel Hempstead: Harvester, 1989); K. M. Newton (ed.), *Theory into Practice* (London: Macmillan, 1992); Steven Lynn, *Texts and Contexts: Writing about Literature with Critical Theory* (New York: HarperCollins, 1994); Keith Green and Jill Le Bihan (eds), *Critical Theory and Practice: A Coursebook* (London: Routledge, 1995); Peter Brooker and Peter Widdowson, *A Practical Reader in Contemporary Literary Theory* (London: Harvester Wheatsheaf, 1996); Michael Ryan (ed.), *Literary Theory: A Practical Introduction* (Oxford: Blackwell, 1999).

Nigel Wood entitled 'Theory in Practice' was launched by Open University Press and in 1995 a competing series was launched by Routledge under the editorship of Rick Rylance. Although the trend towards the integration of theory and practice is on the theoretical level associated with deconstruction, the pull towards practical application may be related to British empiricism (to which Newton alludes in his introduction), the Leavisite suspicion of the abstract, and the institutional position of practical criticism. Even in those British universities where Continental theory has a high profile this distrust of unfettered abstraction lingers. In a survey of university English teaching Colin Evans writes, 'According to the head of school in Cardiff, post-graduates at the Centre for Cultural and Critical Theory are not encouraged to write theoretical work, but to apply theory to literature.'[86]

The 'mission statements' found in the introductions to the theory-in-practice Readers indicate consistent ideals. Their editors share with those of the straight theory Readers the aim to make theory more accessible (indeed the editors are often the same), but the unique selling point of the new pedagogic genre obviously rests in the claim of these textbooks to negotiate between literary theory and critical practice. The preface to *The Waste Land* (a volume in the 'Theory in Practice' series), declares the editors' objective 'to help bridge the divide between the understanding of theory and the interpretation of individual texts'.[87] Selden remarks that it is 'more sensible to grasp a theory and its potential value by observing it at work'.[88] The contributors to *Literary Theory at Work* 'insist that theory is most illuminating . . . when dealing with a literary text'.[89] These Readers are all marketed as 'introductory' texts and expend considerable effort in wooing the theory-shy student. Although their aims are identical, however, there are sometimes minor disagreements as to the most effective means of accomplishing them. Both Newton and Lynn conceive their volumes as *Which?* guides to theory; Newton likens students to 'inexperienced shoppers in a supermarket who are confronted by numerous brands of the same type of products', and offers a trial pack of various competing named brands from Leavis to Spivak.[90] Lynn compares himself to a holiday tour guide: 'Although wandering around is always an option, travelers who know what they're looking for and have a plan for getting there are more likely to have a satisfying and interesting visit.'[91] He undertakes to provide a comprehensive travel guide. Only Selden declares worthily from the Left: 'I am not a salesman or broker and I reject a

---

[86]   Colin Evans, *English People: The Experience of Teaching and Learning English in British Universities* (Buckingham: Open University Press, 1993), p. 174.

[87]   Tony Davies and Nigel Wood (eds), *The Waste Land* (Buckingham: Open University Press, 1994), p. ix.

[88]   Selden, *Practising Theory and Reading Literature*, p. 6.

[89]   Tallack, *Literary Theory at Work*, p. 1.

[90]   Newton, *Theory into Practice*, p. 2.

[91]   Lynn, *Texts and Contexts*, p. xvii.

"market economy" attitude towards critical theory.'[92] There are two basic ways in which the theory-in-practice Readers could be said to function: either by simply demonstrating the encounter between text and theory, or by positively arguing for the value of a particular theoretical model. *The Waste Land* operates on the first principle, while the latter motivates Newton's and Lynn's 'consumer guides'. Closer inspection reveals a definite discrimination against New Criticism. Selden is the most obviously biased, but at least foregrounds his prejudice: 'My own critical orientation cannot and should not be suppressed . . .. I regard the dislodging of both "Old" and "New" criticism from dominant positions as a positive and progressive development.'[93] He nevertheless includes a section on Leavisite and New Criticism. *The Waste Land*, however, does not include a New Critical section and continually snipes against what it regards as the ideological and political failings of New Criticism. In research at least, New Criticism has been eclipsed by poststructuralism in its diverse forms. But by dismissing New Criticism, these Readers are simply exchanging one sort of critical orthodoxy for another equally intractable.

The formats of these textbooks vary widely and range from Newton's simple selection of essays by 'canonical' theorists, to Lynn's rather fussy authored book in which each chapter is divided into an exposition of the theoretical approach, a 'How to Do' section, 'A Sample Essay', and a final section comprising extracts from primary texts and helpful questions. Selden includes a chapter of 'Exercises' at the end of his book, while the theory-in-practice volumes include a section, entitled 'Supplement', in which the editor interviews the contributor providing the reader with a model theoretically informed debate. The first major stumbling-block faced by editors and authors is the difficulty of theory; Newton makes the point that 'much literary theory operates at such a high level of abstraction that students find it difficult to grasp'.[94] One of the genre's rationales is making the esoteric accessible, but there is a conflict built in to *all* student theory Readers in that a choice has to be made between over-simplifying complex ideas and alienating the projected readership. Compromises between elitism and populism are attempted but not always achieved. Selden warns that 'conceptual difficulty cannot always be avoided'.[95] *Practising Theory* is written in clear, accessible prose but Selden remarks that he 'would not wish readers to accept such thin theoretical presentations as adequate preparation'.[96] Lynn jovially chaffs the nervous reader of deconstructive criticism thus: 'If the room starts spinning, or you find yourself getting dizzy, take a deep breath or put the book on the floor so you can read with your head between your legs. Seriously, the next little stretch

[92] Selden, *Practising Theory*, p. 7.
[93] Ibid., p. 5.
[94] Newton, *Theory into Practice*, p. 1.
[95] Selden, *Practising Theory*, p. 4.
[96] Ibid., p. 6.

is a bit theoretical and even strange . . .'!⁹⁷ Lynn's book fails due to a desire to spoon-feed the student and cater for an unfeasibly wide readership ('courses that require students to write about literature'), to say nothing of its horrible matey tone. *The Waste Land*, on the other hand, in spite of its attempt to locate and explicate theories, is far too sophisticated for an introductory guide. Although the reader is forewarned against 'knotty thought', he is not always forearmed. Harriet Davidson, for example, presumes a working knowledge of sophisticated philosophical and linguistic theories when she asserts, without further explanation, that 'structuralism provides a critique of the priority of consciousness in phenomenology, and phenomenology provides a critique of the scientistic objectivity of structuralism'.⁹⁸ Such rebarbative professional language would undoubtedly frighten the theoretical novice.

Objections have been raised to the rationale of these Readers; a note in the *TLS* vilifies the editors of the 'Theory in Practice' series for their denigration of the literary text. The 'gruesome preface' is deplored for implying that 'Theory . . . needs to be "understood", as a whole', while 'Those poor things, "individual texts" . . . require to be "interpreted" to come into their own'.⁹⁹ It should be recorded that the relegation of literature is certainly not the intention of this genre and often an explicit attempt is made to forestall any criticism on this account. Wood et al. undoubtedly do uphold the concept of literary value and this is apparent both in their policy of selecting canonical literary texts (each volume is named after the literary work), and their warning of theory's various dangers. They thus note their intention to avoid

> two major difficulties which commonly arise in the interaction between literary and theoretical texts: the temptation to treat theory as a bloc of formulaic rules that could be brought to bear on any text with roughly predictable results; and the circular argument that texts are constructed as such merely by the theoretical perspective from which we choose to regard them.¹⁰⁰

This is symptomatic of a fairly deferential approach to literature as is the tendency of contributors to *The Waste Land* also to point to the inadequacies of particular theories. Davidson, for example, criticizes the 'totalizing' effect and ahistoricism of Lacanian theory, while Tony Pinkney admits to the limitations of Bakhtin's 'Discourse in the Novel' when related to poetry.¹⁰¹ Such statements

---

⁹⁷   Lynn, *Texts and Contexts*, p. 88.

⁹⁸   Harriet Davidson, 'The Logic of Desire: The Lacanian Subject of *The Waste Land*' in *The Waste Land*, ed. Tony Davies and Nigel Wood (Buckingham: Open University Press, 1994), p. 60.

⁹⁹   D. S., 'NB', *TLS* (23 July 1993), p. 14.

¹⁰⁰   Ibid., p. 14.

¹⁰¹   Davidson, 'The Logic of Desire', pp. 79–80; Tony Pinkney, '*The Waste Land*, Dialogism and Poetic Discourse' in *The Waste Land*, ed. Tony Davies and Nigel Wood (Buckingham: Open University Press, 1994), p. 132.

accede, at least in theory, both to the limitations of theory and to the power of the literary text.

Newton declares his suspicion of the idea 'that theory precedes and therefore occupies a superior position to practice' and asserts that theory cannot be simply 'applied'.[102] Both he and the editors of the 'Theory in Practice' series refer instead to readings from a particular 'theoretical perspective'.[103] But one idea entertained neither by theory-in-practice editors, nor by their critics, is that theory-in-practice subordinates theory *to* practice. As Lawrence Lipking notes, one objection to theory in the classroom in that 'the truth of a difficult idea . . . does not depend on its accessibility to undergraduates or its ability to generate plausible "readings".'[104] The argument for unapplied theory, divorced from the interpretation of the literary text, is one born of practical considerations; some concepts have value only in the context of theoretical discourse and cannot be addressed properly by way of literary interpretation – this applies most obviously to metaphysical theories such as deconstruction. It is likely that many queries provoked by applied theory would still need to be addressed at the level of abstraction alluded to by Newton. Such considerations mean that the editors and authors are obliged to perpetuate the breach they mean to heal. Newton admits the incommensurability of theory and practice, noting that 'it is often not clear from theoretical discourse alone what form of critical practice it would entail'.[105] Nor is it necessarily clear what theory, if any, underpins literary criticism. Consequently all the Readers, except Newton's, which is an anthology of canonical theorists rather than an application of the ideas of these theorists, divide essays into a theoretical and a practical section – in that order. Furthermore, they are often designed and marketed as companion volumes to 'straight' theory Readers.[106] One can draw from this tendency the implication that the student requires prior knowledge or at least an independent account of any theory in order to gauge its full significance and potential for critical practice. Not only can theory-in-practice not do justice to the complex metaphysical theories which often deal with ideas about literature rather than literary texts, the majority of first-year students are simply unequipped to deal with such theories, applied or otherwise. The consequences of hitting critically 'naïve' students with Derrida, Kristeva and Barthes are often negative for both student and teacher. The most appropriate course of action in teaching theory is initially to take an empirical (inductive) rather than metaphysical (deductive) approach to theoretical issues by

---

[102] Newton, *Theory into Practice*, pp. 3, 1.

[103] Davies and Wood, *The Waste Land*, p. ix; Newton, *Theory into Practice*, p. 1.

[104] Lipking, 'The Practice of Theory', p. 22.

[105] Newton, *Theory into Practice*, p. 1.

[106] Selden's and Newton's texts are described as 'supplements' to their earlier books: *A Reader's Guide to Contemporary Literary Theory* and *Twentieth-century Literary Theory* respectively. *Literary Theory at Work* is marketed as a companion volume to Jefferson and Robey's *Modern Literary Theory* (both published by Batsford).

focusing on particular literary texts, thus consolidating close reading skills, and then working outwards to address general concepts via the preconceptions of the students themselves. In this way students are better prepared for a subsequent introduction to 'pure' or abstract theories and after this to apply such theories to the literary text.

Researchers, on the other hand, should not feel embarrassed about returning to traditional literary criticism once they have mastered poststructuralist theory. Lois Tyson regards the proliferation of literary theories in a positive light, suggesting that 'The most useful conclusion we can draw from this state of affairs is not that every methodology is . . . correct or that all methodologies are equally useful, but that, no matter how correct or useful any methodology is, it is incomplete.'[107] She believes that the value of different methodologies lies in their interrogation of each other, in other words the production of metatheory (theory about theory). According to Culler,

> Most of what we call theory does work to direct and influence critical practice, not because it reveals principles that are logically prior to interpretive practice, but because it provides redescriptions that seem attractive and productive, because it generalizes from other cases in ways that suggest how to deal with further cases (even though there is always the possibility that they might prove to be exceptions).[108]

This is an oddly empiricist notion of theory for a poststructuralist and in any case misrepresents the state of contemporary theory. Culler also states that the postmodern loss of foundations has combined with a retention of the metadiscursive function to produce a self-conscious criticism.[109] He elsewhere refers to deconstructive essays which 'suggest the infinite regress of correction and make critics more inclined to situate readings than to correct them'.[110] There is currently a predilection for those literary theories – reader-response, revisionist Marxist, poststructuralist – which are just as likely to encourage metatheoretical as critical responses to the literary text, and which follow metaphysics by moving from the general to the particular. The current predilection for metaphysical theory draws attention away from the particular literary text. As Thomas Kavanagh puts it, 'the contemporary preoccupation with theory has had as one of its effects the displacing of interest away from what is specific to any individual

---

[107] Lois Tyson, 'Teaching Deconstruction: Theory and Practice in the Undergraduate Literature Classroom' in *Practicing Theory in Introductory College Literature Courses*, ed. James M. Cahalan and David B. Downing (Urbana: National Council of Teachers of English, 1991), p. 237.

[108] Jonathan Culler, 'Poststructuralist Criticism', *Style* 21, 2 (1987), p. 177.

[109] Ibid., p. 175; see Fredric Jameson, foreword, *The Postmodern Condition: A Report on Knowledge* by Jean-François Lyotard (Manchester: Manchester University Press, 1984), pp. xi–xii.

[110] Culler, *On Deconstruction*, pp. 268–9.

work and toward the presuppositions and systemic cogency of the theoretical constructs that allow us to carry out our analyses'.[111] Self-conscious theorizing is not inherently valuable – intellectually, ethically or politically – and the intrusion of metatheory into literary criticism has already resulted in the attenuation of the latter. This need not occur if literary theories, including formalisms, were once again valued for their provision of critical methods and metatheory was again distinguished from criticism since its object is criticism itself. Nor need this result in the return to an unexamined critical orthodoxy. As Fish suggests, our 'texts, standards, norms, criteria of judgment' exist 'within a set of institutional assumptions that can themselves become the objects of dispute'.[112] It is the function of metatheory to examine and dispute these assumptions and the function of criticism to analyse and judge literary texts.

Even Turnell felt obliged to admit that while 'It is tempting to make a theoretic distinction between the two "moments" of the critical act – the critic's response to this text and the philosophical analysis of that response . . . we may doubt whether in practice there can be complete separation between the two.'[113] In 'The Resistance to Theory', de Man states that 'A general statement about literary theory should not, in theory, start from pragmatic considerations.'[114] In practice, as he also notes, it may have to. There is no absolute distinction between literary theory and critical practice, but in order to thwart the impracticable attempt to integrate or 'collapse' these discourses, it is necessary to qualify the assertion that all criticism is inherently theoretical, a notion whose prevalence justifies Patrick Parrinder's accusation that the 'concept of theoretical reading has hardened into a dogma'.[115] This orthodoxy was perhaps instituted when René Wellek asked Leavis to defend his position 'more abstractly and to become conscious that large ethical philosophical and . . . aesthetic choices are involved'.[116] Gerald Graff asserts that 'any teacher of literature is unavoidably a literary theorist. Whatever a teacher says about a literary work, or leaves unsaid, presupposes a theory'.[117] Derrida maintains that 'literary criticism has already been determined, knowingly or not, as the philosophy of literature'.[118] Although

---

[111] Thomas M. Kavanagh (ed.), *The Limits of Theory* (Stanford: Stanford University Press, 1989), pp. 2–3.

[112] Stanley Fish, *Is There a Text in This Class?* (London: Harvard University Press, 1980), p. 367.

[113] Turnell, *Literary Criticism in France* (II), p. 297.

[114] Paul de Man, *The Resistance to Theory* (Manchester: Manchester University Press, 1986), p. 4.

[115] Patrick Parrinder, *The Failure of Theory: Essays on Criticism and Contemporary Fiction* (Brighton: Harvester, 1987), p. 11. See also Lipking, 'The Practice of Theory', p. 22.

[116] René Wellek, 'Literary Criticism and Philosophy', *Scrutiny* 5, 4 (1937), 376.

[117] Gerald Graff, 'The Future of Theory in the Teaching of Literature' in *The Future of Literary Theory*, ed. Ralph Cohen (London: Routledge, 1989), p. 250.

[118] Derrida, *Writing and Difference*, p. 28.

Leavis loudly proclaimed his refusal to formulate a literary theory, much of what he wrote, including his critical principles, could reasonably be classed as theoretical and clearly informed his critical practice. But while criticism is always open to a critique of its implicit metaphysical or ideological assumptions, such assumptions do not make criticism inherently *theoretical*. Ideology, which may be an unformulated and even unconscious set of beliefs, is not identical to theory, which is systematic and explicit. The difference between knowing and not knowing, as Derrida puts it, is significant.

Chapter 5

Literary Studies and Cultural Studies

Chaucer with chips? Milton with mayonnaise? I want William Shakespeare in the classrooms, not Ronald McDonald (John Patten).[1]

Literary studies and cultural studies are not opposites; they are both disciplines whose objective is the analysis of cultural forms. While cultural studies originally defined itself in opposition to English, English's incorporation of theory, various kinds of politically informed criticism, and attention to popular and non-literary cultural forms has eroded the old distinction. The historical antagonism between English and cultural studies has been exacerbated by the combination of increasingly large areas of disciplinary overlap and limited institutional resources. There is some quite virulent opposition to what is regarded as an aggressive takeover of English by cultural studies. In *The Western Canon* Harold Bloom predicts the annexing of English and its traditional practices by cultural studies with some distaste:

> I do not believe that literary studies as such have a future, but this does not mean that literary criticism will die. As a branch of literature, criticism will survive, but probably not in our teaching institutions. The study of Western literature will also continue but on the much more modest scale of our current Classics departments. What are now called 'Departments of English' will be renamed departments of 'Cultural Studies' where *Batman* comics, Mormon theme parks, television, movies, and rock will replace Chaucer, Shakespeare, Milton, Wordsworth, and Wallace Stevens.[2]

This pessimism is to a certain extent justified. Since the 1980s literary studies has been in a state of accelerated transition and disruption which warrants the often applied label 'crisis' and renders it vulnerable.[3] The most obvious 'internal' cause

---

[1]   'Patten to abolish NUS closed shop', *The Guardian* (8 October 1992).

[2]   Harold Bloom, *The Western Canon: The Books and School of the Ages* (*London: Harcourt Brace*, 1994), p. 519.

[3]   See Peter Widdowson (ed.), *Re-reading English* (London: Methuen, 1982); William E. Cain, *The Crisis in Criticism: Theory, Literature, and Reform in English Studies* (London: Johns Hopkins University Press, 1984); John L. Kijinski, 'Securing Literary Values in an Age of Crisis: The Early Argument for English Studies', *English Literature in Translation* 31, 1 (1988), 38–52; Stuart Hall, 'The Emergence of Cultural Studies and the Crisis of the Humanities', *October* 53 (1990), 11–23; Bernard Bergonzi, *Exploding English: Criticism, Theory, Culture* (Oxford: Clarendon, 1991); Piero Boitani and Robert Clark (eds), *English Studies in Transition* (London: Routledge, 1993);

of this disorder is the Continental theory which undermined the relative methodological stability associated with New Criticism. While theory initially caused the well-documented schism between traditionalists and theorists, it has subsequently produced the less dramatic but more pervasive fragmentation of critical method into diverse factions, sometimes politically driven. English is currently fundamental to the national curriculum and a hugely popular subject at university level; however it has come under attack, from within and without, as outmoded and elitist. The view taken by Alvin Kernan is that traditional English – that is the analysis of canonical, high cultural texts – has little relevance in the modern world of the mass media and is merely self-perpetuating: 'serious literary activity, as well as most of the audience for literature, is concentrated in the universities. Courses in literature provide almost the only markets for literary works.'[4] A similar view is held by John Frow, who maintains that 'High culture, we might say, is no longer "the dominant culture" but is rather a pocket within commodity culture. Its primary relationship is not to the ruling class but to the intelligentsia, and to the education system which is the locus of their power and the generative point for most high-cultural practices.'[5] Colin MacCabe argues for the inclusion of film and television on the (English) curriculum because to omit such subjects would be to 'ignore the fact that the book's supremacy within our culture . . . is now challenged by the image'.[6] MacCabe is effectively saying that literature no longer has the cultural significance to warrant a discipline to itself. It would seem on the face of it quite logical and even sensible for literary and cultural studies to join forces, but while the disciplines complement each other and even share some values, there are pressing objections, both practical and intellectual, to a 'merger'.

An examination of the origins and history of cultural studies foregrounds its links with English and explains their shared values and methods. Just as early lecturers in English were often trained in classics, those trained in English staffed early cultural studies. The rise of cultural studies is associated in particular with three figures (two from English and one from History) and their seminal texts of the late 1950s and early 1960s: Richard Hoggart, author of *The Uses of Literacy* and founding director of the Centre for Contemporary Cultural Studies (CCCS) at Birmingham University, Raymond Williams, who wrote *Culture and Society*

Josephine M. Guy and Ian Small, *Politics and Value in English Studies: A Discipline in Crisis?* (Cambridge: Cambridge University Press, 1993), p. 1; Simon Frith, 'Literary Studies as Cultural Studies: Whose Literature? Whose Culture?', *Critical Quarterly* 34, 1 (1992), 3; Robert J.C. Young, *Torn Halves: Political Conflict in Literary and Cultural Theory* (Manchester: Manchester University Press, 1996), p. 87.

[4]   Alvin B. Kernan, *The Imaginary Library: An Essay on Literature and Society* (Princeton: Princeton University Press, 1982); quoted in Cain, *The Crisis in Criticism*, p. 7.

[5]   John Frow, *Cultural Studies and Cultural Value* (Oxford: Clarendon, 1995), p. 86.

[6]   Colin MacCabe, 'Towards a Modern Trivium: English Studies Today', *Critical Quarterly* 26 (1984), 69–82.

and *The Long Revolution*, and E.P. Thompson, maverick historian and author of *The Making of the English Working Class*. The common ground shared by these rebel figures was a Left-political leaning, an interest in the social context of literature and popular culture, and a dissatisfaction with the dominant formalism of English. Cultural studies is therefore correctly presented as a breakaway movement from English, but the break was messy and is not yet final. The CCCS was initially housed in the English department at Birmingham and Stuart Hall, Hoggart's assistant and later director of the CCCS, describes from first-hand experience the hostility of both English and sociology to the cuckoo in the nest which was cultural studies.[7] Graeme Turner writes of later university pressure on the CCCS to be reabsorbed into the department of English.[8] This pressure was resisted and the CCCS reinforced its identity by maintaining its distance from English.

But because of this connection cultural studies had inevitably inherited certain concepts and values from English. An early essay by Hoggart, 'Why I Value Literature', indicates a faith in aesthetic value, an unselfconscious empiricism, and a subscription to F.R. Leavis's literary criterion of 'felt life': 'No other art . . . bodies out so wholly and many dimensionally "the felt sense of life".'[9] Hoggart was an unapologetic humanist, insisting 'on the importance of the inner, the distinctive and individual, life of man', and he argued for the historical transcendence of the literary text which, if 'imaginatively penetrating . . . will go beyond particular time and place and speak about our common humanity, will become – as we used to say more readily – universal'.[10] He also retained the New Critical concept of organic unity and a certain Romantic sensibility: 'It is of the essence of . . . the poem's meaning that all its elements simultaneously co-exist . . . so that you feel them all at once as you would in heightened moments of life, if you were sufficiently sensitive.'[11] While Hoggart wrote this essay as a professor of English rather than cultural studies, it was reproduced in his two-volume *Speaking to Each Other* (1970) and he continues to promote these values today (see below).

Hoggart's evident sympathy with Leavis is no aberration since Leavis shared significant critical and even political ideals with the disciplinary migrants. In *The Common Pursuit* he writes belligerently of 'the Marxizing decade' and its demands on 'the literary historian to explain literary history as the reflection of changing economic and material realities'.[12] However, he claims that his opinion

---

  [7] Hall, 'The Emergence of Cultural Studies', pp. 12–13.

  [8] Graeme Turner, *British Cultural Studies: An Introduction* (London: Unwin, 1990), pp. 79–80.

  [9] Richard Hoggart, 'Why I Value Literature' in *The Critical Moment* (London: Faber, 1964), p. 34.

  [10] Hoggart, 'Why I Value Literature', pp. 32, 34.

  [11] Ibid., p. 34.

  [12] F.R. Leavis, *The Common Pursuit* (Harmondsworth: Penguin, 1963), p. 182.

of Marxist criticism is low 'not because I think of literature as a matter of isolated works of art, belonging to a realm of pure literary values (whatever they might be)'.[13] In the same work he writes that 'the understanding of literature stands to gain much from sociological interests and a knowledge of social history'.[14] In *Education and the University* he proposes 'integrating study', addresses the need 'to relate a literary training to other disciplines and studies', and advocates the 'study in concrete terms of the relations between the economic, the political, the moral, religion, art and literature, [which] would involve a critical pondering of standards and key-concepts'.[15] While Leavis regarded himself as marginalized by the establishment (Cambridge), and is cited by many historians of cultural studies, he cannot be appropriated entirely to that history largely because he continued to identify with English, albeit resentfully, and because English continued to identify with him.[16]

One of the founding differences between English and cultural studies is thought to lie in their attitudes to popular culture: according to the picture painted by cultural studies, English ignores or denigrates the popular while cultural studies actively promotes it. English's distaste for the popular was clear from the start; for Matthew Arnold, popular fiction was positively dangerous: 'Plenty of people will try to give the masses, as they call them, an intellectual food prepared and adapted in the way they think proper for the actual condition of the masses. The ordinary popular literature is an example of this way of working on the masses.'[17] In *Fiction and the Reading Public*, Q.D. Leavis quotes Edgar Rice Burroughs's own account of his technique, which was 'to draw action pictures which permit my reader to visualise scenes without great effort'.[18] For Leavis, popular fiction was a 'detrimental diet', which encouraged the 'habit of fantasying' and would 'lead to maladjustment in real life'.[19] *Tarzan* compares unfavourably with modernist texts such as *Heart of Darkness*: 'Conrad is engaged in expressing an infinitely more complex sense of the irony of human aspirations' – in other words, popular culture is pap.[20] The denigration of popular culture by English was reinforced by the belief in a causal connection between high art and moral improvement. However, early cultural studies was at times

---

[13]   Ibid., p. 183.

[14]   Ibid., p. 203.

[15]   F.R. Leavis, *Education and the University: A Sketch for an 'English School'* (London: Chatto & Windus, 1943), pp. 48, 49.

[16]   See Fred Inglis, *Cultural Studies* (Oxford: Blackwell, 1993), pp. 37–46; Hall, 'The Emergence of Cultural Studies', pp. 14–15.

[17]   Matthew Arnold, *Culture and Anarchy*, ed. J. Dover Wilson (Cambridge: Cambridge University Press, 1932), pp. 69–70.

[18]   Q.D. Leavis, *Fiction and the Reading Public* (London: Chatto & Windus, 1932), p. 53.

[19]   Ibid., pp. 53–4.

[20]   Ibid., p. 266.

equally scathing about popular culture. Although Hoggart's attention to popular culture was what made *The Uses of Literacy* a groundbreaking study, he condemned the 'newer mass art' in terms identical to those of Q.D. Leavis:

> This regular, increasing, and almost entirely unvaried diet of sensation without commitment is surely likely to help render its consumers less capable of responding openly and responsibly to life, is likely to induce an underlying sense of purposelessness in existence outside the limited range of a few immediate appetites.[21]

Whatever their political persuasion or disciplinary location, early twentieth-century critics had at best an ambivalent attitude to popular culture. English traditionalists decried the loss of a civilizing high culture, cultural studies retained a nostalgia for the idea of the organic community and its cultural forms, while Marxist critics regarded popular culture as a form which disseminated bourgeois ideology while delivering an addictive fix of easy pleasure.

This shared negative attitude towards the mass media can be explained by the prevalence of the modernist aesthetic which operated across disciplinary and political boundaries and which persists today. It was an ascetic rather than a hedonistic philosophy, privileging difficulty over ease and complexity over simplicity and there was a tendency, susceptible to a Freudian interpretation, to prioritize deferred gain over immediate pleasure. In fact a negative attitude to the 'consumption' of art can be traced back to Hegel. In his lectures on the fine arts, Hegel argued that a work of art could not be 'tasted as such, because taste does not leave its object free and independent but deals with it in a really practical way, dissolves and consumes it'.[22] The critical theorists of the Frankfurt School, who do 'belong' to the history of cultural studies, shared a low opinion of the new forms of entertainment. In the *Dialectic of Enlightenment* (1944), Adorno and Horkheimer roundly attacked the culture industry for its failure to achieve aesthetic sublimation of the more basic instincts:

> The secret of aesthetic sublimation is its representation of fulfilment as a broken promise. The culture industry does not sublimate; it represses. By repeatedly exposing the objects of desire, breasts in a clinging sweater or the naked torso of the athletic hero, it only stimulates the unsublimated forepleasure which habitual deprivation has long since reduced to a masochistic semblance. There is no erotic situation which, while insinuating and exciting, does not fail to indicate unmistakably that things can never go that far. [. . .] Works of art are ascetic and unashamed; the

---

[21]   Richard Hoggart, *The Uses of Literacy* (Harmondsworth: Penguin, 1958), p. 246.

[22]   G.W.F. Hegel, *Aesthetics: Lectures on Fine Art* II, trans. T.M. Knox (Oxford: Clarendon, 1985), p. 621.

culture industry is pornographic and prudish. Love is downgraded to romance.[23]

Henry James was demonstrating his superior literary sensibilities when he declared of the earlier nineteenth century that 'there was a comfortable, good-humoured feeling abroad that a novel is a novel, as a pudding is a pudding, and that our only business with it could be to swallow it.'[24] In 'Art as Technique', Shklovsky takes his predecessor Potebnya to task for the assertion that 'Poetry . . . permits what is generally called "economy of mental effort", a way which makes for "a sensation of the relative ease of the process".'[25] Shklovsky argues precisely the opposite, that 'The technique of art is to make objects "unfamiliar", to make forms difficult, to increase the difficulty and length of perception because the process of perception is an aesthetic end in itself and must be prolonged.'[26] Shklovsky's concept of defamiliarization has certain affinities with Barthes' 'Text . . . which goes to the limit of the rules of enunciation (rationality, readability, etc.)'.[27] And while Barthes warns that 'the tendency must be avoided to say that the work is classic, the text avant-garde; it is not a question of drawing up a crude honours list in the name of modernity', it is clear that it is modernist and postmodernist texts which most often exhibit 'Textual' characteristics. Barthes values 'pleasure without separation' (Text) over the 'pleasure of consumption' (Work) and blames 'The reduction of reading to a consumption . . . for the "boredom" experienced by many in the face of the modern ("unreadable") text'.[28]

In English today, modernist literary criteria are promoted most vociferously by the traditionalists. Frank Kermode suggests that 'the classic must display a capacity to be indefinitely plural'.[29] Bloom's criteria for canonicity in *The Western Canon* are 'strangeness' and 'a mode of originality'.[30] Bloom asserts that 'Contra certain Parisians, the text is there to give not pleasure but the high unpleasure or more difficult pleasure that a lesser text will not provide.'[31] However, he is clearly *with* Barthes in his assertion that 'The correct test for the

---

[23]   Theodor W. Adorno and Max Horkheimer, *Dialectic of Enlightenment*, trans. John Cumming (London: Verso, 1979), p. 140; quoted in Fred Inglis, *Cultural Studies* (Oxford: Blackwell), pp. 71–2.

[24]   Henry James, *Partial Portraits* (London: Macmillan, 1888), p. 376.

[25]   Victor Shklovsky, 'Art as Technique' in *Russian Formalist Criticism: Four Essays*, ed. Lee T. Lemon and Marion J. Reis (London: University of Nebraska Press, 1965), p. 5.

[26]   Ibid., p. 12.

[27]   Roland Barthes, *Image-Music-Text*, ed. Stephen Heath (London: Fontana, 1977), p. 157.

[28]   Barthes, *Image-Music-Text*, p. 163.

[29]   Frank Kermode, 'Old wine in new bottles', *The Guardian* (23 February 1996).

[30]   Bloom, *The Western Canon*, p. 3.

[31]   Ibid., p. 30.

new canonicity is simple, clear, and wonderfully conducive to social change: it must not and cannot be reread, because its contribution to societal progress is its generosity in offering itself up for rapid ingestion and discarding.'[32] James's 'pudding' and Barthes's 'object of consumption' produced what Adorno labelled the *kulinarische Rezeption*.[33] Hoggart retains his admiration for literature and distaste for mass culture in *The Way We Live Now* (1995), where the alimentary metaphor goes into overdrive; mass culture is 'a small voracious creature whose belly has little capacity but can and must all the time and rapidly digest small items and as rapidly void them'.[34] The tabloids are compared to an unhealthy snack, high in calories and low in nutrition: 'From those one doesn't put pages aside, for a careful reading of a particular article. That would be like setting aside on Saturday a half-opened packet of salt-and-vinegar-flavoured crisps for your Sunday dinner.'[35] Literature, however, still represents the textual equivalent of meat and two veg. for Hoggart, being 'irredeemably of the earth and so bound up all the time with possible meanings, hints of meanings, with the weighed creative and creaturely life; bacon and eggs, fish and chips . . .'.[36]

Non-literary values – ethical, social, political – have always informed English and are not incompatible with aesthetics. For Arnold good literature was anti-revolutionary and improving, a force for levelling upwards: 'It does not try to teach down to the level of inferior classes; it does not try to win them for this or that sect of its own, with ready-made judgments and watchwords. It seeks to do away with classes; to make the best that has been thought and known in the world current everywhere.'[37] For the Leavises, literature taught us how to live better while popular culture encouraged moral laziness. But politics has always been to the fore in cultural studies. The analysis of cultural forms promoted by Adorno and Horkheimer was designed not to make a better *citizen*, but to provide an understanding of the workings of capitalist ideology which would facilitate its displacement. The teleological Marxism of the Frankfurt school has been undermined by deconstruction, but cultural studies is still associated with an explicit left-wing politics and continues to defend the political value of cultural critique. Terry Eagleton, who although nominally a professor of English literature is one of its severest critics, has kept alive a certain revolutionary enthusiasm and in *Literary Theory* asserts: 'Any method or theory which will contribute to the strategic goal of human emancipation, the production of "better people", through the socialist transformation of society, is acceptable.'[38] He clearly endorses his

---

32   Ibid., p. 30.
33   Barthes, *Image-Music-Text*, p. 161; quoted in Varsava, *Contingent Meanings*, p. 60.
34   Richard Hoggart, *The Way We Live Now* (London: Chatto & Windus, 1995), p. 99.
35   Ibid., p. 99.
36   Ibid., p. 75.
37   Arnold, *Culture and Anarchy*, p. 70.
38   Terry Eagleton, *Literary Theory: An Introduction* (Oxford: Blackwell, 1983), p. 211.

own method, which he refers to variously as rhetoric, discourse theory and cultural studies. Cultural studies associates English with Conservatism and English clearly does retain some strategic value for Tory politicians (see epigraph).

Although modernist Marxists maintained the connection between high art and political insight, cultural studies' subsequent rejection of aesthetics is partly a rejection of English values and hence the value of English. Aesthetic value is clearly relevant to literature; the fine arts are by definition those which appeal to 'the mind and the sense of beauty' and what characterizes the fine arts in general is the importance of form. Poetry, which prioritizes linguistic form over content, is classed as a fine art and it is significant that New Criticism focused largely upon this genre. But since aesthetic value has traditionally underwritten English it is expedient for critics of the discipline to demystify and deconstruct this concept. Eagleton asserts that art has no autonomous value: 'There is no such thing as a literary work or tradition which is valuable *in itself*, regardless of what anyone might have said or come to say about it. "Value" is a transitive term: it means whatever is valued by certain people in specific situations.'[39] Although taking issue with Eagleton on certain points, Antony Easthope, professor of English and cultural studies, also sets out to devalue literary value which is ascribed, he argues, to those texts which have 'functioned intertextually to give a plurality of different readings transhistorically' (this is precisely the conclusion reached by traditionalists such as Bloom and Kermode).[40] Easthope undertakes an analysis of *Tarzan* and *The Heart of Darkness* which is designed to dispel the illusion of literary value and although he does not cite Q.D. Leavis, is clearly responding to her comparison of Conrad and Rice Burroughs in *Fiction and the Reading Public*. He first admits the persistence of the modernist binary and states his aim to 'inhabit the opposition without too much prejudgement at first'.[41] He then produces a table of textual attributes: *Heart of Darkness* is abstract, complex, figurative; *Tarzan* is concrete, simple, literal.[42] Again, he concedes the vestiges of conventional literary valuation inherent in these adjectives, but asserts that if the terms are 'relativised in relation to each other', this will allow the 'serious' (high cultural) consideration of popular culture. He maintains that a 'modernist' analysis is inappropriate to *Tarzan*, because of its formal qualities, that is the 'visual' features (as described in *Fiction and the Reading Public*) produced by privileging action and event over language or psychology. Attending to the particularity of each text will allow 'an analysis of each kind of text in terms of the position it offers to its reader, and on this basis it becomes possible to deconstruct the high/popular opposition by demonstrating both high and

---

[39]   Eagleton, *Literary Theory*, p. 11.
[40]   Antony Easthope, *Literary into Cultural Studies* (London: Routledge, 1991), p. 59.
[41]   Ibid., p. 80.
[42]   Ibid., p. 89.

popular cultural discourse have a *common origin* in textuality of which the way each hails the reader is an effect'.[43] More simply stated this means that both texts are written, and since they are written differently they produce different effects.

Although the high art/popular culture binary has been inhabited and then deconstructed, it stubbornly persists. Eagleton declares that 'The catch-word "postmodernism" just means that culture and social life are no longer opposites', and that postmodernist 'art has climbed off its pedestal . . . only to become a commodity.'[44] For Fredric Jameson,

> What has happened is that aesthetic production today has become integrated into commodity production generally: the frantic economic urgency of producing fresh waves of ever more novel-seeming goods . . . at ever greater rates of turnover, now assigns an increasingly essential structural function and position to aesthetic innovation and experimentation.[45]

Postmodern art may be obviously commodified, particularly in the cases of pop-art, video and advertising, but Jameson's terms indicate the persistence, not the destruction of the modernist aesthetic. Innovation and experimentation, particularly in literature, produce inaccessible and structurally complex works which fulfil modernist literary criteria.

Cultural studies declares its superiority over English by claiming to analyse *all* values, not merely the outmoded aesthetic. Fred Inglis states that 'Making distinctions of value is *the* form of all human practices, and it is the vocation of the public-spirited student of culture to understand this practice as accurately and sympathetically as will make possible intelligent and upright action in the present.'[46] He imagines that an understanding of cultural value will encourage the same moral rectitude that the Leavises associated with the study of literature. Cultural studies tends to disparage literary value because of its association with modernist elitism. In *Popular Fictions*, Peter Humm et al. repudiate the distinction between good and bad literature and suggest that literature should simply not be considered using aesthetic criteria.[47] Although one must, in good faith, assume that Easthope and Humm have a fundamental belief in the textual equality they promote, the transvaluation of aesthetic value has not yet been effected and for cultural studies to deny this value will hardly facilitate 'intelligent and upright action' or even adequate cultural critique.

Far more viable a strategy on the part of cultural studies is the endorsement

[43]   Ibid., p. 90.
[44]   Terry Eagleton, 'A culture in crisis', *The Guardian* (27 November 1992).
[45]   Fredric Jameson, 'Postmodernism, or the Cultural Logic of Late Capitalism', *New Left Review* 146 (1984), 56.
[46]   Inglis, *Cultural Studies*, p. ix.
[47]   Peter Humm, Paul Stigant and Peter Widdowson (eds), *Popular Fictions: Essays in Literature and History* (London: Methuen, 1986), p. 12.

of non-formal aesthetic values, such as pleasure. The equation of beauty and pleasure recalls Aristotle, for whom that which pleased the senses was beautiful.[48] The modernist aesthetic, while it produced literary works of great lyrical beauty, clearly promoted the cerebral aspect of art over the sensual. Cultural studies does not seek to rejoin beauty and pleasure by creating a neo-Aristotelian hedonist aesthetic, but promotes hedonism as an *alternative* to aesthetics. Although in *The Uses of Literacy*, Hoggart reviled the mass media, he was indulgent towards what he presented as a working-class tendency to prioritize immediate gratification over long-term advantage.[49] In *Postmodernism and Popular Culture* Angela McRobbie rejects conceptions of postmodernist culture as nihilistic and suggests that the accelerated cycle of production and consumption frequently unites both positive pleasure and agency for the consumer (the overthrow of capitalism is clearly no longer the goal of cultural studies for some of its theorists).

Arnold defined the project of *Culture and Anarchy* as the recommendation of culture, culture being the pursuit of 'the best which has been thought and said in the world'.[50] However, the combined effects of external attack from cultural studies and undermining from postmodern theory has meant that English is embarrassed by its traditional values (moral, aesthetic and political) and the evaluative function of literary criticism has become attenuated.[51] Those who criticize the elitism of English are right to the extent that the market for literature (as high art) clearly is reliant on an educated readership and literary values are disseminated and perpetuated by educational institutions. New Critical methods were designed to explicate complex poetic forms and those modernist works which were largely inaccessible to the uneducated.[52] However, the populism of cultural studies is only superficial; while popular cultural forms may be more immediately accessible to the uneducated than literary texts, the professional discourse of cultural studies is just as esoteric as that of English. This inaccessibility is compounded by the divisiveness of a university education which is not universal. It is just as easy to argue for the value of literature from the Left as it is from the Right. The texts of high culture are frequently interpreted as subversive of the dominant ideology. And although some sub-cultural forms may be explicitly anarchic (punk rock), popular genres such as romantic fiction tend to ratify bourgeois or patriarchal ideology. Both disciplines appear to have failed in their traditional objectives: English to 'save' society; cultural studies to bring down capitalism. The ideal of literary studies as a social or moral educator,

---

[48]   See *Topics* {146a}.

[49]   Hoggart, *The Uses of Literacy*, pp. 132–6.

[50]   Matthew Arnold, *Culture and Anarchy*, ed. J. Dover Wilson (Cambridge: Cambridge University Press, 1932), p. 6.

[51]   I have described the relation between postmodern theory and evaluative criticism in 'Postmodern Value' in *Postmodern Surroundings*, ed. Steven Earnshaw (Amsterdam: Rodopi, 1994), pp. 23–37.

[52]   See Cain, *The Crisis in Criticism*, p. 2.

producing a sensitive morally responsible person and shared cultural values (propounded variously by Arnold, Leavis, and more recently Iris Murdoch and Martha Nussbaum) is equally under threat. One has only to look at the personal lives and moral conduct of literary critics and lecturers to see that refined literary sensibilities do not necessarily correlate with sensitive ethical conduct.

One of the most pressing criteria of value imposed on disciplines from outside is the economic: governments Right and Left assess direct contributions by research and indirect contributions by graduates to the national economy and the university is concerned with the related level of government funding, other external funding from industry, and overseas recruitment. English wins over cultural studies in terms of its recruitment figures, and is aided in this by its position within secondary education, although funding for interdisciplinary study is increasing and cultural studies' profile is slowly being raised. However, the humanities in general are overshadowed by the hard sciences, which make a more easily quantifiable contribution to manufacturing and research industries, and are therefore granted more government funding while government funding for the arts and humanities has been progressively squeezed and they hold little interest for industry. The social and political value of literary studies and cultural studies is difficult to ascertain because unquantifiable, it is far easier to assess the relative value of the two disciplines on 'internal' criteria, namely the validity of their theories on empirical as well as metaphysical grounds and the viability, rather than the ideological probity, of their methods.

The forging of English's disciplinary identity was consequent on its separation from philology.[53] However, this schism, precipitated by a post-war loathing of all things German, also deprived English of its methodological backbone.[54] There were early quarrels over what should constitute the discipline – philology, literary history, or literary criticism; such eclecticism is typical of a discipline in its formative years (and of one in crisis). I.A. Richards's practical criticism, which had some pretensions to scientism, provided the requisite systematic method and, combined with the American New Criticism, remained dominant in university English teaching until the 1970s.

After the founding of the CCCS, cultural studies' development of a disciplinary method was hindered somewhat by the diversity of its object. In his inaugural lecture at the CCCS, Hoggart spoke of 'film criticism; television and radio criticism; television drama . . . popular fiction of many kinds – crime, westerns, romance, science fiction, the academic and academic's detective story; . . . the press and journals of all kinds; strip cartoons; the language of advertising

---

[53] Although the University College Chair was first occupied by Thomas Dale, who was committed to the study of literature as distinct from language, there followed four professors who placed emphasis either on composition (rhetoric) or philology. At Oxford, the Merton Chair, established in 1885, was first occupied by the philologist A.S. Napier. See D.J. Palmer, *The Rise of English Studies* (London: Oxford UP, 1965), pp. 18, 22–6.

[54] Ibid., pp. 128–30.

and public relations; popular songs and popular music in all their forms'.[55] This diversity clearly daunted some and a later report from the CCCS still indicated a concern about the lack of focus and 'a problem – which we cannot in any way claim to have solved – as to what the limits of the field of study are'.[56] By contrast, the practitioners of English at this time were not greatly exercised over the limits of their discipline, which had been clearly demarcated by the New Critics, particularly in the sphere of undergraduate teaching. Paul de Man endorses this view of pre-1960 American English: 'There were polemics, no doubt, and differences in approach that cover a wide spectrum of divergencies, yet the fundamental curriculum of literary studies as well as the talent and training expected for them were not being seriously challenged.'[57]

As befits its diverse object, cultural studies was conceived of as interdisciplinary in opposition to monolithic (New Critical) English. Hall, writing in 1990, asserted that cultural studies was conceived as a critique of the humanities rather than as a discipline.[58] Its methods were purloined not only from English and history, but also from sociology, anthropology and then linguistics and semiology. Because New Criticism was the dominant method in English, cultural studies' perception of English as monolithic was not radically awry. Although Leavis and the New Critics were interested in social issues, Simon Frith overstates the case somewhat when he asserts that 'English studies have always been multidisciplinary, drawing on social and art history, on philosophy, on sociology and political theory'.[59]

While Continental theory struck at the empirical heart of English, on the face of it, cultural studies was predisposed towards the assimilation of theory in a way that English was not; as a relatively new discipline its methods would not yet have ossified into a rigid protocol. However, the initial reception of theory by cultural studies was almost as awkward as that of English because of a shared empiricism. According to Graeme Turner, the introduction of Continental theory caused a split in cultural studies between the home-grown 'culturalism' of people like Williams and Thompson and the 'textualist' modernizers, who followed the innovations of the structuralists and poststructuralists.[60] This disagreement informs Hoggart's emphatic disavowal of structuralist principles in 'Why I Value Literature': 'Language is not simply a range of conventional signs'.[61] Turner states that the tension in cultural studies was resolved by Gramsci's theory of

---

[55]   Richard Hoggart, *Speaking to Each Other* (II): *About Literature* (London: Chatto & Windus, 1970), pp. 257–8; quoted in Turner, *Cultural Studies*, p. 159.

[56]   Quoted in Turner, *Cultural Studies*, p. 181.

[57]   Paul de Man, 'The Resistance to Theory' in *Modern Criticism and Theory: A Reader*, ed. David Lodge (London: Longman, 1988), p. 358.

[58]   Hall, 'The Emergence of Cultural Studies', p. 12.

[59]   Frith, 'Literary Studies as Cultural Studies', p. 7.

[60]   Turner, *British Cultural Studies*, p. 72.

[61]   Hoggart, 'Why I Value Literature', p. 33.

hegemony, although it seems more likely that the breach was healed by Althusser's structuralist Marxism. In an overview of language studies at the CCCS in the 1970s, Chris Weedon et al. write that Althusser's 'model of the social formation . . . created the space within Marxism for serious consideration of the importance of signifying practices'.[62] Semiotic theory, particularly that of Roland Barthes, had a lasting impact on cultural studies and informs the shift in attitude towards the mass media. Fulfilling Saussure's vision of a general science of signs, Barthes used the structuralist theory of language as an analytic paradigm for textual and visual cultural forms.[63] Structuralist semiotics managed to oust the culturalism of Hoggart, Williams, and Thompson, and remains fundamentally important to contemporary (anti-foundational) cultural studies.

Contemporary theorists of cultural studies are generally more sanguine than their forebears about diversity and disciplinary fragmentation, both of which fit well with a postmodernist philosophy. Inglis blithely declares that 'culture' is 'a protean, not to say a vacuously inclusive word, which 'can be made to include pretty well everything that is thought and made by human beings'.[64] Leitch contends that 'The polysemy of the word ['culture'] and the perennial contention surrounding the idea reveal less a failure to isolate a discrete object of inquiry than a recurring magnetic pull characteristic of both the concept and the project of studying culture.'[65] John Frow asserts that the focus of his book, *Cultural Studies and Cultural Value*, is 'not on the reality of the Other but on the circumstances of its construction and on the "we" who play and are played by this language game'.[66] However, these theorists of cultural studies are writing for their peers – other theorists – and it is unlikely that such vague and sometimes inane statements are made by those who petition for institutional support. The actual study of any cultural form requires the identification of an object as the CCCS was well aware.

Contemporary cultural studies, however, is still congratulating itself on its disciplinary flexibility and attacking English for its intractability. Henry Giroux, who aims to teach scepticism by means of an *anti*-disciplinary cultural studies, asserts that academics 'must not define themselves exclusively as specific intellectuals' and recommends a 'pedagogy of lived experience and struggle,

[62]   Chris Weedon, Andrew Tolson and Frank Mort, 'Introduction to Language Studies at the Centre' in *Culture, Media, Language: Working Papers in Cultural Studies, 1972–79*, ed. Stuart Hall et al. (London: Hutchinson, 1980), p. 184.
[63]   See Ferdinand de Saussure, *Course in General Linguistics*, trans. Wade Baskin, ed. Charles Bally and Albert Sechehaye (London: Owen, 1959), p. 16; Roland Barthes, 'Rhetoric of the Image' in *Image-Music-Text*, ed. Stephen Heath (London: Fontana, 1977), pp. 32–51.
[64]   Inglis, *Cultural Studies*, p. 109.
[65]   Vincent B. Leitch, *Cultural Criticism, Literary Theory, Poststructuralism* (Oxford: Columbia University Press, 1992), p. x.
[66]   John Frow, *Cultural Studies and Cultural Value* (Oxford: Clarendon, 1995), pp. 3–4.

rather than as the empty, formalistic mastery of an academic subject'.[67] Douglas Kellner asserts that cultural studies has a 'superdisciplinary approach' and Inglis attacks 'discipline' (English) for being authoritarian and commends (cultural) 'studies' for its provisional and flexible nature:

> Cultural Studies curse the conventional idea of an academic *subject* with its implication of scholarly method and clear conceptual framework. They deny the careful boundaries watchfully patrolled by subject specialists in order to prevent poachers and levellers breaking up the fencing and polluting the pure springs of learning.[68]

Inglis describes the disciplinary specialist as a sort of anally retentive autocrat and cultural studies as the romantic outlaw. Easthope presents a similar, though less rhetorically fanciful, picture of literary and cultural studies:

> Beneath the overarching schema of the aesthetic . . . literary study abrogates for itself a place as a coherent, unified and *separated* discipline. No such strategy is possible for cultural studies, which draws on a range of knowledges conventionally discriminated into disciplines: semiotics, structuralism, narratology, art history, sociology, historical materialism, conventional historiography, post-structuralism, psychoanalysis, deconstruction.[69]

The pictures of English painted by the promoters of cultural studies are hopelessly out of date. The 'range of knowledges', which Easthope refers to (most of which are *not* conventionally defined as 'disciplines'), have already been imported into English via Continental theory. Julie Klein has a better understanding of the nature of the contemporary discipline and celebrates its methodological diversity: 'Currently the study of literature is being energized by a wide spectrum of interests, ranging across psychoanalysis, Marxism, history, sociology, and a complex set of interpretive stances that have evolved from structuralism, post-structuralism, and expanding interest in "textualism".'[70] Eagleton points out the number of methods 'involved in literary criticism' in order to attack English's view of itself as a coherent entity. He asserts that these methods 'have more in common with other "disciplines" – linguistics, history, sociology and so on – than they have with each other'.[71]

---

[67]   Henry A. Giroux, 'Academics as Public Intellectuals: Rethinking Classroom Politics' in *PC Wars: Politics and Theory in the Academy*, ed. Jeffrey Williams (London: Routledge, 1995), pp. 299, 305.

[68]   Douglas Kellner, 'Toward a Multiperspectival Cultural Studies', *Centennial Review* 36, 1 (1992), p. 5; Inglis, *Cultural Studies*, p. 227.

[69]   Easthope, *Literary into Cultural Studies*, p. 172.

[70]   Julie Thompson Klein, *Interdisciplinarity: History, Theory, and Practice* (Detroit: Wayne State University Press, 1990), p. 32.

[71]   Eagleton, *Literary Theory*, p. 197.

Some resistance to the new interdisciplinarity in English is put up by entrenched disciplinarians. Bloom regards it as symptomatic of a lack of interest in the literary text:

> Precisely why students of literature have become amateur political scientists, uninformed sociologists, incompetent anthropologists, mediocre philosophers, and overdetermined cultural historians, while a puzzling matter, is not beyond all conjecture. They resent literature, or are ashamed of it, or are just not all that fond of reading it.[72]

This is a curious response from a critic whose most famous work comprises a post-Freudian theory of literary influence. Richard Levin, another traditionalist, argues that the new interdisciplinarians simply adopt theories from other disciplines and proceed to apply these with no particular appreciation or knowledge of their disciplinary provenance.[73] Levin cites various Freudian and post-Freudian psychoanalytic theories as adopted by Coppélia Kahn, Catherine Belsey and Toril Moi. An example of this kind of 'transference' is the criticism informed by Lacan's psychoanalytic theory of gendered language acquisition. One Lacanian term which is enjoying widespread currency in literary criticism is the 'Other', cited above in Frow's introduction. This concept has its origins in Hegel's philosophy of consciousness and for Lacan 'If I have said that the unconscious is the discourse of the Other (with a capital O), it is in order to indicate the beyond in which the recognition of desire is bound up with the desire for recognition.'[74] Frow follows Lacan when asserting 'I capitalize the word to indicate the making of a mythical One out of many'.[75] Harriet Davidson states of *The Waste Land*, that

> At the end of the poem, the desire to control desire through the ego and the unconscious disrupting force of desire remain. In redefining 'my lands' as a series of allusions, the subject seems to accept his desire as the desire of the other. But that Other is not benign; the great cultural achievements of our symbolic system are also scenarios of despair and destruction.[76]

The Waste Land does address human despair, even alienation (the sense that life has no meaning and that the world is mechanistic and unsympathetic), but

---

[72] Bloom, *The Western Canon*, p. 521.

[73] Richard Levin, 'The New Interdisciplinarity in Literary Criticism' in *After Poststructuralism: Interdisciplinarity and Literary Theory*, ed. Nancy Easterlin and Barbara Riebling (Evanston: Northwestern University Press, 1993), pp. 14–15.

[74] Jacques Lacan, *Ecrits: A Selection*, trans. Alan Sheridan (London: Tavistock, 1977), p. 172.

[75] Frow, *Cultural Studies and Cultural Value*, p. 3.

[76] Harriet Davidson, 'The Logic of Desire: The Lacanian Subject of *The Waste Land*' in *The Waste Land*, ed. Tony Davies and Nigel Wood (Buckingham: Open University Press, 1994), p. 79.

Lacanian theory tends to overdetermine a literary reading and produce a criticism as formulaic as more conventional formalism. Shoshana Felman writes of Balzac's 'The Girl with the Golden Eyes': 'The principle of identity is subverted along with the principle of opposition when Henri discovers, in the recognition scene, that the Same is uncannily Other and the Other is uncannily the Same: what he had expected to be Other – his rival's face – is Same; what he had expected to be Same – his rival's sex – is Other.'[77] The argument that New Criticism internalized theoretical precepts such as the organic unity of the text can also be applied to Lacanian criticism. Whenever the 'Other' is used in critical analysis, Lacan's psycho-linguistic theory may implicitly be endorsed without being understood. The term has been over-used and consequently debased. Easthope regards 'The concept of the other [as a] diffuse, flexible, a relatively "deep" term able to gain analytic purchase in parts of texts that the more traditional accounts of ideology and gender cannot reach.'[78] Without the capital 'O', it signifies more generally difference but it is not the Heineken of literary criticism and is often simply used an alternative to New Critical paradox or ambiguity.

The new interdisciplinarity means that English can compete with cultural studies, but also renders it vulnerable to charges of methodological incoherence and simple ignorance. Eagleton sounds a warning note to this effect: 'Before we become too euphoric . . . we should notice that there are certain problems . . . . For one thing, not all of these methods are mutually compatible.'[79] Interdisciplinarity may also encourage superficiality and dilettantism over depth of knowledge. Hegel supports disciplinary specialization in the *Logic* for precisely this reason:

> There is a host of interesting things in the world: Spanish poetry, chemistry, politics, and music are all very interesting and if any one takes an interest in them we need not find fault. But for a person in a given situation to accomplish anything, he must stick to one definite point, and not dissipate his forces in many directions {80 n.}.[80]

Although Plato's subject matter was diverse, he also advocated rigorous philosophical training; in the *Parmenides*, the young Socrates is admonished: 'you are undertaking to define "beautiful", "just", "good", and other particular forms, too soon [. . .] you must make an effort and submit yourself, while you are still young, to a severer training in what the world calls idle talk and condemns as useless' {135c–d}.[81] But interdisciplinary study need not result in 'dissipation'

---

[77]   Shoshana Felman, *What Does a Woman Want? Reading and Sexual Difference* (London: Johns Hopkins University Press, 1993), p. 63.

[78]   Easthope, *Literary into Cultural Studies*, p. 133.

[79]   Eagleton, *Literary Theory*, p. 198.

[80]   Hegel's *Logic*, trans. William Wallace (Oxford: Clarendon, 1975).

[81]   Aristotle, *The Complete Works of Aristotle*, ed. Jonathan Barnes (Oxford: Princeton University Press, 1984).

as the dictionary definition, 'of or between different branches of learning' suggests, foregrounding the obvious fact that disciplinarity is a precondition of interdisciplinarity.[82] Interdisciplinary study can produce work of genuine merit when different disciplinary perspectives are brought to bear on the same object. This kind of interdisciplinarity often takes the form of collaborative works between practitioners of different disciplines, such as Peter Lamarque and Stein Olsen's *Truth, Fiction, and Literature*.[83] Like Wimsatt and Beardsley's 'The Intentional Fallacy', this text is the result of collaboration between a literary critic and a philosopher. The two disciplinary perspectives combine to produce a novel angle on the philosophical nature of literature. But this kind of fruitful synthesis is hardly exemplified by the Lacanian criticism cited above.

While contemporary cultural studies tends to posit the value of a fragmented discipline, this value is endorsed by anti-foundational philosophies rather than by any practical considerations. Disciplinary methods are not written in stone, as the incorporation of Continental theory by both English and cultural studies shows, and disciplinary boundaries are not impermeable. However, the very possibility of a radically fragmented or deconstructed discipline is doubtful. Even on a metaphysical level, Derrida is unwilling to deconstruct notional boundaries out of existence and in the context of the academic institution and its practical constraints, deconstruction is effectively defused. In spite of deconstruction, according to George Levine, 'The disciplinary divisions are almost absolute. Scientists don't talk to philosophers of science; philosophers of science don't talk to literary theorists; literary theorists – while implying their right through the study of language and discourse to tread on everyone's turf – seem not to talk to anybody but like-minded theorists.'[84] The institutional pull towards discipline is evident in the fact that although interdisciplinarity was becoming institutionalized at the time that the CCCS was founded, particularly in the polytechnic sector, attracting increasing interest and funding from educational organisations, a 1971 report declared that 'Interdisciplinary work . . . is poorly placed and supported . . . in practice it runs up against the boundaries between disciplines'.[85] Inglis asserts that cultural studies is only able to take an iconoclastic stance against disciplinarity because it is *new*.[86] The dissolution of

---

[82]   *The Concise Oxford Dictionary of Current English*, 7th edn, ed. J. B. Sykes (Oxford: Clarendon, 1982).
[83]   See Peter Lamarque and Stein Haugom Olsen, *Truth, Fiction, and Literature: A Philosophical Perspective* (Oxford: Clarendon, 1994)
[84]   George Levine, 'Looking for the Real: Epistemology in Science and Culture' in *Realism and Representation: Essays on the Problem of Realism in Relation to Science, Literature, and Culture*, ed. George Levine (Madison: University of Wisconsin Press, 1993), p. 15.
[85]   Klein cites British organizations as UNESCO and the Society for Research into Higher Education in Interdisciplinarity, p. 36; quoted in Turner, *Cultural Studies*, p. 180.
[86]   Inglis, *Cultural Studies*, pp. 8–10.

the disciplinary system itself, as required by idealists such as Giroux, is extremely unlikely. Inevitably cultural studies has turned into a discipline with departments and degrees. Institutional requirements have also meant that this cultural studies has found it expedient to formulate its methods.

In a chapter entitled 'How to Do Cultural Studies', Inglis asserts that the object of cultural studies is 'to discern historical narrative wherever one can, and let those stories . . . intertwine as theories'.[87] A rather more detailed programme for contemporary cultural studies is formulated by Easthope in *Literary into Cultural Studies*. This is designed as a positive act of 'political intervention' against the humanist presumptions of empirical literary study.[88] However, he rejects the 'over-arching concept of hegemony' as an analytic tool since it subsumes textuality.[89] He defines six terms of analysis: sign system, institution, ideology, gender, subject position, and 'the other'. These terms are 'imbricated' (overlap) so that none is 'foundational', although one or several may be prioritized in a particular analysis. This anti-foundational or decentred method-ology, he claims, prevents the subject from claiming a position of superiority over the object of study: 'Nor, considered as a pedagogic practice, does the proposed methodology, though it remains critical, seek to maintain itself as a mode of academic discourse promising its subject a position of theoretical mastery.'[90] To give weight to this claim, Easthope recruits deconstruction, asserting that his paradigm breaches 'that inside/outside opposition, installing its subject in a different position altogether'.[91] This effectively forestalls the criticism that might be levelled against any metadiscourse by a poststructuralist critic – that it claims to stand outside its object in a quasi-scientific manner. However, Easthope's egalitarian ideal is hopelessly compromised by the fact that even the unwilling subject cannot escape the position of 'mastery' consequent on the proficiency in a critical model (even if it is decentred, deconstructive and anti-foundational) and its subsequent application. The designer of the paradigm, although scrupulously pointing out his historical location, is even less able to escape this embarrassing position. In addition, to design a critical model for cultural studies radically undermines Easthope's disavowal of disciplinary identity.

Furthermore, in practice 'mastery' is exactly what the paradigm delivers. Easthope sets it to work on a film thriller, modernist novel, cigarette advertisement, and nineteenth-century ballad. Barthes asserted that linguistic and non-linguistic signification are analogous and Easthope agrees that the advertisement 'must work as text, at the level of signification'.[92] He concludes that in decoding the cryptic symbolism of the advert, 'My imaginary security is

[87] Ibid., p. 234.
[88] Easthope, *Literary into Cultural Studies*, p. 138.
[89] Ibid., p. 129
[90] Ibid., p. 138.
[91] Ibid., p. 139.
[92] Ibid., p. 154.

confirmed both by my identification with Western imperialism as it imposes itself on its Oriental other and the operation of decoding by which I master the exciting and pleasurable otherness of this textuality.'[93] The stress on textuality leads Easthope to undertake a *literary* reading of an advertisement, that is one which explores its connotative complexity.

The analysis of Woolf's *To the Lighthouse* prioritizes sign system and gender. The modernist text is read quite sympathetically for the masculine/feminine discourse of Mr and Mrs Ramsay, modernist ambiguity, and the psychological drama played out between the Ramsays and their son, James. Less convincing, however, is the interpretation of Mr Ramsay's interior monologue on his own intelligence. This monologue reads:

> It was a splendid mind. For if thought is like the keyboard of a piano, divided into so many notes, or like the alphabet is ranged in twenty-six letters all in order, then his splendid mind had no sort of difficulty in running over those letters one by one, firmly and accurately, until it had reached, say, the letter Q. He reached Q. Very few people in the whole of England ever reach Q . . . But after Q? What comes next? . . . Still, if he could reach R it would be something . . . Q he was sure of. Q he could demonstrate. If Q then is Q – R – Here he knocked his pipe out . . .[94]

For Easthope, this 'enacts' Lacan's structuralist psychoanalysis; Mr Ramsay's 'position of security and mastery is confirmed by the seemingly transparent access signifier gives to the signified [as Easthope's is confirmed by decoding the Benson and Hedges advertisement] but undermined when he finds he cannot bring the effortless movement forward along the syntagmatic chain'.[95] Although Easthope's privileging of language is appropriate to the modernist text, the poststructuralist analogy is redundant to explain a passage which more simply depicts the sterile linear logic of the masculine imagination in opposition to Mrs Ramsay's more fertile feminine mind. There is little discussion of the institutional and ideological context of modernism and the assertion that 'formal features are *always* ideological' makes this omission unaccountable.[96] The loss of the disciplinary perspectives of sociology and history (Easthope himself was trained in traditional English), informs a method which appears as intransigent and as mystical as New Criticism.

Neither does Easthope's model seem entirely appropriate when applied to non-literary cultural forms. The paradigm formulated in *Literary into Cultural Studies* clearly underpins the comparative analysis of one of Wordsworth's Lucy

---

93   Ibid., p. 156.
94   Quoted ibid., p. 150.
95   Ibid., p. 150.
96   Ibid., p. 148.

poems and Madonna's 'Like a Prayer' in *Wordsworth Now and Then*.[97] In his reading, Easthope prioritizes the sign-system and the 'Other' and points to thematic links between the two texts. Both present a dream of self-fulfilment by means of an 'Other': for Wordsworth's speaker this Other is Lucy; for the singer of 'Like a Prayer', an unnamed addressee. Easthope also compares the voice: 'In both cases language is to be wholly expressive, full speech, completely rendering a self which is only itself.'[98] Easthope foregrounds the ideological link – bourgeois individualism – between Romantic ideas of self-presence in Wordsworth's poem and the modern theme of isolation in 'Like a Prayer'. However, not only does he privilege ideological content over poetic form, he again ignores specific context-ual factors, such as the production and consumption of the popular culture 'text'.

A broader analysis of Madonna's cultural significance actually undermines Easthope's argument for coherent bourgeois ideology. Madonna's success is founded not on her lyrical art or musical talent but on her skill as self-publicist and image constructor. She is famous for her serial self-creation, with reference to iconic cultural figures such as Marilyn Monroe ('Material Girl'), and cultural stereotypes of femininity ('Like a Virgin'). Like a mass-marketed Cindy Sherman, Madonna literally embodies not the 'myth' of coherent self-presence, but the postmodern *fragmented* self and constructed identity, thus contradicting Easthope's interpretation of the lyrics. Commentaries such as Camille Paglia's, which focus on Madonna's status as cultural icon and her manipulation of the virgin-whore stereotype, are likely to produce more germane conclusions than a poststructuralist analysis of her pop songs. This is the view taken by Paglia herself, debunking cultural studies in no uncertain terms:

> Current academic writing on Madonna . . . is of deplorably low quality. It is marked by inaccuracy, bathos, overinterpretation, overpoliticization, and grotesquely inappropriate jargon borrowed from pseudotechnical semiotics and moribund French theory. Under the misleading rubric 'cultural studies', intensely ambitious but not conspicuously talented, learned, or scrupulous humanities professors are scrabbling for position by exploiting pop culture and sensitive racial and sexual issues for their own professional purposes.[99]

It is clear that English methods still comprise a significant part of cultural studies' disciplinary make-up. However, Easthope's critical technique is inappropriate because it is a version of close reading applied to the diverse forms of popular culture. Eagleton asserts that 'literary theory can handle Bob Dylan just as well

---

[97]   Antony Easthope, *Wordsworth Now and Then: Romanticism and Contemporary Culture* (Buckingham: Open University Press, 1993).

[98]   Ibid., p. 126.

[99]   Camille Paglia, *Vamps and Tramps* (London: Penguin, 1995), p. 372.

as John Milton', but the application of literary-critical methods to non-literary forms marks a failure to engage with significant contextual *and* formal differences in the object of analysis.[100] Although Easthope mentions the fact that 'Like a Prayer' is not a poem but a song with accompanying video, this is merely an aside and does not inform his analysis to any significant extent. Although song lyrics, unlike a cigarette advertisement, do have textual form, to 'read' a pop song in this way is to neglect significant differences. The practice of referring to non-literary cultural forms, visual or aural media, even *events* as texts, is misnomic, the product of an undiscriminating textualism. Video, pop music, film, dance, fashion, are *not* written or literary texts and warrant specific forms of analysis reflecting their technical composition and cultural/social context, rather than a blanket semiological or *literary* approach. The methodologies developed by one discipline, such as English, may be inappropriate or useless when applied to the objects and endemic problems of another. The accessibility of popular culture does not justify the waiving of specialist knowledge and forms of analysis. The yoking together of disparate cultural forms extends the realm of cultural studies manifesting the colonizing impulse more often imputed to English. Easthope concedes that 'there is nothing inherent in the intellectual schema which would stop the kind of paradigm, method and object of study I've advocated leading to no more than the cultural imperialism Fish foresees, no more than the growth and perpetuation of a revised form of literary studies'.[101] Colonization is an appropriate metaphor in that imported infrastructures have often proved both inadequate and inappropriate in a different context. The ideal of early cultural studies as an interdisciplinary *field* should not be forgotten. Cultural studies would function better as an umbrella term, like the humanities, operating as a faculty, centre, or field, supporting interdisciplinary research in the arts and social sciences.[102]

Although cultural studies has an anti-disciplinary rationale, it has already been institutionally validated as a discipline and because of its overlap with English represents a real threat since institutions are unlikely to have the resources to support two departments. English should answer the criticisms of cultural studies where relevant, although criticisms of monolithic imperialism are unjust. Easthope makes a dismissive reference to the 'conventional literary studies account' of *To the Lighthouse* which would mistakenly privilege the unified text over gendered discourse, but this is again founded on an outmoded conception of English. English is already capable of producing a reading which surpasses his in terms of addressing historical context and ideology, as well as sign-system and gender, but is clearly in a state of methodological confusion.

---

[100]   Eagleton, *Literary Theory*, p. 205.

[101]   Easthope, *Literary into Cultural Studies*, p. 178.

[102]   Although Birmingham now offers undergraduate degrees in cultural studies, the CCCS initially supported only postgraduate work.

The ethos and history of different universities will inform their attitudes towards English and cultural studies; ex-polytechnics favour interdisciplinary cultural studies, while older universities have an established English tradition. The future of English, which is a consistently good recruiter, will depend upon institutional funding, policies and politics. But for the sake both of intellectual rigour and disciplinary coherence, literary studies should reject the more impracticable ideals of postmodernism such as 'non-mastery' and continue to promote knowledge acquisition and competence in disciplinary methods (as well as the institutionally required 'transferable skills'). It should re-establish itself as a discipline with a distinct and coherent methodology, while selecting what is relevant from postmodern theory and engaging with the world outside the text. This model for contemporary literary studies is formulated as a strategic response to Easthope's aggressive cultural studies, although actually it overlaps with his paradigm because of the historical connections between the two disciplines and the fact that post-New Critical English has already incorporated alternative theories and approaches. Where the literary studies paradigm differs most obviously from Easthope's model is in citing a foundational practice, that is close reading and formal analysis. The literary critic should also be equipped to analyse the historical context and ideological content of the literary text but should consider social identity not only as a rhetorical construction, as textualist cultural studies tends to do, but also in relation to political, economic and social conditions and historical events. The English degree associated with the proposed paradigm would require a competence in grammar, rhetoric and composition after the traditional American model. But while this would mean that the student possessed the requisite skills to analyse 'government proclamations, diplomatic communiqués and advertising copy', as Easthope recommends, and to undertake an authoritative comparative analysis of literary and non-literary texts, practical disciplinary constraints and historical convention mean that the literary text would take priority over the non-literary.[103] And although an understanding of the complex interrelation between literature as high culture and popular fiction *is* relevant to English, the persistence of modernist criteria of literary value means that the high cultural form should still be privileged. English should retain its traditional disciplinary identity and object and be extremely wary when approaching the non-textual forms with which neither it nor textualist cultural studies is fully equipped to cope.

Many of those who theorize and teach English are aware of the need for a disciplinary overhaul. In *The Crisis in Criticism*, William Cain argues for a reformed English studies which 'draw[s] on many disciplines, dispute[s] the barriers between the literary and non-literary, contest[s] the opposition between the canonical and non-canonical, and exhibit[s] critical skills in a variety of

---

[103] Easthope, *Literary into Cultural Studies*, p. 177.

culturally oriented ways'.[104] This is too vague, betrays the influence of metaphysical deconstruction, and goes too far towards cultural studies. Leavis's agenda in *The Common Pursuit* is still germane:

> to insist that literary criticism is, or should be, a specific discipline of intelligence is not to suggest that a serious interest in literature can confine itself to the kind of intensive local analysis associated with 'practical criticism' – to the scrutiny of the 'words on the page' in their minute relations, their effects of imagery and so on: a real literary interest is an interest in man, society and civilization, and its boundaries cannot be drawn; the adjective is not a circumscribing one.[105]

Adjectives may not circumscribe the boundaries of literary criticism but institutions do. In *Politics and Value in Literary Studies*, Guy and Small argue more pragmatically that English must stop regarding itself as a special case and compete with other disciplines; it should 'possess a clearly defined object of study, a set of specialist practices appropriate to explaining it, a theory (or theories) of those practices, and ways of evaluating theories'.[106] English need neither uphold New Critical methods, canonical literature, and conservative values for their own sake, nor accept literary theory uncritically. What is required is a mediation between the two extremes.

---

104 Cain, *The Crisis in Criticism*, p. xvii.
105 Leavis, *The Common Pursuit*, p. 200.
106 Guy and Small, *Politics and Value in Literary Studies*, p. 156.

PART III

Chapter 6

Reason and Rhetoric

. . . to crack the wind of the poor phrase, Running it thus . . . (*Hamlet* I iii 108–9)

For postmodern philosophers and literary theorists, rhetoric is in vogue and formal logic distinctly unfashionable. A number of factors have conspired to favour rhetoric throughout the twentieth century. Traditionally, philosophy was thought to transcend the vagaries of natural language, but in the most recent twist of the linguistic turn, deconstruction has cast suspicion over such pretensions. Enfeebled rational argument is now presented as leaning heavily on rhetoric and poststructuralists reveal and revel in the literary figures in 'neutral' philosophical texts. Postmodern anti-foundationalism and poststructuralist anti-logocentrism dictate that truth, the traditional objective of logic, is no longer a fitting goal for the philosopher. Formal logic aside, it is undeniable that reason and rhetoric are interdependent since philosophy is mediated through language. However, for the purposes of critical analysis the classical distinction between rational argument and literary style should be reinstated because the 'collapse' of the reason/rhetoric binary can function both to diminish the precision of critical analysis and to endorse logically faulty or specious argument. Classical distinctions are necessary to analyse the abuses of rhetoric in postmodern theory.

Michel Meyer asserts that metaphysics from Plato to Heidegger 'forgot rhetoric'.[1] It is clear, however, that philosophy and rhetoric are entangled even in Plato's hierarchical scheme. For the Plato of the *Gorgias* rhetoric was vastly inferior to philosophy because while philosophy's purpose was to establish truth, rhetoric was concerned solely with persuasion and was therefore susceptible to political corruption. In the *Phaedrus* the state of contemporary rhetoric is epitomised by the Attic orator, Lysias; Socrates asserts that his discipline cannot be a true art since it has no respect for truth and the good, but is concerned merely with effect {260*e*}. The Sophists, with whom Lysias is identified, were concerned with the art of persuasion (primarily the pleading of a case in court), irrespective of any moral dimension, and it was this amoral aspect which was particularly repugnant to Plato. Socrates ridicules rhetoric and the 'niceties of the art', but he is at the same time concerned to elevate rhetoric by infusing it with the ideals and methods of philosophy: the pursuit of the true and the good by means of the dialectic {266*e*}.

The dialectic is presented in the *Republic* as a form of deductive reasoning by which metaphysical knowledge may be attained:

---

[1]   Michel Meyer (ed.), *From Metaphysics to Rhetoric* (London: Kluwer, 1989), p. 1.

that which the reason itself lays hold of by the power of dialectic, treating
its assumptions not as absolute beginnings but literally as hypotheses . . .
to enable it to rise to that which requires no assumption and is the starting
point of all, and after attaining to that again taking hold of the first
dependencies from it, so to proceed downward to the conclusion, making
no use whatever of any object of sense but only of pure ideas moving on
through ideas to ideas and ending with ideas {511*b–c*}.

In the *Phaedrus*, the dialectic is described as a method of classification:
'divisions and collections' {266*b*}. The procedure is twofold: first, 'bring a
dispersed plurality under a single form . . . and thus to make plain whatever may
be chosen as the topic for exposition; second, 'divide into forms' {265*d–e*}. The
dialectic is designed to map and classify the objective structure of reality and in
both the *Republic* and the *Phaedrus* represents the epitome of logocentrism. The
primary object of both the dialectic and 'good' rhetoric is the soul: 'if we are to
address people scientifically, we shall show them precisely what is the real and
true nature of that object on which our discourse is brought to bear. And that
object . . . is the soul' {270*e*}. With an understanding of the different types of
soul, achieved by the application of the dialectic, the orator can then select the
most suitable and influential mode of discourse. Socrates summarizes:

The conditions to be fulfilled are these: first, you must know the truth
about the subject that you speak or write about: that is to say, you must be
able to isolate it in definition, and having so defined it you must next
understand how to divide it into kinds, until you reach the limit of division;
secondly, you must have a corresponding discernment of the nature of the
soul, discover the type of speech appropriate to each nature, and order and
arrange your discourse accordingly, addressing a variegated soul in a
variegated style that ranges over the whole gamut of tones, and a simple
soul in a simple style{277*b–c*}.

It was Aristotle, influenced by Plato's dialectical method, who formalized
both logic and rhetoric. In the *Prior Analytics*, which is regarded as the first
treatise on the science of formal logic, Aristotle defines deduction as a 'discourse
in which, certain things being stated, something other than what is stated follows
of necessity from their being so' {24*b*}.[2] In the language of formal logic, that
which is stated is the premiss and that which follows is the conclusion. The
simplest form of logical deduction formulated by Aristotle is the syllogism which
can be illustrated as follows: all dogs smell (major premiss); Rex is a dog (minor
premiss); therefore Rex smells (conclusion). The syllogism is governed by the
law of non-contradiction: it is not possible to assert the premiss and deny the
conclusion without contradicting oneself. If I deny the conclusion, that Rex

---

[2]		*The Complete Works of Aristotle*, ed. Jonathan Barnes (Oxford: Princeton
University Press, 1984).

smells, it then follows that I am also contradicting either the major premiss, that all dogs smell, or the minor premiss, that Rex is a dog.

The main criticism levelled at Aristotle's system of deductive inference by modern commentators is that it cannot account for all properties and relations. Michael Bybee, for example, suggests that Aristotle's exclusion of induction and his ignorance of abduction (form of syllogism of which the major premiss is true but the minor premiss is only probable) accounts for the paucity of his system.[3] One irreconcilable difference between postmodern and classical philosophers appears to be their respective attitudes towards truth. For Plato, truth is the ultimate good and end of the dialectic, while for Derrida logocentrism is the object of deconstruction. For Aristotle, truth is desirable, but not the inevitable outcome of logical reasoning. In the *Prior Analytics* he states that in philosophy, 'We must look for the attributes and the subjects of both our terms . . . in the pursuit of truth starting from an arrangement of the terms in accordance with truth . . . while if we look for dialectical deductions we must start from plausible propositions' {46a}. However, the truth value of the logical conclusion is always contingent on the truth of the premisses: 'It is clear then that if the conclusion is false, the premisses of the argument must be false, either all or some of them; but when the conclusion is true, it is not necessary that the premisses should be true . . . yet it is possible, though no part of the deduction is true, that the conclusion may none the less be true; but not necessarily' {57a–b}. So although logic theoretically represents an infallible means to establish the truth, valid reasoning provides only a conditional guarantee and depends ultimately on the truth of the stated premisses. Deductive reasoning is therefore technically 'absolved' from logocentrism by means of this truth/validity distinction.

Aristotelian logic continues to inform modern philosophical logic; however, its schematic, abstract, and mathematical form means that not only is it uncongenial to literary theorists as a highly complex and specialized branch of philosophy, it is also inaccessible to many. This is not true of rhetoric, which historically has comprised a part of English education, particularly in America. For Aristotle, the first part of rhetoric consisted of the finding of arguments or proofs and the second the arrangement of these arguments: 'the only necessary parts of a speech are the statement and the argument. These are the essential features of a speech; and it cannot in any case have more than introduction, statement, argument, and epilogue' {1414b}. The third part of rhetoric is style and there are three levels: plain or low, middle or forcible, and high or florid. Each has appropriate choices of vocabulary, tropes, grammar, syntax and rhythm. It is the third division of rhetoric which is closest to the literary or dramatic art discussed in the *Poetics* and in the *Rhetoric* Aristotle states, 'It was naturally the poets who first set the movement going; for words represent things' {1404a}. This division is described as 'having a small but real importance' since 'speeches

---

[3]   Michael D. Bybee, 'Logic in Rhetoric – And Vice Versa', *Philosophy and Rhetoric* 26, 3 (1993), 169–90.

of the written kind owe more of their effect to their language than to their thought' {1404a}. The fourth division of rhetoric is *memoria* – simply the memorizing of speeches – and the fifth, regarded by Aristotle as minor but necessary, is delivery (voice projection and gesture). Classical rhetoric includes an element of logic. In addition to the five divisions of rhetoric, there are three modes of persuasion considered to be properly rhetorical. The first of these is *ethos* (ethical appeal), which 'depends on the personal character of the speaker' {1358a}. The second is *pathos* (emotional appeal), 'when the speech stirs their emotions' {1358a}. It is the third mode of persuasion, *logos* (rational appeal), which most clearly draws on the *Prior Analytics*: 'through speech itself when we have proved a truth or an apparent truth by means of the persuasive arguments suitable to the case in question' {1358a}. The emphasis throughout is on propriety: the appropriate argument, form, devices and mode of persuasion should be chosen for the particular situation, subject and audience.

Aristotle did not posit a rigid demarcation between logic and rhetoric, quite the reverse: 'rhetoric is a combination of the sciences of logic and of ethics; and it is partly like dialectic, partly like sophistical reasoning' {1359b}. Logic is an essential component of rhetoric because to be in command of the three modes of rhetorical persuasion a man must 'be able to reason logically' {1358a}. Like Plato, Aristotle is dismissive of empty rhetoric; according to Jonathan Barnes, 'one of Aristotle's main claims in the *Gryllus* [not extant] was that rhetoric should not excite the passions by fine language but should rather persuade the reason by fine argument'.[4] However, unlike Plato, Aristotle recommends incorporating logic in the service of persuasion rather than truth and in this sense his rhetoric approaches sophism or bad rhetoric. He advises in rhetorical discourse the substitution of the syllogism by the *enthymeme*, a form of partial syllogism where either one of the premises or the conclusion is left unstated: 'he who is best able to see how and from what elements a deduction is produced will also be best skilled in the enthymeme, when he has further learnt what its subject-matter is and in what respects it differs from the deductions of logic' {1355a}. It is significant that Aristotle also advises the logician on rhetorical strategies in the *Prior Analytics*:

> In order to avoid being argued down, we must take care, whenever an opponent sets up an argument without disclosing the conclusions, not to grant him the same term twice over in his propositions, since we know that a deduction cannot be drawn without a middle term, and that a term which is stated more than once is the middle {66a}.

Not only does classical rhetoric incorporate logical reasoning, then, but logic is at times supplemented by rhetoric.

Aristotle refers frequently to both the *Analytics* and *Poetics* throughout the

---

[4]	Jonathan Barnes, *Aristotle* (Oxford: Oxford University Press, 1982), p. 20.

Rhetoric and in disciplinary terms rhetoric has shuttled between literature and philosophy.[5] In the early twentieth century there was an attempt to reinstate classical rhetoric within the American English degree.[6] In the 1920s rhetoric enjoyed a revival at Cornell University and the New Critics, or 'new rhetoricians' including Cleanth Brooks and Robert Penn Warren, followed this revival in seeking to reintroduce the rational element of rhetoric, following its near obliteration in literary studies. In *The Philosophy of Rhetoric*, a collection of lectures originally delivered at Harvard University, I.A. Richards referred to rhetoric as the 'dreariest and least profitable part of . . . freshman English!'[7] Richards advocates a revised discipline which is 'a persistent, systematic, detailed inquiry into how words work'. This 'must be philosophic' in that it should 'take charge of the criticism of its own assumptions', something not often associated with close reading.[8] Richards draws on Plato's dialectic (without naming it): 'The theorem holds that we *begin* with the general abstract anything, split it, as the world makes us, into sorts and then arrive at concrete particulars by the overlapping or common membership of these sorts.'[9] He continues, 'All thinking from the lowest to the highest . . . is sorting.'[10] Richards not only salvaged classical rhetoric but modernized it by drawing on contemporary developments in psychology and linguistics.

In Britain rhetoric was not such an important element of university English, in spite of Richards's influence. But as classical rhetoric was being revived in America, British philosophy was undergoing its linguistic turn. This, at least in the early stages, did not mark a turn to rhetoric, but rather the persistence of a logical-mathematical ideal instituted by Descartes. Descartes had wished for a discipline which would provide a surety equivalent to that of mathematics: 'a form of "knowledge" which should "attain a certitude equal to that of the demonstrations of Arithmetic and Geometry"'.[11] Logic itself became increasingly

---

[5]   In the Middle Ages, rhetoric was an essential component of education as part of the trivium: the university course of grammar, rhetoric and logic. But because of this demarcation, rhetoric was confined mainly to epideictic display and letter-writing. In the Renaissance Peter Ramus, a French philosopher, divided logic and rhetoric while the seventeenth century generally saw the blurring of the boundaries. Rhetoric was also adopted by literary studies; critics as early as Horace claimed for poetry the instructive function of rhetoric (Art of Poetry). With Romanticism there was a revival of interest in *elocutio* (delivery) but the stress on the expressive meant that the logical element of rhetoric was largely ignored.

[6]   See Edward P.J. Corbett, *Classical Rhetoric for the Modern Student* (New York: Oxford University Press, 1965), pp. 535–68.

[7]   I.A. Richards, *The Philosophy of Rhetoric* (London: Oxford University Press, 1936), p. 3.

[8]   Ibid., p. 23.

[9]   Ibid., p. 31.

[10]   Ibid., p. 30.

[11]   *The Philosophical Works of Descartes* I, trans. E. Haldane and G.R.T. Ross, 2nd edn (Cambridge: Cambridge University Press, 1931), p. 5.

mathematical in the nineteenth century with Gottlob Frege's attempt to establish the logical form of language and the development of predicate calculus, which turned logic into a form of algebra. In a professional relationship mimicking that of Plato and Aristotle, Frege's theories were then fully systematized by Bertrand Russell, who presented pure mathematics as a development from logic, most notably with A.N. Whitehead in *Principia Mathematica*. Russell was interested in the logical properties of language and in the *History of Western Philosophy* affirmed that the methods of modern analytic empiricism, with 'its incorporation of mathematics and its development of a powerful logical technique', would render 'many ancient problems . . . completely soluble'.[12] This faith in the ability of logic to solve philosophical problems without residue is very much in the classical vein. Wittgenstein, a pupil of Russell at Cambridge, regarded logic in a less rosy light and in the *Tractatus Logico-Philosophicus* chose instead to foreground its self-referential nature in a thoroughly logical fashion: 'The propositions of logic are tautologies. The propositions of logic therefore say nothing [about the world]' {6.1–6.11}.[13] Aristotle's introduction of schematic letters enabled the formulation of a truly abstract system. Although the syllogism *may* be applied, it does not have to be and its 'algebraic' terms do not necessarily refer to anything outside the system. If the terms of logic are neither connotative *nor* denotative but self-referential, then logic can be said to escape rhetoric whereas 'ordinary-language' ontology, epistemology or metaphysics may not. Wittgenstein was preoccupied with the bounds of language and the implications of these limitations for the philosopher; in *Philosophical Investigations* he anticipated aspects of poststructuralist theory by rejecting the possibility of an all-encompassing philosophical metalanguage.

Twentieth-century philosophers and literary critics have been increasingly willing to admit that there is no possibility of philosophy escaping rhetoric entirely. In *Anatomy of Criticism* Northrop Frye denounces 'conceptual rhetoric' which he construes as an attempt to avoid the emotive and the literary in order to achieve 'the direct union of grammar and logic'.[14] He states that 'all structures in words are partly rhetorical, and hence literary, and . . . the notion of a scientific or philosophical verbal structure free of rhetorical elements is an illusion.'[15] This is clearly not the case with formal logic. Brooks and Warren distinguish between poetic and scientific language, upholding the possibility of 'strictly notational statement', such as mathematical or geometrical proposition, which does not require metaphor. Such statements, they claim 'are (or aspire to be) pure

	[12]	Bertrand Russell, *History of Western Philosophy*, 2nd edn (London: Unwin, 1979), p. 788.
	[13]	Ludwig Wittgenstein, *Tractatus Logico-Philosophicus* (London: Routledge & Kegan Paul, 1922).
	[14]	Northrop Frye, *Anatomy of Criticism: Four Essays* (London: Penguin, 1957), p. 331.
	[15]	Frye, *Anatomy of Criticism*, p. 350.

denotations'.[16] However when abstract logic is applied, natural language and figurativity necessarily return. As Frye puts it, 'Anything which makes a functional use of words will always be involved in all the technical problems of words, including rhetorical problems.'[17] Descartes's geometric ideal was doomed to failure since the transition from mathematical to natural language means that the self-referential quality of formal logic is lost. It is precisely the transcendence of formal language which explains its conspicuous failure as philosophy and its irrelevance for humanities intellectuals – not merely is it, technically speaking, tautologous, it is sterile and fails to 'speak' to the human condition.

A positive turn towards philosophical rhetoric has been taken by another set of New Rhetoricians, who share Wittgenstein's distaste for reductive formal logic but promote instead 'informal', 'non-formal' or 'fuzzy' logic (something like Aristotle's rhetorical *logos* or appeal to reason).[18] Chaïm Perelman, a figurehead for this movement, favours informal logic (argumentation) over formal logic because of the essential limitations of the latter to the axioms and rules of deduction.[19] Jean-Blaise Grize compares 'non-formal' arguments favourably with formal logic whose 'conclusion must contain nothing that was not already present in the premises. It is for this very reason that logic lays itself open to the criticism of sterility'.[20] Martin Warner follows Pascal's rejection of Descartes' 'geometric ideal' and suggests as an alternative 'philosophical finesse', which he defines as 'a term of art introduced, after the manner of Pascal, to designate a certain range of patterns of ratiocination which do not easily fit the geometric model'.[21] In *Rhetoric, Language, and Reason* Meyer asserts that logic on its own 'works only with the answers and their links, while rhetoric concentrates on the relationship between questions and answers'.[22] Meyer argues that rhetoric or 'argumentation' has the ethical edge over formal logic since it is required to argue its case rather than simply relying on the rules of deduction. He constructs a Platonic hierarchy by distinguishing between '*evil rhetoric*' (persuasion), which suppresses questioning and is 'little more than manipulative discourse', and a positive,

[16] Cleanth Brooks and Robert Penn Warren, *Modern Rhetoric*, shorter 3rd edn (New York: Harcourt Brace Jovanovich, 1972), p. 319.

[17] Frye, *Anatomy of Criticism*, p. 331.

[18] See Chaïm Perelman and L. Olbrechts-Tyteca, *The New Rhetoric: A Treatise on Argumentation*, trans. John Wilkinson and Purcell Weaver (Notre Dame: University of Notre Dame Press, 1971) and Chaïm Perelman, *The New Rhetoric and the Humanities* (Dordrecht: Reidel, 1979).

[19] Chaïm Perelman, 'Formal Logic and Informal Logic' in *From Metaphysics to Rhetoric*, ed. Michel Meyer (London: Kluwer, 1989), p. 9.

[20] Jean-Blaise Grize, 'To Reason While Speaking' in *From Metaphysics to Rhetoric*, ed. Michel Meyer (London: Kluwer, 1989), p. 40.

[21] Martin Warner, *Philosophical Finesse: Studies in the Art of Rational Persuasion* (Oxford: Clarendon, 1989), pp. 361, 333.

[22] Michel Meyer, *Rhetoric, Language, and Reason* (University Park: Pennsylvania State University Press, 1994), pp. 155, 156.

interrogative rhetoric – 'problematology' – which foregrounds questioning.[23] He proposes that this form of rhetoric will overcome the opposition of metaphysics and rhetoric and encourage 'a new rhetoric and a metaphysics which would no longer be ontological'.[24] Problematology is a modest scheme designed 'to integrate argumentation and logic, figurative and literal language, knowledge and literature, into one overall conception of thinking as it actually takes place, without favouring any *a priori* norm of reason.'[25] Meyer claims that not only does problematological rhetoric transcend the opposition between metaphysics and rhetoric, it also 'transcends the classical opposition between the rhetoric of *figures* (or literary rhetoric) and the rhetoric of *conflict* (or argumentation, legal or not)'.[26] These New Rhetoricians combine classic and poststructuralist traits, seeking to transcend classical oppositions but retaining a Platonic logocentrism. Meyer, for example, still appeals to truth as the ultimate good: 'rhetoric has reemerged as a new form of truth of language and reasoning, the truth of man as an individual'.[27] Jean Ladrière argues that the establishment of truth by means of deduction must always have recourse to argumentation in order to persuade of the truth of the propositions or premises: 'Validity, in an axiomatized system, is precisely nothing more than a representation of the truth of the represented propositions. And, finally, it is this truth which counts. The discovery of truth is never *entirely* analytic.'[28] Enlightenment notions such as truth and reason are not placed within the obligatory scare quotes of anti-foundational postmodernism and since the New Rhetoric suffers from that metaphysical complaint, nostalgia for truth, it cannot be classed as postmodernist.

The philosophical New Rhetoric of Perelman et al., with its commitment to truth and reason, should be distinguished from an equally 'serious' but ultimately specious postmodern rhetoric which substitutes argument for epideictic display. Ian Angus and Lenore Langsdorf, editors of *Unsettled Borders: Envisioning Critique at the Postmodern Site*, maintain that postmodernism has blurred the boundaries between rhetoric and philosophy, producing instead a (Hegelian) dialectic: 'Rather than each limiting and devaluing the other, both extend into and require the other. The very means for conceptualizing dualities of reason and speech, knowledge and persuasion, truth and opinion – in short, mind and body – are annulled.'[29] Following Derrida, Angus asserts that postmodern discourse is *neither* local *nor* universal, neither internally nor externally legitimated, but

---

[23]   Ibid., p. 155.
[24]   Meyer, *From Metaphysics to Rhetoric*, p. 7.
[25]   Meyer, *Rhetoric, Language, and Reason*, p. 4.
[26]   Ibid., pp. 155–6.
[27]   Ibid., p. 5.
[28]   Jean Ladrière, 'Logic and Argumentation' in *From Metaphysics to Rhetoric*, ed. Michel Meyer (London: Kluwer, 1989), p. 22.
[29]   Ian Angus and Lenore Langsdorf (eds), *The Critical Turn: Rhetoric and Philosophy in Postmodern Discourse* (Carbondale and Edwardsville: Southern Illinois University Press, 1993), p. 14.

hovers somewhere between the two. He sets rhetoric against metaphysics (rather than logic), the totalizing discourse which attempts to incorporate ('translate') all other discourses. However, there is always an untranslatable remainder and the identification of this remainder is the job of rhetorical criticism, which 'operates at the moment of translation' to recover plurality.[30] There is still an obstinate 'philosophical nodal point that cannot be inscribed within rhetoric'.[31] This 'nodal point' is *silence*, which marks the traditional closure of philosophic discourse on a transcendental signified (truth) and thereby the escape from the condition of discourse. Such postmodern rhetorics have simply lost interest in logic, formal or otherwise, preferring to manufacture an endlessly proliferating 'discourse', which in this case leans heavily on an over-used metaphor (see below). It is perhaps significant that Perelman was a philosopher who wrote his doctoral thesis on Frege while Angus is a lecturer in communications.[32]

Even though ordinary language philosophy is necessarily rhetorical, this does not mean it has been granted a full poetic licence. It has always been expected to follow the rules of logic and the conventions of argumentation. Calvin Schrag and David Miller state that in 'White Mythologies', 'Derrida . . . appears ready to embrace the collapse of philosophy into rhetoric'.[33] He certainly jettisons the logocentric ideal of both logic and rhetoric and co-implicates reason and rhetoric, but categorically excludes mathematical logic and all 'purely formal' discourses from the rule of metaphor: 'Outside the mathematical text – which it is difficult to conceive as providing metaphors in the strict sense, since it is attached to no determined ontic region and has no empirical sensory content'.[34] Commentators are divided on Derrida's commitment to argumentative rigour, but most concede that there is a noticeable shift from the relatively conventional early work to the increasingly experimental texts such as *Glas*. Richard Rorty asserts that since 1975, Derrida's work 'has . . . become much less easy to interpret as argumentative', ascribing this change to a desire to evade the charge of 'negative theology'.[35] Peggy Kamuf likewise notes the difference between 'early' and 'late'

[30]   Ian Angus, 'Learning to Stop: A Critique of General Rhetoric' in *The Critical Turn: Rhetoric and Philosophy in Postmodern Discourse*, ed. Ian Angus and Lenore Langsdorf (Carbondale and Edwardsville: Southern Illinois University Press, 1993), p. 199.
[31]   Ibid., p. 184.
[32]   See James L. Golden and Joseph J. Pilotta (eds), *Practical Reasoning in Human Affairs: Studies in Honour of Chaïm Perelman* (Dordrecht: Reidel, 1986), p. 3.
[33]   Calvin O. Schrag and David James Miller, 'Communication Studies and Philosophy: Convergence Without Coincidence' in *The Critical Turn: Rhetoric and Philosophy in Postmodern Discourse*, ed. Ian Angus and Lenore Langsdorf (Carbondale and Edwardsville: Southern Illinois University Press, 1993), p. 129.
[34]   Jacques Derrida, *Margins of Philosophy*, trans. Alan Bass (London: Harvester Wheatsheaf, 1982), p. 227.
[35]   Richard Rorty, 'Two Meanings of "Logocentrism": A Reply to Norris' in *Redrawing the Lines: Analytic Philosophy, Deconstruction and Literary Theory*, ed. Reed Way Dasenbrock (Minneapolis: University of Minnesota Press, 1989), p. 215. See also

Derrida, although she still claims a certain philosophical rigour for *Glas* and *The Post Card*:

> Although it would be misleading to understand these earlier works as in some simple way more systematic than his later work, Derrida himself recognizes in 'The Time of a Thesis' that they conform perhaps more readily to some standard expectations governing discursive exposition of a thesis. In subsequent writings, most notably *Glas* (1974), *The Truth in Painting* (1978), and *The Post Card* (1980), these constraints are greatly loosened as Derrida moves beyond thematic considerations of writing as formal spacing and attempts new, active determinations of the relation between theme and form.[36]

Christopher Norris argues along the same lines that Derrida's work, particularly his early work, is rigorous and analytical by the strictest philosophical standards. Norris admits that later texts, such as *Glas* and *The Postcard*, are the most appealing for those who wish to maintain the textuality of philosophy. He states that although in recent work Derrida 'seems less concerned with arguments and more inclined to exploit the various possibilities of noncommunication and cross-purpose exchange. Even here . . . Derrida is resuming issues and problems that are worked over with meticulous care in his more "philosophical" texts'.[37] Although this implies that the later texts lack this 'meticulous care', Norris still wishes to claim such texts for the philosophical, rather than the literary-critical camp and attacks those critics who cannot see past Derrida's rhetoric: 'Their mistake is to suppose that first-rate philosophy – analytic work of the highest order – cannot be conducted in a style that partakes of certain "literary" figures and devices, or which makes its point through a skilful interweaving of constative and performative speech-act genres.'[38] Norris is in no doubt that *all* Derrida's writing can sustain a rigorous philosophical critique. He attacks the idea, propagated by certain Anglo-American detractors of poststructuralism such as John Ellis, that deconstruction constitutes a hermeneutic licence, maintains that this idea is totally refuted by an examination of Derrida's texts and suggests that Ellis's interpretation results from an insufficient acquaintance with the actual texts. In summing up Derrida's 'three greatest virtues', Norris remarks that he:

Reed Way Dasenbrock (ed.), *Redrawing the Lines: Analytic Philosophy, Deconstruction and Literary Theory* (Minneapolis: University of Minnesota Press, 1989), p. 15.

[36] *A Derrida Reader: Between the Blinds*, ed. Peggy Kamuf (London: Harvester Wheatsheaf, 1991), p. 5.

[37] Christopher Norris, 'Philosophy as Not Just a "Kind of Writing": Derrida and the Claim of Reason' in *Redrawing the Lines: Analytic Philosophy, Deconstruction and Literary Theory*, ed. Reed Way Dasenbrock (Minneapolis: University of Minnesota Press, 1989), p. 195.

[38] Christopher Norris, *What's Wrong with Postmodernism: Critical Theory and the Ends of Philosophy* (London: Harvester, 1990), p. 145.

combines a quite extraordinary range and depth of philosophical thought with a keen analytical intelligence *and* (by no means incompatible with these) a degree of stylistic virtuosity that allows his writing to reflect at every point on its own performative aspect, or on issues raised in and through the practice of an answerable 'literary' style.[39]

Such defences of Derrida rely upon the separation of argument and performance, style and content, rhetoric and logic. Although Norris asserts that logic, grammar and rhetoric are 'co-implicated', he nevertheless retains clear lines of demarcation between these different orders; the term 'interweaving' suggests that it is possible to 'unravel' these elements. In fact this metaphor has already been worked extensively in a similar context by Derrida himself. In a reading of Husserl's phenomenology Derrida uses one of Husserl's own metaphors to pick holes in his argument. Summarizing Husserl, Derrida states: 'The "strata" [form and meaning] are "woven", their intercomplication is such that the warp cannot be distinguished from the woof.'[40] Furthermore, 'what is woven as language is that the discursive warp cannot be construed as warp and takes the place of a woof which has not truly preceded it'.[41] However, the phenomenologist's 'patience and scrupulousness must, in principle, undo the tangle'.[42] Derrida's own practice is to tangle 'warp' and 'woof', logic and rhetoric, literature and philosophy, in a distinctive way.

While it would be ridiculous to state that Derrida's texts comprise conventional models of philosophical argumentation, it is obvious that the later, more performative work moves further in the direction of rhetorical 'excess' and the unconventional philosophical style proves problematic for the critic. Lee Brown asserts that the 'Separation of important persuasive strategies from eccentricities and ornaments in Wittgenstein, Nietzsche, and Heidegger have posed well-known hermeneutic difficulties.'[43] In the case of Derrida it is necessary to address the concept of 'enactment' whereby the deconstructive style (elliptical, 'excessive', difficult to decipher) is designed to express certain principles of deconstruction such as the polysemic nature of language, anti-logocentrism, *différance*. Derrida appears to conflate the poles of applied deconstructive logic and rhetoric, leaving little space for conventional argumentation. But although it is necessary to appreciate the importance and function of Derrida's style and his deliberate transgression of classical logical and rhetorical conventions, since he declares his necessary subscription to metaphysics and its logical laws, it is not inappropriate to reapply these laws in the analysis of his writing.

[39] Ibid., p. 160.
[40] Derrida, *Margins of Philosophy*, p. 160.
[41] Ibid., p. 160.
[42] Ibid., p. 161.
[43] Lee B. Brown, 'Philosophy, Rhetoric, and Style', *The Monist* 63, 4 (1980), 429.

Différance obviously transgresses the Aristotelian law of contradiction, as formulated in the *Metaphysics*, which dictates that it is impossible 'for the same thing to be and not to be' {1006*a*}. For Aristotle, presence (existence) cannot be predicated of something, it is rather the condition of predication. Derrida quotes Benveniste to this effect in 'The Supplement of Copula': '"Beyond the Aristotelian terms, above that categorization, there is the notion of 'being' which envelops everything. Without being a predicate itself, 'being' is the condition of all predicates".'[44] His assertion that *différance* has no identity at all (no essence or existence) may therefore be designed to exempt it from Aristotelian law. If Derrida can remove *différance* from the realm of being or existence then he can claim it as a non-logocentric (non-)concept. David Wood notes a contradiction in Derrida's work 'between different texts on the subject of the status of différance' and compares Derrida's position on non-conceptuality in 'Différance' with that in *Positions*.[45] Paradox is, of course, the very essence of *différance*: 'Here we are touching upon the point of greatest obscurity, on the very enigma of *différance*, on precisely that which divides its very concept by means of a strange cleavage.'[46] Gayatri Spivak leaps to the defence of this 'strange cleavage' in deconstruction in her preface to *Of Grammatology*:

> The deconstructive reader exposes the grammatological structure of the text . . . by locating the moment in the text which harbors the unbalancing of the equation, the sleight of hand at the limit of a text which cannot be dismissed simply as a contradiction.[47]

In fact, for Spivak, the very 'word "Grammatology" thus appropriately *keeps alive* an unresolved contradiction'.[48] The imposition of a logical analysis upon the text of 'Différance' is likely to produce just such a dismissal and Derrida therefore discourages this type of analysis: 'If *différance* is unthinkable in this way, perhaps we should not hasten to make it evident, in the philosophical element of evidentiality which would make short work of dissipating the mirage and illogicalness of *différance*.'[49] In a defence of Nietzsche's self-contradictory metaphysical critique of metaphysics, Derrida advises, 'This is not an incoherence for which a *logical* solution is to be sought, but a textual strategy and stratification that must be analyzed in *practice*.'[50] This allusion to Nietzschean

---

[44]   Derrida, *Margins of Philosophy*, p. 195.

[45]   David Wood, 'Différance and the Problem of Strategy' in *Derrida and Différance*, ed. David Wood and Robert Bernasconi (Evanston: Northwestern University Press, 1988), p. 65.

[46]   Derrida, *Margins of Philosophy*, p. 19.

[47]   Jacques Derrida, *Of Grammatology*, trans. Gayatri Chakravorty Spivak (London: Johns Hopkins University Press, 1974), p. xlix.

[48]   Ibid., p. l.

[49]   Derrida, *Margins of Philosophy*, p. 19.

[50]   Ibid., p. 179.

'enactment' proscribes the logical critique of Nietzsche and, by implication, of Derrida himself. In one sense, Derrida's logical reasoning *is* valid and internally coherent since it is founded on the principle of the paradox – the Derridean law of contradiction.

One of the textual strategies Derrida employs to give weight to his assertion regarding the ambiguous ontological status of *différance* is that of placing certain words under erasure (*sous rature*). This is designed to indicate metaphysical concepts which are under suspicion but nevertheless inescapable: 'Now if *différance* ~~is~~ (and I also cross out the "~~is~~") what makes possible the presentation of the being-present, it is never presented as such'.[51] However, *différance*'s existence as a metaphysical concept is not really affected by this; as David Wood points out, placing metaphysical concepts under erasure does nothing to deprive them of their power.[52] Derrida takes pains to state that his account of *différance* does not amount to the reification/deification of a negative concept, even though 'the detours, locutions, and syntax in which I will often have to take recourse will resemble those of negative theology, occasionally even to the point of being indistinguishable from negative theology'.[53] However, negative theology comprises an argument for the existence of God through negation, since to negate a concept already implies its existence. This particular negation relates to the avowed non-conceptuality of *différance*: as *différance* has no signified, it cannot then be elevated to the status of transcendental signified. Derrida is obviously concerned to dissociate himself from this process since he wishes to avoid the necessary existence of *différance*. For Derrida, then, 'différance' is not a counter-argument against an original assertion of the existence/essence of *différance*, but an ('original') assertion of the non-existence of a non-concept/entity – a double negative seeking to evade the grammatically analogous logical positive. Richard Rorty in fact refuses to accept Derrida's assertion that although his account of *différance* may be 'indistinguishable' from 'negative theology' it is *not* the same thing. He asks, 'How can Derrida's "trace", "*différance*", and the rest of what Gasché calls "infrastructures" be more than the vacuous nonexplanations characteristic of a negative theology?'[54] An apparently less exorbitant but equally unjustifiable claim made by Derrida is that *différance* is not a foundational metaphysical term, even in the negative sense: 'Reserving itself, not exposing itself, in regular fashion it exceeds the order of truth at a certain precise point, but without dissimulating itself as something, as a mysterious being, in the occult of a nonknowledge . . . '.[55] The importance and function of *différance* in Derrida's scheme makes it very obviously foundational and Derrida's attempts to claim for it a peculiar ontological status make of it precisely such 'a mysterious being'. It

---

[51]   Ibid., p. 6. NB: Derrida actually uses a cross.
[52]   See Wood, '*Différance* and the Problem of Strategy', pp. 63–70.
[53]   Derrida, *Margins of Philosophy*, p. 6.
[54]   'Two Meanings of "Logocentrism"', p. 208.
[55]   Derrida, *Margins of Philosophy*, p. 6.

is indeed difficult to see how Derrida's negation can convince the reader that he avoids the deification or even conceptualization of *différance* unless this is simply accepted as an *a priori* truth, act of faith, or the sort of founding concept which Derrida seeks to avoid. So while Derrida rejects the idea that *différance* or any of his other 'quasi-concepts' have the status of *a priori* or transcendental concepts, these concepts function in exactly the same way. In a footnote Wood qualifies his criticism by saying that *différance* is not a concept but rather produces 'conceptual effects'.[56] The fact that *différance* produces 'conceptual effects' means that logically one must infer its existence as a metaphysical concept.

To turn to rhetoric, in 'The Principle of Reason', Derrida describes a fictional university lecturer in order to mock notions of rhetorical propriety: 'People indulgently close their eyes to the schematic, drastically selective views he has to express in the rhetoric proper to an academic lecture about the academy. But they may be sorry that he spends so much time in a prolonged and awkward attempt to capture the benevolence of his listeners.'[57] Although Derrida predictably balks at Aristotle's notion of rhetorical propriety, his style of writing is nevertheless governed by a certain rhetorical protocol, albeit one which deliberately flouts classical rules. In the *Rhetoric*, Aristotle distinguishes between three kinds of oratory: the first is persuasive and deliberative and is associated with public affairs and politics; the second is forensic, and is used to condemn or defend a person's actions; the third is *epideictic* and is associated with performance. For Aristotle it is the *epideictic* (performative) which 'is most literary, for it is meant to be read' {1414a} and this term best describes Derrida's writing which tends to be ludic rather than lucid. However, classical rhetoric was primarily a verbal form and although Derrida consistently attacks the historical prioritizing of speech over writing, many of his important texts were originally lectures. For Aristotle, a different style suits oratory and written prose and failure to observe these distinctions will result in rhetorical failure:

> the speeches of professional writers sound thin in actual contests. Those of the orators, on the other hand, look amateurish enough when they pass into the hands of a reader. This is just because they are so well suited for an actual tussle, and therefore contain many dramatic touches, which, being robbed of all dramatic rendering, fail to do their own proper work, and consequently look silly. Thus strings of unconnected words, and constant repetitions of words and phrases, are very properly condemned in written speeches: but not in spoken speeches – speakers use them freely, for they have a dramatic effect {1413b}.

Much of Derrida's work contains strings of words, connected only by semantic

---

56   Wood, '*Différance* and the Problem of Strategy', p. 69, n. 6.
57   Jacques Derrida, 'The Principle of Reason: The University in the Eyes of Its Pupils', trans. Catherine Porter and Edward P. Morris, *Diacritics* 19 (1983), 6–7.

nuance, frequent repetition, and other 'dramatic touches' but he is evidently unworried by his speeches passing into the hands of the reader or about looking 'silly'.

Aristotle proclaims, 'It is a general rule that a written composition should be easy to read and therefore easy to deliver. This cannot be so where there are many connecting words or clauses, or where punctuation is hard' {1407b}. He proceeds to outlaw a type of prose which appears to be the model for deconstruction:

> 'By 'free-running' style I mean the kind that has no natural stopping places, and comes to a stop only because there is no more to say of that subject. This style is unsatisfying just because it goes on indefinitely – one always likes to sight a stopping-place in front of one: it is only at the goal that men in a race faint and collapse; while they see the end of the course before them, they can keep going. Such, then, is the free-running kind of style; the compact is that which is in periods. By a period I mean a portion of speech that has in itself a beginning and an end, being at the same time not too big to be taken in at a glance. Language of this kind is satisfying and easy to follow. It is satisfying because it is just the reverse of indefinite; and moreover, the hearer always feels that he is grasping something and has reached some definite conclusion {1409a–b}.

Aristotle says of the free-running style that it is outmoded; whereas 'Every one used this method formerly; not many do so now' {1409a}. As he puts it, 'If . . . you go on too long, you make him [the listener] feel left behind, like people who pass beyond the boundary before turning back' {1409b}. Derrida uses the free-running style as if it never went out of fashion but since he actively wishes to produce writing the meaning of which is difficult to grasp and which enacts *différance*, this style is entirely appropriate.

Aristotle advises that 'Strange words, compound words, and invented words must be used sparingly and on few occasions . . . . The reason for this restriction [is] . . . that they depart from what is suitable, in the direction of excess' {1404b}. In addition, 'Words of ambiguous meaning are chiefly useful to enable the sophist to mislead his hearers. Synonyms are useful to the poet' {1404b}. At one point (following a semantic explanation) Derrida warns that in fact it is not possible to establish the meaning of *différance*, which is 'irreducibly polysemic'.[58] Compound words, such as *différance*, and verbal ambiguities are Derrida's stock-in-trade. Aristotle also advocates 'naturalness', suggesting that to be persuasive 'a writer must disguise his art and give the impression of speaking naturally and not artificially. Naturalness is persuasive, artificiality is the contrary; for our hearers are prejudiced and think we have some design against them, as if we were mixing their wines for them' {1404b}. Even Derrida's earlier essays such as 'Différance' flaunt their rhetoricity by means of punning, word-play and

---

[58] Derrida, *Margins of Philosophy*, p. 8.

etymological excavation. By Aristotle's standards, Derrida is a conspicuous
rhetorical failure since his prose is hardly natural, but it is quite possible that he
wishes to incite the reader's prejudice.

Aristotle dictates that appropriate language fits itself to its medium; prose
should avoid both absurdity, or excess, and 'frigidity', since 'when the sense is
plain, you only obscure and spoil its clearness by piling up words' {1406a}. This
is precisely what Derrida wants to do in order to demonstrate the fallacy of
logocentrism. In a sense the question whether Derrida's rhetoric obscures his
argument is irrelevant, for where the 'flowers of rhetoric' flourish so abundantly,
the intent is not to appeal to reason but to enact a principle. Derrida makes
explicit that it is *différance* itself which necessitates the elliptical mode of
writing:

> In the delineation of *différance* everything is strategic and adventurous.
> Strategic because no transcendent truth present outside the field of writing
> can govern theologically the totality of the field. Adventurous because this
> strategy is not a simple strategy in the sense that strategy orients tactics
> according to a final goal, a *telos* or theme of domination, a mastery and
> ultimate reappropriation of the development of the field.[59]

The implication here, then, is that a conventional philosophical critique is not an
appropriate response to the text. However, Derrida does not want it thought that
his strategy should be identified with anything *less* worthy than philosophy:
'Finally, a strategy without finality, what might be called blind tactics, or
empirical wandering if the value of empiricism did not itself acquire its entire
meaning in its opposition to philosophical responsibility.'[60] Derrida, then, accepts
the onus of 'philosophical responsibility', while claiming that the writing of
différance is something different to philosophy. There is a sort of rhetorical
propriety to Derrida's work, which is classical in spirit, though not *strictly*
classical.

In 'Différance' Derrida asserts: 'What I will propose here will not be
elaborated simply as a philosophical discourse, operating according to principles,
postulates, axioms or definitions, and proceeding along the discursive lines of a
linear order of reasons.'[61] He asserts that it is *différance* itself which requires this
and at one point notes the significance of the Latin origin of the word: 'this will
not be without consequences for us, linking our discourse . . . to a language that
passes as less philosophical, less originally philosophical than the other'.[62] Since
Derrida admits that he is working within metaphysics, then his own discourse
operates within its laws notwithstanding his attempts at transgression (the double

---

59   Ibid., p. 7.
60   Ibid., p. 7.
61   Ibid., pp. 6–7.
62   Ibid., p. 7.

bind). Derrida's claim to transgress Aristotelian law does not rest simply on an alternative logic, but on an argument which exploits etymological evidence and distinctive textual strategies. There is no reason why the concept of enactment should excuse deconstruction from a more conventional philosophical critique. Logic or rhetoric alone would not be adequate to explain Derrida's strategies but combined they provide the means to dissect deconstruction.

The idea that reason depends on rhetoric, reasonable and innocuous enough in itself, has lead to clear abuses of rhetoric, particularly by poststructuralist enthusiasts who lack philosophical training. The rhetorical trope which is most often exploited by these theorists is the metaphor. In 'The Statesman's Manual' Coleridge wrote that he regarded it as among the miseries of his time that it recognized no medium between the literal and the metaphorical.[63] It is among the miseries of the postmodern age that it recognizes little *distinction* between the two. In the *Rhetoric*, metaphor is categorized as part of style, its function to present things in a fresh way or, in Russian Formalist idiom, to make the stone stony, and Aristotle makes a clear distinction between 'the proper or regular and the metaphorical use' {1404b}. Against the classical opposition of metaphorical and ordinary language use goes the conception of metaphor as intrinsic to language. Richards writes in *The Philosophy of Rhetoric* that 'a word is normally a substitute for . . . not one discrete past impression but a combination of general aspects', and offers this as the general principle of metaphor.[64] He thereby conflates metaphor, which forcibly yokes concepts together, with the connotation of ordinary language.

Another consequence of the extended concept of metaphor is the denial of metaphorical mortality. The 'death' of metaphor occurs when a figure becomes conventional and leached of its metaphoricity. Other terms used to designate this process are 'literalization' (Donald Davidson) and 'lexicalization' (Paul Ricoeur), but however labelled, it is flatly refuted by Derrida.[65] In 'White Mythology', Derrida describes the conventional understanding of metaphorization as the transformation of the sensible to the intelligible, but denies that original meaning can be entirely effaced. For Derrida, a spark of life always 'remains active and stirring'.[66] It is part of his crusade to revive etiolated metaphors and this is achieved in several ways: by foregrounding the etymology of a word; by listing its connotations; and most esoterically, by means of graphic illustration. These procedures demonstrate Derrida's fondness for the pun, verbal and visual. While

[63] *The Collected Works of Samuel Taylor Coleridge* VI, ed. R.J. White (London: Routledge & Kegan Paul, 1972), p. 30.
[64] Richards, *The Philosophy of Rhetoric*, p. 93.
[65] Donald Davidson, 'What Metaphors Mean', *Critical Inquiry* 5 (1978), 37; Paul Ricoeur, *The Rule of Metaphor: Multi-Disciplinary Studies of the Creation of Meaning in Language*, trans. Robert Czerny (London: Routledge & Kegan Paul, 1978), p. 291.
[66] Derrida, *Margins of Philosophy*, p. 213.

they display the peculiar metaphysical logic of deconstruction, Derrida, like Richards, overlooks the actual workings of language. Although ordinary language is always potentially connotative, decisions between literal and figurative interpretation are nevertheless made. The idea that philosophical terms (philosophemes) are necessarily *still* metaphorical arises from a blindness to the literal meaning of dead metaphor and a refusal to recognize that the etymon is often lost without a trace. Ricoeur argues cogently that 'dead metaphors are no longer metaphors, but instead are associated with literal meaning, extending its polysemy'.[67] Ricoeur defines the 'literal' as *current usage*, thereby incorporating connotation while excluding metaphor, and it is this pragmatic distinction which informs the following reading of postmodernist texts.

The problem with 'universal' theories of metaphor is that they operate with too wide a definition, suppressing significant differences which operate in ordinary language use. The fact that non-formal language is necessarily rhetorical, does not mean that it is necessarily metaphorical. The historical development of meaning can also be telescoped as the often tenuous link between current usage and etymon is artificially reinforced. However, there is a commonly perceived (common-sense) distinction between literal and metaphorical use which is not simply illusory. Where texts are metaphorical, it is possible to abstract and analyse the metaphor *qua* metaphor, and to see exactly how it works in conjunction with the chain of reason, a procedure endorsed by Aristotelian rhetoric.

Thanks in large part to Derrida, long-dead metaphors are now being disinterred to reveal patriarchy, imperialism and logocentrism. In postmodern theory there is a prevalence of topographical and cartographic imagery: centres and margins, spaces, locations, positions, frames, edges, boundaries and borders.[68] Terms such as 'boundary' and 'margin' are not ordinarily metaphorical when used to refer to concepts since they have passed into common usage. They differ from the philosophemes examined by Derrida by virtue of the fact that their 'physical' origins are not lost but remain current. While extant parallel meaning makes for obvious connotative force, it does not entail metaphor. But in many postmodernist texts, the rhetorical weight accruing to 'dead' metaphors clearly indicates what Ricoeur defines as re-metaphorization: 'The reanimation of a dead metaphor . . . is a positive operation of de-lexicalizing that amounts to a new production of metaphor and, therefore, of metaphorical meaning.'[69] This rhetorical loading operates in contemporary narratives of liminal identities and

---

[67]   Ricoeur, *The Rule of Metaphor*, p. 290.

[68]   Philip Brian Harper, *Framing the Margins: The Social Logic of Postmodern Culture* (Oxford: Oxford University Press, 1994); bell hooks [*sic*], *Feminist Theory: From Margin to Centre* (Boston: South End, 1984); Donald Preziosi, 'Between Power and Desire: The Margins of the City' in *Demarcating the Disciplines: Philosophy Literature Art*, ed. Samuel Weber (Minneapolis: University of Minnesota Press, 1986), pp. 237–53.

[69]   Ricoeur, *The Rule of Metaphor*, p. 291.

literatures, transgressed boundaries, and blurred borders, but in these accounts metaphors are often used to buttress questionable logic.

Steven Connor notes the totalizing effect of postmodern imagery and worries that 'the exploited and managed Other, may in a sense be programmed by the conceptual map of centre and margin'.[70] In spite of this warning, the boundary lexicon continues to exert considerable appeal for postmodern theorists and is *de rigueur* for discourses such as post-colonialism which has a particular interest in geo-political boundaries.[71] The ontological status of the geo-political boundary slides between the conceptual and the physical – it may be geologically indicated by a coastline or merely politically demarcated – and it is because of this indeterminacy that the slide between literal and metaphorical reference can appear seamless. A concealed slide between literal and metaphorical reference allows the postmodern theorist to implicate those who maintain disciplinary difference in an oppressive political programme. At the same time, spatial rhetoric can work in postmodernism's favour to consolidate implicit claims to political efficacy and professional competence.

The metaphor of the border is also employed in Angus's account of postmodern rhetoric. The postmodern philosopher is obliged to qualify all absolute entities and Angus identifies a border or transition point (such liminal entities are familiar from Derrida's thought) at which translation (totalization) succumbs to deconstruction and re-translation: 'in the postmodern condition, at the border, there is neither leave-taking from discourse nor a completion of discourse – only a moment of switching from silence to babble'.[72] Along with a deconstructive logic, Angus employs what has become a clichéd postmodernist rhetoric, leaning heavily on the deconstructive geographical motif of the transgressed boundary or border and eschewing rigorous argumentation.

The margin is a similarly potent metaphor for postmodern theorists. Although Gayatri Spivak refuses the label of marginal in favour of 'the institutional appellation, "teacher"', she regards herself as confined within the centre-margin model.[73] The principle of the double bind dictates that the postcolonial is *constituted by* Western modes of representation and must therefore critique the 'discursive system of marginality' from within. Spivak deconstructs the centre/margin binary, asserting that '"postcoloniality", far from being marginal,

---

[70] Steven Connor, *Postmodernist Culture: An Introduction to Theories of the Contemporary* (Oxford: Blackwell, 1989), p. 231.

[71] For an account of the post-colonial obsession with mapping see Graham Huggan, 'Decolonizing the Map: Post-Colonialism, Post-Structuralism and the Cartographic Connection' in *Past the Last Post: Theorizing Post-Colonialism and Post-Modernism*, ed. Ian Adam and Helen Tiffin (London: Harvester Wheatsheaf, 1991), pp. 125–38.

[72] Angus, 'Learning to Stop', p. 202.

[73] Gayatri Chakravorty Spivak, 'Poststructuralism, Marginality, Postcoloniality and Value' in *Literary Theory Today*, ed. Peter Collier and Helga Geyer-Ryan (Cambridge: Polity, 1992), p. 221.

can show the irreducible margin in the centre'.[74] The revised model functions to endorse Spivak's 'politically correct' identification with the 'radical academic', by suggesting that the marginalized can speak from the centre and retain her authentic voice. However, the rhetorical double bind is seriously compromised by alternative schemes to overhaul imperialist rhetoric. Bill Ashcroft, for example, rejects the literary categorisation of migrant and native writings which 'act as branches of the main tree of English literature and thus maintain its centrality and stature'.[75] After Deleuze and Guattari, he discards the 'arborised paradigm' in favour of the 'rhizomatic'. 'Rhizomatic figures', as defined by Deleuze and Guattari, are 'acentered systems, networks of finite automatons, chaoid states'.[76] The rhizome, whose significance lies in the fact that it has no centre, no origin or end, is unambiguously metaphorical since it is a transference that has not yet become idiomatic or literalized. But in terms of descriptive propriety, it marks no progression from Foucault's network model. In fact, neither Spivak nor Ashcroft is trapped within spatial representation of any kind, as Spivak's initial rejection suggests.

In spite of the evident crudity of the centre-margin model and the existence of alternatives, there is a general disinclination to abandon it.[77] Connor suggests that the margin is an ideal location from which would-be political subversives launch guerrilla-type attacks on the centre. This romantic view certainly informs Susan Sellers' suggestion that 'perhaps there is something positive – and perhaps something revolutionary – in the impetus a position on the margins can give'.[78] Jane Marcus stakes a claim to this position, stating that 'feminism . . . in its explicit articulation of otherness . . . places the critic in the position of exile, aware of her own estrangement from the center of her discipline . . . edgily balancing on boundaries and testing limits' – a claim severely compromised by her 'institutional appellation' of 'Distinguished Professor of English' at the City

---

[74]	Spivak, 'Poststructuralism, Marginality, Postcoloniality and Value', p. 228.

[75]	Bill Ashcroft, abstract, 'Post-Colonial Literatures and the Contemporary', *Literature and the Contemporary* (University of Hull, 1994).

[76]	Gilles Deleuze and Félix Guattari, *What Is Philosophy?*, trans. Hugh Tomlinson and Graham Burchell (New York: Columbia University Press, 1994), p. 216. Ironically, in *A Thousand Plateaus* (1986) Deleuze and Guattari perceive the map as 'open and connectable' and liken it to the rhizome. Quoted in Huggan, 'Decolonizing the Map', p. 132. According to *The Concise Oxford Dictionary* a rhizome is a 'prostrate or subterranean rootlike stem emitting both roots and shoots'.

[77]	See Diana Brydon, 'Commonwealth or Common Poverty?: The New Literatures in English and the New Discourse of Marginality' in *After Europe: Critical Theory and Post-Colonial Writing*, ed. Stephen Slemon and Helen Tiffin (Sydney: Dangaroo, 1989), pp. 1–16.

[78]	Susan Sellers, 'Learning to Read the Feminine' in *The Body and the Text: Hélène Cixous, Reading and Teaching*, ed. Helen Wilcox et al. (London: Harvester Wheatsheaf, 1990), p. 193.

University of New York.[79] In 'Sorties', Hélène Cixous vigorously rejects the implications of marginality but implicitly endorses the rhetoric, asserting that 'woman' should 'not have the margin . . . foisted on her as her domain!'[80] The evident drawback of both the rhizome metaphor and network model is that they appear to decentre power and therefore immediately make it more difficult to attack. In political terms, therefore, the more concrete the margin can be made to seem, the better.

Mary Mellor opens *Breaking the Boundaries*, an argument for eco-feminist socialism, with an anecdote about the barbed wire fences surrounding the nuclear base at Greenham Common. She concludes: 'We must transform both society and ourselves by breaking down the false boundaries within ourselves.'[81] There is a concealed slide here between conceptual and physical boundaries which lends Mellor's eco-feminism an undeserved dynamism. Maggie Humm takes a different tack in *Border Traffic: Strategies of Contemporary Women Writers*, admitting at the outset that 'These borders are, in most cases, metaphoric'.[82] This leaves Humm free to exploit the metaphor to its full potential: 'In solving the enigma of the woman writer who vaults over the boundaries of her literary landscape, criticism quickly contains literary athleticism inside a fence crosshatched from periods and genres and glued together with consistency.'[83] But while she forestalls objection to a concealed slide between physical and metaphysical levels of discourse, her rhetoric still works to create a romantic picture of the heroic woman writer eluding the trap of repressive period and genre criticism.

Boundary rhetoric is also conscripted by those theorists wishing to deconstruct the high art/popular culture binary. Angela McRobbie adopts this vocabulary to ambiguous effect when summarizing the achievements of Stuart Hall: 'Culture is a broad site of learning, and perhaps we learn best and are most open to ideas when the barriers between the discipline and the academy and the experiences of everyday life are broken down. There is a sense in which Stuart Hall is . . . speaking from the other side, from the space of difference.'[84] If Hall, who incidentally favours the network model, is speaking from the 'other side', he can hardly be said to have broken down any barriers, but McRobbie's intention is clear enough – to invest his theories of culture with a concrete force by means of

---

[79] Quoted in Mae G. Henderson (ed.), *Borders, Boundaries and Frames: Essays in Cultural Criticism and Cultural Studies* (London: Routledge, 1995), p. 6.

[80] Hélène Cixous and Catherine Clément, *The Newly Born Woman*, trans. Betsy Wing (Manchester: Manchester University Press), p. 93.

[81] Mary Mellor, *Breaking the Boundaries: Towards a Feminist Green Socialism* (London: Virago, 1992), p. 284.

[82] Maggie Humm, *Border Traffic: Strategies of Contemporary Women Writers* (Manchester: Manchester University Press, 1991), p. 1.

[83] Humm, *Border Traffic*, p. 4.

[84] Angela McRobbie, *Postmodernism and Popular Culture* (London: Routledge, 1994), p. 66.

the boundary metaphor.[85] And in spite of his criticism of the postmodern map, Connor uses the same metaphor when describing the hegemonic operation of power in the pop music business. He suggests that rather than 'decentring or undermining the structures of the rock industry, each eruption of cultural difference only serves to stabilize this culture, by spreading and diversifying its boundaries'.[86] This expansionist tendency is presented as the paradigm of capitalism which is thereby rhetorically linked to the imperialist nation-state. The effect is to imply that capitalism is morally dubious without Connor having explicitly to argue this case. Mae Henderson, in a recent collection of essays in cultural studies entitled *Borders, Boundaries and Frames*, foregrounds the difference between what she calls 'intellectual border crossings' and the enforced transit of the dispossessed, but maintains that 'there are nonetheless professional risks incurred when one lives and works "on the borders"'.[87] As the publication of an increasing number of such texts indicates, these risks can pay dividends and boundary rhetoric can materially benefit those working in the field of cultural studies. Breaking down the metaphorical barriers between high art and popular culture expands the field of professional competence and works to consolidate professional power.[88]

The current popularity of spatial representation may be a legacy of structuralism, with its predilection for schematic diagrams and neglect of history. The boundary is also a highly productive term for deconstruction, and its analogues – margin, border, tympanum, hymen, parergon – litter the Derridean corpus. It could be said that in examining the metaphors and etymology of philosophy, Derrida addresses its founding principles. While one must give credit to this as a serious scholarly exercise, 'Tympan' and *Glas* can also be interpreted as harmless rhetorical games. Something rather more sinister is going on in 'The Law of Genre', where Derrida engages with the politics of genre theory. He declares that 'as soon as genre announces itself, one must respect a norm, one must not cross a line of demarcation, one must not risk impurity, anomaly or monstrosity'.[89] The consequences of crossing this 'line' are dirt, infection and sexual transgression. The statement: 'if it should happen that they do intermix . . . then this should confirm . . . the essential purity of their identity', has

[85] See Stuart Hall, 'Brave New World', *Marxism Today* 32 (February 1988), p. 28. Cf. Michel Foucault, *The History of Sexuality* (Harmondsworth: Penguin, 1978), pp. 92–102.

[86] Connor, *Postmodernist Culture*, pp. 189–90.

[87] Henderson, *Borders, Boundaries and Frames*, p. 2.

[88] Cf. Henderson: 'scholars . . . in fields such as Black Studies, Women's Studies, and Gay and Lesbian Studies may feel that the integrity of their newly constituted disciplines have [*sic*] been threatened by aggressive border crossings entailed in the professionalization and legitimation of culture studies'. *Borders, Boundaries, and Frames*, p. 26.

[89] Jacques Derrida, *Acts of Literature*, ed. Derek Attridge (London: Routledge, 1992), pp. 224–5.

discomfiting allusion to theories of racial purity and eugenics.[90] By foregrounding the connotations of boundary rhetoric and aided by the fact that the French *genre* denotes grammatical gender, literary genre and biological genus, Derrida manages to ascribe Nazi ideology to traditional genre theorists.[91]

A similar procedure is followed by Robyn Ferrell in an essay entitled 'Xenophobia: At the Border of Philosophy and Literature'. Ferrell milks the metaphor of 'border' for all it is worth, reeling off lists: 'country, boundary, territory and field, state, empire, King and country, sovereignty, title, currency, trade, import, exchange and quarantine'; 'frontier, foreign, enemy state, border patrol, defence, smuggling, contraband, illicit dealing, espionage, treason.'[92] She asserts of this tactic that,

> It is not a literary flourish but a measuring out of the ground. If there can be said to be a border between philosophy and literature, then what territory/territories could be said to be defended in drawing the same. Borders are not natural but political occurrences, held in place by a tacit xenophobia, the logic of 'us-and-them'[.][93]

Very few people want to be called xenophobic, but if the reader is persuaded by this highly emotive language, then to distinguish between literature and philosophy equates with the worst kind of nationalism. However, that the linguistic connotation of jingoism should inculpate the genre theorist, or indeed anyone using the word 'boundary' in anything but its strictest literal sense, should be regarded with some scepticism. Ferrell quite deliberately foregoes logical cogency for rhetorical display, equating disciplinary boundaries with geo-political borders simply by pointing out connotations. As suggested by Mae Henderson, distinguishing between literature and philosophy, high art and popular culture, or literal and figurative modes of discourse, does not have the same consequences as the forced expulsion of groups of people in the service of territorial expansion. It is as well to be aware of the links between power politics and cultural representation, but to suggest that the distinction between literature and philosophy is racist is crude in the extreme. It is understandable that those of a literary bent should lean so heavily on metaphor, but etymological excavations and rhetorical acrobatics should supplement rather than replace rigorous argumentation.

---

[90]   Derrida, *Acts of Literature*, p. 225.

[91]   Rather than endorsing the 'edge' as he does in 'Living On: Border Lines', Derrida here replaces it with the fold: 'The trait that marks [generic] membership inevitably divides, the boundary of the set comes to form, by invagination, an internal pocket larger than the whole'. *Acts of Literature*, pp. 227–8.

[92]   Robyn Ferrell, 'Xenophobia: At the Border of Philosophy and Literature' in *On Literary Theory and Philosophy: A Cross-Disciplinary Encounter*, ed. Richard Freadman and Lloyd Reinhardt (London: Macmillan, 1991), p. 142.

[93]   Ferrell, 'Xenophobia', p. 142.

While rhetorical exposition does not justify the wholesale censure of English, philosophy or any other traditional academic discipline, spatial terms undoubtedly do have a reifying effect, and this is true of rhizomes, networks and folds, no less than of centres, margins and edges. This effect is compounded by postmodernist re-metaphorization and means that the term 'boundary' is fraught with rhetorical (rather than political) difficulty for those who wish to uphold disciplinary difference. In an essay entitled 'The Epistemology of Metaphor', Paul de Man considers Locke's promotion of the idea of regulated language and concludes that

> We have no way of defining, of policing, the boundaries that separate the name of one entity from the name of another; tropes are not just travellers, they tend to be smugglers and probably smugglers of stolen goods at that. What makes matters even worse is that there is no way of finding out whether they do so with criminal intent or not.[94]

De Man suggests that we turn Locke's rhetoric against his assertions and the deconstructive method can equally well be applied to 'The Epistemology of Metaphor'. De Man's ascription of 'intent' to the literary figure implies that the writer has no control over his language, but this abnegation is compromised by the deliberately extended metaphor which represents the trope as romantic outlaw and the classical rhetorician as policeman. It would be a fruitless task to attempt the scientific categorization of literary language or to expunge metaphor from theoretical or philosophical discourse, but 'classical' distinctions between the literal and the figurative, between current usage and etymon, provide the means to separate the ethical appeal (*ethos*) of postmodern rhetoric from its appeal to reason (*logos*). The common distinction made between reason and rhetoric may be metaphysically problematic, but should not be discarded for this reason alone. Without such distinctions, acquiescence to flawed argument may be extorted by underhand means and the appreciation of significant cultural differences, such as those between logic and rhetoric themselves, mistakenly cast beyond the (metaphorical) boundaries of intellectual good taste and political probity.

---

[94]   Paul de Man, 'The Epistemology of Metaphor', *Critical Inquiry* 5 (1978), 19.

Chapter 7

Poetics and Politics

For poetry makes nothing happen (W.H. Auden, 'In Memory of W.B. Yeats').

There is a widespread assumption among literary and cultural theorists that their pronouncements are politically relevant and, in some cases, politically effective. This is not in itself dangerous, but it is misguided. For academics in France, Britain and America, the 1960s was a decade marked by the high-profile political activism which has ever since been remembered with nostalgia by left-wing intellectuals in the humanities. Since this period, particularly in Britain and America, there has been a concerted attempt by these same intellectuals to politicize literary studies which had formerly been dominated by the ostensibly politically neutral New Criticism. The politicizing impetus has been successful in that the Left now represents the orthodox, though not unchallenged, political position for humanities intellectuals in Britain and America. The shift from formalist criticism to ideological critique has been linked with the assimilation of the poststructuralist theory, which was expressly formulated but signally failed to facilitate the social revolution predicted by Marx. Although some twenty years later the full-blooded revolutionary is now a rare animal, politicized literary and cultural studies still claim to reach outside the academy and assist in political and social change. It is precisely because of the continuing influence of poststructuralist theory that these claims remain unjustified. Although there is presumably some filter-down effect from philosophy to popular thinking, humanities intellectuals should recognize both the essential limitations of metaphysical discourse and the value of empirical study if they claim to address reality and not merely its representation.

Even Marx, the single most influential figure on the Western intellectual Left in the twentieth century, got it wrong. One reason for Marx's enduring appeal for intellectuals may be the fact that by training he was a philosopher. Marx's work, which was always informed by Hegelianism, combined metaphysics with empirical study in a way which is instructive when considering the limitations of poststructuralist critique. He presented history as the concretization of the dialectic: 'is it at all surprising that a society founded on the *opposition* of classes should culminate in brutal *contradiction*, the shock of body against body, as its final denouement?'[1] Marx took a critical view of contemporary philosophical idealism, however, and in *The German Ideology* with Engels, described it as 'the

---

[1]   Karl Marx and Frederick Engels, *Collected Works* VI (London: Lawrence & Wishart, 1976), p. 212.

putrescence of the absolute spirit'.[2] In *The Poverty of Philosophy*, he castigated 'the metaphysicians' and criticized Proudhon for reducing the dialectic to its 'meanest proportions', affirmation, negation, and negation of negation.[3] Marx and Engels always stressed their prioritization of actual material conditions over abstract theories: 'The premises from which we start are not arbitrary ones; not dogmas, but real premises from which abstraction can only be made in the imagination. They are the real individuals, their activity, and the material conditions under which they live . . . . These premises can thus be verified in a purely empirical way.'[4] This claim to attend to the material was to a certain extent justified and informs Bertrand Russell's accusation that (for a philosopher) Marx 'is too practical, too much wrapped up in the problems of his time'.[5] For a political analyst, however, Marx's interpretation of and predictions for society were overdetermined by the Hegelian dialectic, and reliance on this model arguably prompted a wilful misreading of contemporary historical events. In 1848 there was an uprising in Paris as the working-class National Guard forced the abdication of King Louis Philippe and the formation of a provisional government. In June 1849 Marx wrote to Engels: 'never has a colossal eruption of the revolutionary volcano been more imminent than it is in Paris today'.[6] But although the incipient revolution fizzled out later the same month, faith in the dialectic allowed Marx to interpret this failure as merely one small step in the creation of the necessary conditions for the inevitable revolution. In 1850 he wrote in the *Neue Rheinische Zeitung*:

> only the June defeat has created all the conditions under which France can seize the *initiative* of the European revolution. Only after being dipped in the blood of the *June insurgents* did the tricolour become the flag of the European Revolution – *the red flag!*
> And we exclaim: *the revolution is dead! Long live the revolution!*[7]

The overthrow of capitalism by the working class in Britain predicted by Marx and Engels in the nineteenth century never materialized in Western Europe, while revolutions later took place in industrially underdeveloped Russia and feudal China.[8]

---

[2]   Karl Marx and Frederick Engels, *The German Ideology*, ed. C.J. Arthur (London: Lawrence & Wishart, 1970), 1932, p. 39.
[3]   Marx and Engels, *Collected Works* VI, pp. 163, 165.
[4]   Marx and Engels, *The German Ideology*, p. 42.
[5]   Bertrand Russell, *History of Western Philosophy*, 2nd edn (London: Unwin, 1979), p. 753.
[6]   Karl Marx and Frederick Engels, *Collected Works* XXXVIII (London: Lawrence & Wishart, 1982), p. 199.
[7]   Karl Marx and Frederick Engels, *Collected Works* X (London: Lawrence & Wishart, 1978), p. 70.
[8]   Following the October Revolution, the Communist Party of the Soviet Union (CPSU) exercised autocratic rule. In Marxist theory this is socialism, the period between

Although British intellectuals flirted with communism proper, British left-wing politics was always characterized by gradualism. In France, however, communism was a real political option; the *Parti Communiste Français* (PCF) which, like the Communist Party of Great Britain, had been founded in 1920, was relatively hard-line Stalinist for a Western European party, but unlike its British equivalent had achieved significant electoral success. France also preceded Britain and America in infusing its *literary* criticism with radical Left politics and the *avant garde* of this literary-political movement was the journal *Tel Quel*, also instrumental in the advancement of poststructuralist theory.[9] When *Tel Quel* was founded in 1960 it dealt primarily with developments in literature – the *nouveau roman*, Alain Robbe-Grillet's experiments with literary language. However, as the decade proceeded, it increasingly engaged with contemporary political issues.

In May 1968 the famous student protests and sit-ins in Paris spread to factory workers, resulting in widespread disruption and a general strike.[10] In the same month, *Tel Quel* declared its political commitment to this struggle, outlining a course of supportive 'textual' action which would 'bring the social revolution to its conclusion in the realm of language'.[11] This action comprised the development of a branch of Marxist-Leninist theory, which would integrate philosophy, linguistics, semiology, psychoanalysis, literature, and history of science, and would be capable of avoiding 'the pattern of a teleologico-transcendental humanistic and psychologistic mystification, the abettor of the terminal obscurantism of the bourgeois state'.[12] For the perpetrators of poststructuralist theory to accuse another body of 'terminal obscurantism' is a case of the pot calling the kettle black. According to Bernard Brown, the May 'revolution' failed in spite of its intellectual support because the workers were neither organized nor coherent in their demands and public support waned.[13] General de Gaulle diffused the situation by dissolving the National Assembly, the PCF supported parliamentary democracy, and in the subsequent election there was a drop in support for both communist and non-communist Left and a decisive Gaullist majority. The next issue of *Tel Quel* opened not with a rallying editorial, but with an article by Julia Kristeva on semiology in the USSR.

There are illuminating comparisons to be drawn between *Tel Quel* and a

---

the overthrow of capitalism and communism proper when the party acts at once as the vanguard and dictatorship of the proletariat.

    9   The following discussion of *Tel Quel* is indebted to Patrick ffrench's *The Time of Theory: A History of Tel Quel* (1960–1983) (Oxford: Clarendon, 1995).

    10   These protests had somewhat inauspicious beginnings in student demands for dormitory-visiting privileges, but were fed by a renewed political interest (after Algeria) in the Vietnam war.

    11   Jean-Louis Baudry et al., 'La Révolution ici maintenant', *Tel Quel* 34 (1968), 3. Translation by John Burgass.

    12   Ibid., p. 4.

    13   Bernard E. Brown, *Protest in Paris: Anatomy of a Revolt* (Morristown: General Learning Press, 1974), ch. 1.

British journal founded in 1959, the *New Left Review*, not least the inverse ratio between theoretical sophistication and direct political action. In spite of an indigenous Left politics which was characterized by moderation, British intellectuals were impressed by Marx's political theory and also by the prospect of communism.[14] However, according to Michael Kenny, the revelations after Stalin's death in 1953 and the Soviet invasion of Hungary in 1956 'engendered a profound political and ethical crisis for communists around the world' and caused the exodus of intellectuals from the Party.[15] In Britain these intellectuals included E.P. Thompson, Stuart Hall, Raymond Williams and Richard Hoggart who rejected Party orthodoxy and formed a breakaway movement, subsequently labelled the 'New Left'. This New Left occupied the political ground between communism and social democracy and disseminated its ideas through the *New Left Review*.[16] In 'Revolution', Thompson rejects both violent revolution and Fabian gradualism, suggesting that 'It is possible to look forward to a peaceful revolution in Britain, with far greater continuity in social life and institutional forms than would have seemed likely even 20 years ago'.[17] In the first issue of *New Left Review* (1960), Hall set out its aims in an editorial whose tone was moderate rather than hard-line. New Left thinking was predicated upon the idea that social change would be precipitated by intellectuals; the new journal sought to 'bring to life a genuine dialogue between intellectual and industrial workers' and Hall maintained that 'The humanist strengths of socialism . . . must be developed in cultural and social terms, as well as in economic and political.'[18] The link between theory and political action is made explicit: 'We have spoken of the New Left as a "movement of ideas": the phrase suggests both the place we accord to socialist analysis and polemic, and the natural growth of ideas, through people, into socialist activity.'[19] However, Thompson was more emphatic that theory alone was not enough: 'it is necessary to *find out* the breaking-point, not by theoretical speculation alone, but in practice by unrelenting reforming pressures in many fields'.[20] The moderate political position was complemented by the

---

[14]   The Labour Representation Committee, the forerunner of the Labour Party, was founded in 1900 as a coalition of political movements which included the Independent Labour Party, the trade union movement, and the Fabians. The Fabian Society had itself been set up in 1884 by a group of left-wing intellectuals and advocated peaceful political progress towards socialism through electoral and constitutional politics.

[15]   Michael Kenny, *The First New Left: British Intellectuals After Stalin* (London: Lawrence & Wishart, 1995), p. 4. The following account of the New Left is indebted to this book.

[16]   The *New Left Review* was formed by a merger of *The New Reasoner*, edited by Thompson and Paul Saville, and the *Universities and Left Review*, edited by Stuart Hall et al.

[17]   E.P. Thompson, 'Revolution', *New Left Review* 3 (1960), 7.

[18]   Stuart Hall, editorial, *New Left Review* 1 (1960), 1.

[19]   Ibid., p. 2.

[20]   Thompson, 'Revolution', p. 8.

empiricism favoured by Williams, Hoggart and Thompson. However, the journal clearly attracted the idealist spirit; Kenny reports the dismay of a contemporary at the fact that the *New Left Review* was printed on glossy paper, 'a selling out to the consumer society that we were all against'.[21] (In spite of, or perhaps because of, this rampant consumerism the journal ran into financial difficulties.)

From 1962, under the editorship of Perry Anderson, *New Left Review* moved away from the empiricism of Thompson et al. to a Marxism which drew upon the European tradition of Lukács, Gramsci, Sartre, Marcuse, Adorno and Althusser. This caused a schism between 'old' and 'new' New Left; in 1963 Williams wrote disapprovingly in an internal memorandum: 'we strain to catch the idioms of the Third World, or Paris, of Poland, of Milan'.[22] Thompson publicly attacked Anderson in the *Socialist Register* (1965) and Anderson responded in *New Left Review* by reaffirming his commitment to European theory and accusing Thompson of ignorance, insularity and a 'pseudo-empiricism'.[23] It is clear that since the first editorial, the revolutionary fervour of the journal had also increased; *New Left Review* celebrated the Paris failure with a special issue in which Anderson wrote that 'the May events vindicated the fundamental socialist belief that the industrial proletariat is the revolutionary class of advanced capitalism. It has, at the same stroke, made indisputable the vital revolutionary role of intellectuals, of all generations.'[24] This misplaced faith in the inexorable dialectical movement of history towards revolution rivals that of Marx some 120 years before and also indicates the assimilation of Gramsci's intellectual-flattering theory. For Gramsci, 'the study of the role and function of the intellectual is intimately related to the core of revolutionary strategy since a working-class victory can be assured only when working-class hegemony has been achieved over the whole of society'.[25] While Thompson had advocated political activism and is known for his involvement with the Campaign for Nuclear Disarmament, the new New Left largely confined itself to textual action.

The apparent discrepancy between thought and deed for both French and British intellectual Left can be attributed to theory. According to Patrick ffrench, Gramsci's notion of ideology 'permitted a link between cultural practice and political practice' for *Tel Quel*.[26] For Gramsci, ideology was the world-view expressed in and reinforced by language and culture, which maintained the hegemony of the ruling class. Poststructuralist theory reinforced the political

---

[21]   Kenny, *The First New Left*, p. 27.

[22]   Quoted ibid., *The First New Left*, p. 31.

[23]   Perry Anderson, 'Socialism and Pseudo-Empiricism', *New Left Review* 35 (1966), 2–42.

[24]   Perry Anderson, editorial, *New Left Review* 52 (1968), 1, 7.

[25]   Antonio Gramsci, *Letters From Prison*, trans. Lynne Lawner (London: Cape, 1975), p. 43. See also H. Stuart Hughes, *Consciousness and Society: The Reorientation of European Social Thought, 1890–1930* (Brighton: Harvester, 1979), p. 102.

[26]   ffrench, *The Time of Theory*, p. 113.

significance of language, suggesting that the subversion of hegemonic language was itself an inherently revolutionary activity.[27] Ironically, Anderson himself admitted in *Considerations on Western Marxism*, that since 1925, the European tradition (which he had defended in *New Left Review*), had effectively severed the link between theory and practice which is essential to Marxist thought. As Tony Bennett points out, early twentieth-century European theorists 'were either, after an initial period of political involvement, divorced from concrete political pursuits, concerning themselves with theoretical issues . . . or, from the very beginning, had been concerned with Marxism in a purely theoretical sense'.[28] Adorno had written that 'Philosophy, which once seemed obsolete, lives on because the moment to realize it was missed.'[29] Gramsci's notion of ideology and aggrandizement of the intellectual had encouraged the *substitution* of political action with theoretical critique and *Tel Quel* and the New Left justified inaction by stressing the link between language, culture and politics.

Terry Eagleton suggests that poststructuralism was born of the dashing of communist hopes in 1968: 'Unable to break the structures of state power, poststructuralism found in [*sic*] possible instead to subvert the structures of language.'[30] The intellectuals' disillusion with communism also found expression in the deconstruction of Marxist theory. Jean-François Lyotard announces his suspicion of the Marxist metanarrative in *Economie Libidinale* (1974): 'It is clear that . . . European capitalism cannot but collapse soon. (We know that it is not so simple . . .)'.[31] The gap between the doctrinaire politics of the early twentieth-century intellectuals and the iconoclastic poststructuralist approach is clear in this text:

> We must come to take Marx as if he were a writer, an author full of affects, take his text as a madness and not as a theory, we must succeed in pushing aside his theoretical barrier and stroking his beard without contempt and without devotion, no longer the false neutrality which Merleau-Ponty advised in the past . . . no, stroke his beard as a complex libidinal volume, reawakening his hidden desire and ours along with it.[32]

Lyotard explains his rhetorical tactics thus: 'Our politics is of flight, primarily,

---

[27]   For example, Jacques Lacan's revision of Freud suggests that gender positions are constructed and patriarchal society supported by language. In issue 51 of *New Left Review* (1968) both Gramsci and Lacan were 'introduced' to the readers.

[28]   Tony Bennett, *Formalism and Marxism* (London: Methuen, 1979), p. 103.

[29]   Quoted in James Seaton, *Cultural Conservatism, Political Liberalism: From Criticism to Cultural Studies* (Ann Arbor: University of Michigan Press, 1996), p. 148.

[30]   Terry Eagleton, *Literary Theory: An Introduction* (Oxford: Blackwell, 1983), p. 142.

[31]   Jean-François Lyotard, *Libidinal Economy*, trans. Iain Hamilton Grant (London: Athlone, 1993), p. 238.

[32]   Ibid., p. 95.

like our style'.[33] Significantly, he concludes *Economie Libidinale* with what appears to be a call to inaction, a justification of the Marxist intellectual (and a defence of glossy paper):

> We need not leave the place where we are, we need not be ashamed to speak in a 'state-funded' university, write, get published, go commercial. . . . What would be interesting would be to stay put, but quietly seize every chance to function as good intensity-conducting bodies. No need for declarations, manifestos, organizations, provocations, no need for *exemplary actions*. Set dissimulation to work on behalf of intensities. Invulnerable conspiracy . . . with neither programme nor project, deploying a thousand cancerous tensors in the bodies of signs. We invent nothing, that's it, yes, yes, yes, yes.[34]

While Lyotard clearly endorsed the political effectiveness of his rhetorical critique at the time of writing, he later publicly dismissed this text – a judicious if craven gesture as poststructuralist practice had by that time been proved ineffectual.

Lyotard's later work does engage with political issues in a rather less exalted manner, but the flight from politics to poetics was characteristic of much early poststructuralism. In 'Sorties', Hélène Cixous investigates the patriarchal nature of language and advocates, in order to undermine this system and achieve the revolution in language, particular modes of speaking and writing, which she identifies as feminine. To define the feminine is already to violate its principle; feminine writing 'will never be able to be *theorised*, enclosed, coded . . . . But it will always exceed the discourse governing the phallocentric system'.[35] Cixous nevertheless allows that even within this system 'one can begin to speak. Begin to point out some effects'.[36] The strategic practice of *écriture féminine* is apparent in Cixous' own writing ('enactment') and involves the disruption of various linguistic codes by means of characteristic deconstructive style: '*Voice!* That, too, is launching forth and effusion without return. Exclamation, cry, breathlessness, yell, cough, vomit, music. Voice leaves, Voice loses. She leaves. She loses.'[37] In an 'Exchange' with Verena Conley (1984), Cixous also asserted that *écriture féminine* was politically effective: 'To teach upon feminine writing frees, liberates language, word usage. Of course, one cannot imagine a political liberation without a linguistic liberation; that is all very banal.'[38] In the same

---

[33] Ibid., p. 20.
[34] Ibid., p. 262.
[35] Hélène Cixous, 'Sorties' in *The Newly Born Woman*, written with Catherine Clément, trans. Betsy Wing (Manchester: Manchester University Press, 1986), p. 92.
[36] Ibid., p. 92.
[37] Ibid., p. 96.
[38] Hélène Cixous, 'An Exchange with Hélène Cixous', interview by Verena Andermatt Conley in *Hélène Cixous: Writing the Feminine* by Verena Andermatt Conley, expanded edn (London: University of Nebraska Press, 1991), p. 138.

interview, however, Cixous explicitly extricates herself from politics and the 'real': 'I would lie if I said that I am a political woman, not at all. In fact, I have to assemble two words, political and poetic. Not to lie to you, I must confess that I put the accent on poetic. I do it so that the political does not repress, because the political is . . . so rigorously real that sometimes I feel like consoling myself by crying and shedding poetic tears.'[39] According to Conley, Cixous left the feminist publishing house *Des Femmes* in 1982 'in order to enjoy greater poetic freedom, which, she felt, had been reduced by pressures and interpretations of the relation between the poetic and the political'.[40] In theory, feminism, like any positive political movement with particular concrete goals, and the anti-teleological, anti-foundational, and anti-positivist philosophy of deconstruction, make uneasy bedfellows. In practice the conflict is minimized as Cixous gets carried away with her poetic tears, the ecstatic discourse of *écriture féminine*, and leaves quotidian discourse and the 'rigorously real' behind. It is precisely this esoteric style and language which alienates many readers and thereby contains the subversive potential of *écriture féminine* firmly within the academy.

Economic analysis, the foundation of many political theories, was universally derided by the poststructuralist 'poets'. Lyotard, Derrida and Cixous attempted to undermine both the scientific pretensions and disciplinary identity of economics. In 'From Restricted to General Economy' (1967), Derrida considers the economy of 'Hegelian speculation', that is, Hegel's philosophical system. According to Derrida, Hegel is a philosopher who considers that everything can be made sense of, or turned to profit, by means of the *Aufhebung*. Derrida turns the *Aufhebung* against Hegel by suggesting that its radical indeterminacy (it signifies both conservation and negation) means that it is one term which cannot be turned to semantic profit. He is at pains to disassociate *différance* from the *Aufhebung*: 'Contrary to the metaphysical, dialectical, "Hegelian" interpretation of the economic movement of *différance*, we must conceive of a play in which whoever loses wins, and in which one loses and wins on every turn.'[41] Like Lyotard, Derrida is interested in the more general 'libidinal' economy and relates the *Aufhebung* to sexual profit: 'the *Aufhebung*, within enjoyment, inhibits, retains, and relieves pleasure'.[42] In *Glas* he returns to the *Aufhebung* in an analysis of the etymology of economy (*oikos* house, *-nomos* manage) in order to emphasize the nature of economy as a general system rather than a restricted science:

---

[39] Ibid., pp. 139–40. In a later 'conversation' (interviews are obviously patriarchal) she asserts that 'I found the only way I could deal with politics – poetically – was by changing genres'. Cixous, 'Conversations with Hélène Cixous and members of the Centre d'Etudes Féminines' in *Writing Differences: Readings from the Seminar of Hélène Cixous*, ed. Susan Sellers (Milton Keynes: Open University Press, 1988), p. 153.

[40] Conley, *Hélène Cixous*, p. ix.

[41] Derrida, *Margins of Philosophy*, p. 20.

[42] Jacques Derrida, *Glas*, trans. John P. Leavey, Jr and Richard Rand (London: University of Nebraska Press, 1986), p. 123.

The *Aufhebung*, the economic law of absolute reappropriation of the absolute loss, is a family concept.

And so political. The political opposes itself to the familial while accomplishing it. So the political economy is not one region of the general onto-logic; it is coextensive with it.[43]

In interview, Derrida foregrounds the fact that he is preoccupied with economics as a metaphysical discourse rather than an empirical science: 'economic discourse is founded on logocentric philosophical discourse and remains inseparable from it'.[44] The function of deconstruction is to 'teach science that it is ultimately an element of language . . . despite its attempts to justify itself as an exclusively "objective" or "instrumental" discourse'.[45] Deconstruction, however, is an equally restricted system and what happens in both 'From Restricted to General Economy' and *Glas* is that Derrida turns the *Aufhebung* and the concept of economy to philosophical profit by using them to illustrate his theories of unstable reference and co-implicated oppositions.

Lyotard is equally scornful of political economy which he describes as the '"left's" illusion *par excellence*'.[46] Anticipating *The Postmodern Condition*, he describes science itself as 'at first glance research into efficiency, that is, into power, and on the second merely the production of strange and efficient fictions. Not only is there no "economic thing", there is no "scientific thing", either.'[47] He undertakes a performative philosophical exposition, describing Chinese (Taoist) eroticism and Hegel's 'sublation' (the *Aufhebung*) as illustrative of the same desire for augmentation which Derrida ascribes to profit-making philosophy: 'desire as affirmative force becomes reserve and institution'.[48] Unlike Derrida, Lyotard refers to events in economic history such as the Wall Street crash of 1929. He cites Jacques Néré's *La Crise de 1929* as the source of the following facts: 'from June 1918 to December 1920 the value of the commercial portfolio of the Federal Reserve System rises from $435 to $1578 million. In parallel, the percentage of gold reserves falls; at the start of 1921, it is at 42.4 per cent, when the legal minimum is then 40 per cent'.[49] However, economic statistics are similarly turned to rhetorical profit as the relation between gold and paper currency and the process of inflation provide neat metaphors for poststructuralist theories of unstable reference and plural signification.

---

43 Derrida, *Glas*, p. 133.
44 Jacques Derrida, 'Deconstruction and the Other', interview by Richard Kearney in *Dialogues with Contemporary Thinkers: The Phenomenological Heritage*, ed. Richard Kearney (Manchester: Manchester University Press, 1984), p. 115.
45 Ibid., p. 115.
46 Lyotard, *Libidinal Economy*, p. 238.
47 Ibid., p. 215.
48 Ibid., p. 223.
49 Ibid., p. 230.

Cixous uses the same monetary metaphor while eulogizing Lispector: 'There is a slow, cosmic time there, that of the seed and its fruit, of the chicken and the egg, of gestation, and of dripping honey. With monetary "signs", we get away from this time and its space. We go crazy in signs . . . .'[50] In 'Sorties', the feminine economy is intimately related to the feminine libido, both of which oppose their masculine counterparts. Patriarchal economy is capitalist: 'what *he* wants, whether on the level of cultural or of personal exchanges, whether it is a question of capital or affectivity (or of love, of *jouissance*) – is that he gain more masculinity: plus-value of virility, authority, power, money, or pleasure'.[51] The feminine economy is altogether less acquisitive: 'She too, with open hands, gives herself – pleasure, happiness, increased value, enhanced self-image. But she doesn't try to "recover her expenses".'[52] The Hegelian dialectic is initially disparaged for its stake in the masculine economy; Cixous decries 'its syllogistic system, the subject's going out into the other *in order to come back* to itself'.[53] However, this rather idealistic picture of feminine generosity is undermined by the fact that following the description of the feminine economy as one which rejects (negates) profit, *écriture féminine* is advertised as paying large dividends: 'the act that will . . . return her goods, her pleasures, her organs, her vast bodily territories kept under seal'.[54] Such discrepancies, excused in theory by the double bind, could perhaps be forgiven if *écriture féminine* constituted a truly subversive, that is profitable, strategy for female emancipation, but it does not. Subscription to the feminine economy appears to prohibit its backers from the deliberate accumulation of *financial* wealth and reproduces rather than revises an ideal of female self-sacrifice.

The claim to political effectivity and relevance made by *Tel Quel* survived both the failure of the Paris uprising and subsequent blows to Marxist good faith, although it had to be modified. After 1968 *Tel Quel* had turned hopefully to Maoism, whose concept of cultural revolution was extremely congenial. However, a visit to China in 1974 revealed the actual conditions of the regime and produced further disillusion. Julia Kristeva dates her turn away from politics to psychoanalysis from this point: 'I thought that it would be more honest for me not to engage politically but to try to be helpful or useful in a narrow field, where the individual life is concerned'.[55] In spite of this renunciation of political activism,

---

[50]   Ibid., pp. 239–40. Patricia Waugh remarks that the 'Big Bang' in the London stock market of the 1980s meant that 'Post-structuralist commentators could feel vindicated in their analyses of late capitalism as an economy of signs'. *Harvest of the Sixties: English Literature and its Background 1960 to 1990* (Oxford: Oxford University Press, 1995), p. 19. See also Terry Eagleton, 'Discourse and discos: Theory in the space between culture and capitalism', *TLS* (15 July 1994), p. 3.

[51]   Cixous, 'Sorties', p. 87.

[52]   Ibid., p. 87.

[53]   Ibid., p. 78.

[54]   Ibid., p. 97.

[55]   Quoted in *The Kristeva Reader*, p. 7.

in 'A New Type of Intellectual: The Dissident', she asserts: 'It is the task of the intellectual, who has inherited those "unproductive" elements or our modern technocratic society which used to be called the "humanities", not just to produce this right to speak and behave in an individual way in our culture, but to assert its *political value*.'[56] For Kristeva, dissidence itself was critical thought turned on language and institutions and the effects of this thought are 'multiple sublations of the unnameable, the unrepresentable, the void'.[57] In *The Postmodern Condition* (1979), Lyotard makes similarly vague but positive assertions of the political use of cultural critique: 'Let us wage a war on totality; let us be witnesses to the unpresentable; let us activate the differences and save the honor of the name.'[58] Since Marx had been scathing about 'the metaphysicians' in *The Poverty of Philosophy*, it may be that the metaphysicians were paying him back by stroking his beard, though ostensibly 'without contempt'. But although social, economic and political change meant that Marxist theory was in need of radical revision, it is highly debatable whether poststructuralism represented any improvement on 'vulgar' Marxism. The critique of metaphysics, Derrida's in particular, has had some impact on philosophy because it operates within that discipline. However, the attack on political economy and science has left these discourses largely intact because it works at the same level of metaphysical speculation. Although the linguistic dissidents acted in good faith, this was ultimately misplaced since their acts of rebellion had little impact on the social fabric of a liberal democracy.

By the mid- to late 1970s, literary theory from France was being translated into English (although generally without its original political baggage).[59] At the same time, Marxism began to get a foothold in British literary studies, thus ending cultural studies' monopoly on the left-wing political position in the humanities.[60] While the political Right was dominant throughout the 1980s and early 1990s in both Britain and America, the 'literary Left' was consolidating its position within the humanities. During the 1980s literary studies began to diversify, supplementing feminist studies with black and gay studies – all

---

[56]   *The Kristeva Reader*, p. 294.

[57]   Ibid., p. 300.

[58]   Jean-François Lyotard, *The Postmodern Condition: A Report on Knowledge*, trans. Geoff Bennington and Brian Massumi (Manchester: Manchester University Press, 1984), p. 82.

[59]   See Jonathan Culler, *Structuralist Poetics: Structuralism, Linguistics and the Study of Literature* (London: Routledge & Kegan Paul, 1975); Terence Hawkes, *Structuralism and Semiotics* (London: Methuen, 1977); Jacques Derrida, *Of Grammatology*, trans. Gayatri Chakravorty Spivak (London: Johns Hopkins University Press, 1974), published simultaneously in Baltimore; Roland Barthes, *Image-Music-Text*, trans. Stephen Heath (London: Fontana, 1977); Derrida, *Writing and Difference* (1978), published simultaneously in Chicago and London by Routledge.

[60]   See Terry Eagleton, *Marxism and Literary Criticism* (London: Methuen, 1976); Raymond Williams, *Marxism and Literature*; Tony Bennett, *Formalism and Marxism* (London: Methuen, 1979).

explicitly politicized discourses with radical agendas. Deconstruction has been assimilated, although not without difficulty, within these politico-intellectual movements and has contributed to the elevation of the 'other' or 'difference' to a founding principle. Terry Eagleton puts the same interpretation on American poststructuralism as he does on the French variety: the 'reason for making a fetish of discourse is the political paralysis of the North American left which must direct into the sign what it cannot realize in reality'.[61] The political force of poststructuralists has been persistently trumpeted by English-speaking enthusiasts, often by virtue of a rather loose interpretation of the political. In *Criticism in the Wilderness*, Geoffrey Hartman asserts that 'The revisionists challenge the attitude that condemns the writer of criticism or commentary to nonliterary status and a service function. To that extent they are a political movement that attacks the isolation of the critic: isolation within the university and from broader, more public issues'.[62] The deconstruction of theory and practice, inside and outside, underpins this assumption of political relevance, but Hartman remains better known for his rhetorical flights and textual thefts than for his politics.

Fredric Jameson followed the poststructuralists, especially Lyotard, in *The Political Unconscious* in seeking a revolution which involves 'the liberation of desire and of libidinal transfiguration'.[63] However, the sense of impotence induced in the western post-Marxist comes to the fore in 'Postmodernism, or the Cultural Logic of Late Capitalism' when he identifies the double bind of capitalism: 'even overtly political interventions . . . are all somehow secretly disarmed and reabsorbed by a system of which they themselves might well be considered a part, since they can achieve no distance from it'.[64] Jameson argues that whereas the 'psychic experience' of modernism was dominated by categories of time, postmodernism is dominated by categories of space. The action he endorses is cerebral rather than concrete: 'The political form of postmodernism, if there is any, will have as its vocation the intervention and projection of a global cognitive mapping, on a social as well as a spatial scale.'[65] Jameson asserts that cognitive mapping 'seeks to endow the individual subject with some new heightened sense of its place in the global system'.[66] However, James Seaton has recently argued that Jameson's political ineffectiveness is matched only by his

---

[61]   Eagleton, 'Discourse and Discos', p. 3.

[62]   Geoffrey Hartman, *Criticism in the Wilderness: The Study of Literature Today* (London: Yale University Press, 1980), p. 9.

[63]   Fredric Jameson, *The Political Unconscious* (Ithaca: Cornell University Press, 1981), p. 67; quoted in Seaton, *Cultural Conservatism*, p. 150.

[64]   Fredric Jameson, 'Postmodernism, or the Cultural Logic of Late Capitalism', *New Left Review* 146 (1984), 87.

[65]   Ibid., p. 92.

[66]   Ibid., p. 92.

cultural importance.[67] The 'individual subject' who is going to benefit from cognitive mapping would need to be very highly educated indeed in order to decode the 'terminal obscurantism' which follows from Jameson's adoption of the language of poststructuralism.

The two strands of political and literary theory did not merge in the discipline of English until the 1980s.[68] The post(-structuralist)-Marxist critics made the same claims for the transformative power of literary-critical practices as the Parisian poststructuralists. The mind-set of these critics is epitomized by Catherine Belsey's influential text book, *Critical Practice* (1980). Here Belsey asserts that 'Post-Saussurean linguistics . . . undermines common sense in a more radical way and so provides a theoretical framework which permits the development of a genuinely radical critical practice.'[69] Following the teachings of Althusser and Lacan, it was an article of faith with the post-Marxist literary Left that the concept of the transcendent, essential or universal self (itself an article of faith for humanist philosophy) is complicit with bourgeois ideology and capitalism. Theorists sought to dispel the myth of the self by positing a 'subject' which is linguistically and/or ideologically constructed – for Belsey, the subject is 'Initially (and continuously) constructed in discourse'.[70] The deconstruction of the subject was presented as a strategic political weapon against bourgeois, patriarchal, Enlightenment and humanist ideology. Poststructuralist theories of subjectivity are relieved of the burden of empirical truth and required only to demonstrate theoretical coherence or plausibility, an inadequate basis for any kind of political decision-making.[71]

Deconstruction was not universally admired by the intellectual British Left and has been criticized as an apolitical and ahistorical discourse. In *Literary Theory* Eagleton describes Derrida's deconstruction as 'an ultimately *political* practice, an attempt to dismantle the logic by which a particular system of thought, and behind that a whole system of political structures and social institutions, maintains its force'.[72] However, for Eagleton this project signally

---

[67]   James Seaton, *Cultural Conservatism, Political Liberalism: From Criticism to Cultural Studies* (Ann Arbor: The University of Michigan Press, 1996).

[68]   See Terry Eagleton, *The Crisis in Contemporary Culture* (Oxford: Clarendon, 1993), p. 3. He introduced Marx and Engels, Macherey, Lukács and Benjamin to students.

[69]   Catherine Belsey, *Critical Practice* (London: Methuen, 1980), p. 36.

[70]   Ibid., p. 83.

[71]   The idea of the subject in process can be traced back to the pre-Socratic philosopher, Heraclitus, who believed that all things were in a state of flux and that therefore man could not step twice into the same river because neither he nor the river would be the same. Enough scientific evidence can be found to support this hypothesis, but none to show that self-consciousness is constructed by language or ideology. Raymond Tallis argues against Belsey et al. that the sense in which the subject is in process is 'trivial' and cannot be adduced to support the idea that the self is radically fragmented and incoherent. *In Defence of Realism*, p. 69.

[72]   Eagleton, *Literary Theory*, p. 148.

fails and he maintains that in fact 'Derrida's 'work has been grossly unhistorical, politically evasive and in practice oblivious to language as "discourse"'.[73] Christopher Norris asserts that deconstruction serves a reactionary politics by undermining 'the very concept of historical reason as aimed toward a better, more enlightened or accountable version of significant events'.[74] Eagleton and Norris have grounds for their criticism of deconstruction, not least in its schematic approach. In 'Différance' (first published in the very historical year of 1968), Derrida states of history: 'I utilize such concepts . . . only for their strategic convenience and in order to undertake their deconstruction at the currently most decisive point'.[75] Deconstruction cordons off history, like any other metaphysical concept, within quotation marks:

> I am starting, strategically, from the place and the time in which 'we' are, even though in the last analysis my opening is not justifiable, since it is only on the basis of *différance* and its 'history' that we can allegedly know who and where 'we' are, and what the limits of an 'era' might be.[76]

The fact that deconstruction slid, chameleon-like, not only into Yale School formalism but also into the postmodern nihilism which celebrates linguistic play for its own sake rather than as the agent of social change, suggests that its political colour is indeterminate. Some British poststructuralists continue to defend the political relevance of deconstruction. In *Legislations* a collection of essays which are not 'about' politics, but are 'inscribed in a political situation', Geoffrey Bennington defends Derrida's political relevance against those who 'appeal in their criticisms of deconstruction, to the concepts of "history" and/or "politics"'.[77] He counter-attacks by arguing that

> These concepts function in their discourse as uncriticized and uncritical transcendental terms . . . . But as the effort of deconstruction is precisely to question just such transcendental concepts, and more generally the transcendental position itself, then invoking them against it without further clarifying or modifying their status can never constitute a valid criticism.[78]

However, it is clear that neither Eagleton nor Connor think the result worth the effort.

---

[73]   Ibid., p. 148.

[74]   Christopher Norris, *Deconstruction and the Interests of Theory* (London: Pinter, 1988), p. 25.

[75]   Jacques Derrida, *Margins of Philosophy*, trans. Alan Bass (London: Harvester Wheatsheaf, 1982), 1972, p. 12.

[76]   Ibid., p. 7.

[77]   Geoffrey Bennington, *Legislations: The Politics of Deconstruction* (London: Verso, 1994), p. 4.

[78]   Ibid., p. 4.

Some British champions argue that the ethical aspect of deconstruction makes it inherently political. According to Derek Attridge, 'there has always been an ethico-political dimension to Derrida's writing, manifesting itself particularly in a respect for *otherness*, be it textual, historical, cultural, or personal'.[79] Bennington asserts that deconstruction is political because it is open to the 'other'. Derrida himself corroborates this to a certain extent, asserting that 'deconstruction is, in itself, a positive response to an alterity which necessarily calls, summons or motivates it'.[80] However the link between ethics and politics, doubtful in the context of practical politics, is only obscured further by the poststructuralists. Bennington asserts that 'the space of communication is most radically itself, most radically open to the coming of the other, when I am not even sure whether someone has come and said something'.[81] According to Bennington, violence is judgement or legislation by the other, however it is always possible that the legislator is a 'charlatan' and the 'moment at which the legislator always might be a charlatan . . . just is the moment of the political, and it is irreducible because it is undecidable. This is why there is no end to politics.'[82] Because of its openness to the other (as legislator), deconstruction provides a unique access to this irreducible moment and therefore a unique access to the political. Deconstruction's relation to political, or even ethical, practice is obscure; in communication with an 'other', a knowledge of deconstruction does not in any way facilitate good ethical or political behaviour. Furthermore, the accessibility of Bennington's text is effectively limited to those academics with a higher degree in literary theory. He is contributing to the thirty-year tradition of poststructuralist metaphysical philosophy, but the pretensions of such discourse to political relevance are insupportable. Suspicion of political speakers is almost automatic in a cynical modern climate and needs neither encouragement nor support from deconstruction.

Derrida has recently turned deconstruction on political theory in 'Spectres of Marx', first published in *New Left Review*. Here he eschews rhetorical beard stroking and considers Marx's pervasive influence, particularly 'in political philosophy which structures implicitly all philosophy'.[83] He asserts that deconstruction itself 'would have been impossible and unthinkable in a pre-Marxist space' and is a radicalization of Marx.[84] But the double bind is at work since 'a radicalization is always indebted to the very thing it radicalizes'.[85] Derrida is clearly hostile to the capitalism which 'is attempting to install its worldwide hegemony in paradoxical and suspect conditions', helped in this by

---

79   *Acts of Literature*, p. 5.
80   Derrida, 'Deconstruction and the Other', p. 118.
81   Bennington, *Legislations*, p. 2.
82   Ibid., p. 3.
83   Jacques Derrida, 'Spectres of Marx', *New Left Review* 205 (May/June 1994), 56.
84   Ibid., p. 56.
85   Ibid., p. 56.

the media.[86] However, as suggested in Chapter 1, Derrida's basic analytic paradigm has not developed, but has merely been repeatedly applied to different texts in the same formulaic way that Marx applied the dialectic to history.

In 'Spectres of Marx' Derrida asserts that both anti-Communist America and Marx himself relied upon the concept of a 'dividing line'. The Americans wished to use this line to exclude communism and Marx wished to cross the line between theory and actualization by revolution, but both continued to 'believe in the existence of this dividing line as real limit and conceptual distinction'.[87] The 'spectre' of Marx is the mobile force which Derrida uses to deconstruct the binary of linear history: 'Before knowing whether one can differentiate between the spectre of the past and the spectre of the future . . . one must ask oneself whether the *spectrality effect* does not consist in undoing this opposition, or even this dialectic, between actual, effective presence and its other.'[88] He asserts that 'In order to analyse these wars and the logic of these antagonisms, a problematics coming from the Marxian tradition will be indispensable for a long time yet.'[89] Although Derrida *mentions* historical events and contemporary conditions, he is less concerned to analyse these events historically or sociologically than he is rhetorically and logically and the deconstruction of history or politics is still primarily a philosophical/textual exercise.

Nevertheless, unlike Lyotard in *Libidinal Economy*, Derrida asserts that the spirit of Marxism is a promise 'not to remain "spiritual" or "abstract", but to produce events, new effective forms of action, practice, organization, and so forth'.[90] This appears to contradict the metaphysical 'spirit' of deconstruction. In response to an interviewer who asked whether deconstruction translates into 'political praxis', Derrida has also answered that 'the available codes for taking such a political stance are not at all adequate to the radicality of deconstruction' and that 'I try where I can to act politically while recognizing that such action remains incommensurate with my intellectual project of deconstruction.'[91] Many eminent poststructuralists preempt criticism by agreeing that deconstruction and political action are irreconcilable. Gayatri Spivak argues that:

> Deconstruction points out that in constructing any kind of an argument we must move from implied premises, that must necessarily obliterate or finesse certain possibilities that question the availability of these premises in an absolutely justifiable way. Deconstruction teaches us to look at these limits and questions. It is a corrective and a critical movement. It seems to

---

[86] Ibid., p. 38.
[87] Ibid., p. 35.
[88] Ibid., p. 36.
[89] Ibid., p. 46.
[90] Ibid., p. 54.
[91] Derrida, 'Deconstruction and the Other', pp. 19, 20.

2

POETICS AND POLITICS 155

me also, that because of this, deconstruction suggests that there is no
absolute justification of *any* position.[92]

Asked repeatedly how poststructuralism might lead us to *act* politically, Spivak
replies: 'in terms of how it would change one's practice, it would depend on not
believing that the formula for the good end would come if the programme were
adequately represented, because there is in fact no possibility of adequate
representation of any narrative in practice'.[93] Elsewhere, however, she states
categorically that 'Deconstruction cannot found a political program of any kind',
but that if one did want to found a political project based on deconstruction, 'it
would be something like wishy-washy pluralism on the one hand, or a kind of
irresponsible hedonism on the other'.[94] This is an acknowledgement which
effectively preempts such criticisms as Stuart Sim's left-wing critique of
postmodernism, that Derrida's continual reference to the metaphysical double
bind effectively removes him from the 'practico-political dimension'.[95] However,
many poststructuralists are not prepared to admit the political inefficacy of their
textual strategies. While the most common assertion currently being made is that
the deconstruction of metaphysics has political significance, it is clear that there
is simply no common philosophical ground on which poststructuralist
metaphysicians and socialists can thrash out their differences. The relatively
unreconstructed left-wing intellectuals point to the practical irrelevance of
poststructuralist theory, while defensive poststructuralists point to the
metaphysical presuppositions of their critics' discourse. Both are right.

The correlation between Left politics and literary theory in general remains,
as does the tendency of disciplinary conservatives to eschew both political
comment and literary theory. Richard Levin states that 'There is no necessary
connection between critical approaches and political beliefs.'[96] Harold Bloom
admits 'that canons always do indirectly serve the social and political, and indeed
the spiritual concerns and aims of the wealthier classes of . . . Western society',
but resists the reduction of aesthetics to ideology.[97] Hilton Kramer and Roger
Kimball, beleaguered traditionalists, set up a journal, *The New Criterion*,
expressly to attack the left-wing orthodoxy and maintain their 'independent
critical voice' and the 'integrity and independence of artistic activity'.[98] Kramer

---

[92]   Gayatri Chakravorty Spivak, *The Post-Colonial Critic: Interviews, Strategies,
Dialogues*, ed. Sarah Harasym (London: Routledge, 1990), p. 104.
[93]   Ibid., p. 28.
[94]   Ibid., p. 104.
[95]   Stuart Sim, *Beyond Aesthetics: Confrontations with Poststructuralism and
Postmodernism* (London: Harvester Wheatsheaf, 1992), p. 41.
[96]   Richard Levin, 'The New Interdisciplinarity in Literary Criticism' in *After
Poststructuralism: Interdisciplinarity and Literary Theory*, ed. Nancy Easterlin and
Barbara Riebling (Evanston: Northwestern University Press, 1993), p. 24.
[97]   Bloom, *The Western Canon*, pp. 23, 33.

coyly alludes to his politics, but argues that the political crisis represented by the Left's attack on humanism/the humanities is not answered by reducing art to politics. He argues that 'To subordinate art to politics . . . is not only to diminish its power to shape our civilization at its highest levels of aspiration but to condemn it to a role that amounts to little more than social engineering.'[99] The squabble between literary Left and Right in America culminated in the much-hyped 'PC' wars of the early 1990s, where the positions of intellectual radicals and reactionaries were further polarized by the media. More seriously, world events were impinging on the consciousness of the literary Left and apparently dispelling the last shreds of faith in the surviving linguistic dissidents. In 1992 Colin MacCabe asserted that 'The events of 1989 were . . . of such staggering import that they did remove the last vestiges of any supposed link between theory and Marxism.'[100] William Cain, who identifies with the political Left, admits that 'The literary Left has minimal influence on public debate . . . and it has shown no ability to convert people to progressive causes and reverse the momentum of the Right's social policies.'[101] The persistent failure of the intellectual *avant-garde* to transform liberal democracy and overthrow capitalism in the twentieth century makes the credibility of the post-Marxist intellectual extremely weak.

After the debacle of Political Correctness, the liberal Left appears to be reasserting itself in America. This fight back by the moderates, which is also noticeable in Britain, often involves the reaffirmation of certain aspects of humanism or Enlightenment philosophy against poststructuralist theory. Seaton asserts the superiority of culturally conservative journalists, such as Edmund Wilson and Lionel Trilling, over postmodern theorists such as Jameson, Rorty and Fish because of their accessible language: 'Those who avoid an esoteric vocabulary, who write in a public language that allows nonspecialists to understand and judge their arguments, implicitly declare their allegiance to a common culture and thus to what they have in common with other citizens.'[102] He also asserts the democratic concept of human rights over that of 'diversity' (difference). Stanley Fish argues that whereas politicized literary and cultural studies are unable to reach outside the academy because of the inaccessibility of their professional language, the neoconservatives are able to broadcast their ideas

---

[98]   Hilton Kramer and Roger Kimball (eds), *Against the Grain: The New Criterion on Art and Intellect at the End of the Twentieth Century* (Chicago: Dee, 1995), pp. ix, x.

[99]   Hilton Kramer, 'Studying the Arts and Humanities: What Can Be Done?' in *Against the Grain: The New Criterion on Art and Intellect at the End of the Twentieth Century*, ed. Hilton Kramer and Roger Kimball (Chicago: Dee, 1995), p. 77.

[100]   Colin MacCabe, 'Cultural Studies and English', *Critical Quarterly* 34, 3 (1992), 33.

[101]   William E. Cain, 'The Crisis of the Literary Left: Notes toward a Renewal of Humanism' in *After Poststructuralism: Interdisciplinarity and Literary Theory*, ed. Nancy Easterlin and Barbara Riebling (Evanston: Northwestern University Press, 1993), p. 130.

[102]   Seaton, *Cultural Conservatism*, p. 158.

in non-academic publications.[103] Fish also points out that literary and cultural theorists are experts in literary criticism rather than 'arms control, city management or bridge-building' and do not have the ear of policy makers.[104]

The intellectuals' desire for political importance, fostered by Gramsci, remains urgent. Newfield and Strickland are representative of a trend in politicized literary and cultural studies with a new buzzword, the 'public intellectual'.[105] In 'Academics as Public Intellectuals', Henry Giroux combines disciplinary radicalism with political liberalism, and argues 'that higher education must be defended as a vital public sphere . . . whose moral and educative dimensions impact directly on civic life'.[106] What is notable about this sentiment is that it was expressed by Arnold in *Culture and Anarchy*. Where Giroux differs from Arnold is in seeking, in the Marxist intellectual tradition, to educate students as self-conscious 'critical agents', rather than good, that is acquiescent, citizens. Giroux argues that 'Such a mode of self-reflexivity must become part of a wider strategy of crossing and transgressing the borders between the self and others, theory and practice, and the university and everyday life'.[107] However, the public intellectual is a worthy ideal which is still not realized in part because of the literary theory which hermetically seals the academic, like Socrates in the *Phaedrus*, within the metaphorical walls of the academy.

It is not merely the language of political literary and cultural theory which defuses its political potential, but an apparent disinterest in concrete facts. Donald Lazere identifies 'a refreshing trend away from poststructuralist theorizing and toward concrete issues in cultural studies', citing Derrida and Spivak. Spivak herself argues that 'to be a theorist of something, you have to look at the documentation in detail', and asserts that what is read by cultural critics is rather 'ideological stuff in journals and newspapers'.[108] However, her theoretical writing often either makes use of anecdotal narrative or the type of dense poststructuralist discourse which does not stoop to mundane empirical inquiry.[109] In 'Spectres of Marx', Derrida accuses Francis Fukuyama in *The End of History* of a failure to analyse empirical evidence in favour of theory and cites against the assertion that the ideal of liberal democracy has been realized the fact that 'never before, in absolute figures, never have so many men, women, and children been subjugated,

---

[103] Stanley Fish, *Professional Correctness: Literary Studies and Political Change* (Oxford: Clarendon, 1995), p. 90

[104] Fish, *Professional Correctness*, p. 90.

[105] See Henry A. Giroux, 'Academics as Public Intellectuals: Rethinking Classroom Politics' in *PC Wars: Politics and Theory in the Academy*, ed. Jeffrey Williams (London: Routledge, 1995), pp. 294–307.

[106] Ibid., p. 298.

[107] Ibid., p. 302.

[108] Lazere, 'Cultural Studies', p. 351; Spivak, *The Post-Colonial Critic*, pp. 98, 96–7.

[109] For an example of the former see 'Postmarked Calcutta, India', *The Post-Colonial Critic*, pp. 75–94.

starved, or exterminated on the Earth'.[110] Ironically, when theorists do cite data in support of their arguments, it is often without reference to the original research. Lyotard cites both data and sources in *Libidinal Economy*, Derrida cites no figures or sources in support of his emotive statements. Richard Rorty, who (tongue-in-cheek) describes himself as a 'bourgeois liberal', explicitly blames the current 'prestige' of theory on Marx's combination of Hegelian philosophy and economic analysis, maintaining that political situations are clarified by empirical analysis rather than metaphysical theory.[111] However, Marx, whose preoccupation with contemporary material conditions was criticized by Russell, illustrated his economic theory with concrete examples. In *Das Kapital*, Marx's analysis of working conditions in nineteenth-century industrial Britain is supported by references to Acts of Parliament and official reports which describe these conditions in detail. There is one quotation from 'J. Murray, 12 years of age': 'I turn jigger and run moulds. I came at 6. Sometimes I come at 4. I worked all night last night, till 6 o'clock this morning. I have not been in bed since the night before last. There were eight or nine other boys working last night. All but one have come this morning. I get 3 shillings and sixpence.'[112] On the next page Marx cites a doctor's report: 'Although in the district of Stoke, only 36.6% and in Wolstanton only 30.4% of the adult male population above 20 are employed in the potteries, among the men of that age in the first district more than half, in the second nearly 2/5 of the whole deaths are the result of pulmonary diseases among the potters.'[113] What is more, Marx scrupulously cited his sources with full bibliographical details, although as history has shown, such attention to fact does not guarantee a correct interpretation if that interpretation is determined by an erroneous theory.

In response to a criticism that Derrida ignores 'the specificity of politics and of empirical social research', Anselm Havercamp asks rhetorically, 'But is it not the very specificity of politics that asks for a refocusing within the frame given, "democracy", and even of a refocusing of the frame as it is given and too easily taken for granted?' It is clear that poststructuralism has no obligation to empiricism and positively discourages such logocentric practices as fact-finding. While metaphysicians are to some extent absolved from attention to the world of objects and actions, logic is bound by its own rules, and literary criticism can legitimately stop inside the text; immediately cultural theorists claim political purchase they are morally and intellectually bound to take notice of 'hard' (empirically verifiable) fact. Giroux attacks neoconservatives, including Kimball,

---

[110] Derrida, 'Spectres of Marx', p. 53.

[111] Richard Rorty, 'Towards a liberal Utopia', interview by Martyn Oliver, *TLS* (24 June 1994), p. 14.

[112] Karl Marx, *Capital: A Critical Analysis of Capitalist Production* I, trans. Samuel Moore and Edward Aveling, ed. Frederick Engels (London: Lawrence & Wishart, 1961), p. 245.

[113] Ibid., p. 246.

who remonstrate with cultural critics for their failure to 'address the real problems of everyday life', asserting that they are anti-intellectual, market-led, and hostile to scepticism.[114] But ideological critique is leached of significance without reference to the world outside the text and political analysis stands or falls on its ability to point to concrete evidence. One cannot question the sincerity of any Left theorist but there is a certain amount of bad taste in the failure to attend closely to the world outside text or conceptual structure while claiming to address its social, political or economic problems. Historiography and narrative construction are valid areas of study but events in the material world are not merely narrative or ideological constructions. It is the empirical methods of analysis mocked or more often simply ignored by poststructuralist theorists which have a far better purchase on political and practical problems inside and outside the social institution which is the university.

Although poststructuralism has expanded the field of professional competence in literary studies, it has been destructive rather than constructive; within literary studies a coherent methodology has been replaced with a model of internal conflict while the empiricist and positivist philosophies which underpinned the humanities have been shaken and in some cases supplanted by anti-foundational metaphysics so that humanism, liberalism and Enlightenment rationality have taken a battering from which they are struggling to recover. Whether postmodern relativism has permeated through the walls of the academy or whether this relativism is simply a function of a prevailing *Zeitgeist*, there is an increased awareness that reports of historical events or scientific findings are at least partly determined by context. But radical or postmodern relativism is neither practised nor practicable in the real world because it asks for a suspension of judgement. The enthusiasts were and are deluded; although concepts and practices in the humanities have been affected by poststructuralism, such ideas as *différance*, radical indeterminacy or polysemy, the constructed subject, the chaos of contemporary life, and suspicion of metanarratives such as history or truth, simply do not equate with common experience. Most of the population (and indeed most academics outside working hours) continue to communicate meaning with apparent success, to accept and make certain assertions as matters of fact, to exercise free will, to experience self-consciousness, a sense of coherent identity, and so on. These assumptions are of course founded on common sense, the Johnsonian stone-kicking type of assertion based on perception and experience which is much maligned by poststructuralists. But deconstruction is a metaphorical sledge-hammer taken to crack a metaphysical nut – common sense already tells us that genre categories, literary value and disciplinary boundaries are contingent.

The assumption that metaphysical theory can be put into practice and can deconstruct various boundaries within educational and other social institutions

---

[114] Giroux, 'Academics as Public Intellectuals', p. 296.

depends upon a collapse of categories which is tenable only within the realm of metaphysics itself and even within this discourse is tenuous. The differences discussed above have been chosen because they are of particular interest to literary studies at the present time and worth defending, at least against metaphysical attack. Outside metaphysics, the relationship between literary realism and metafiction can be both formally distinct and effectively ignored but subjective experience will always be more than a fictional narrative or linguistic construct. Literature and philosophy have much to say to each other but their disciplinary boundaries are grounded in historical and material practices and (sometimes literally) concrete structures which are not built upon metaphysical foundations and will not be undermined by deconstruction. The effective modernization of literary studies depends not on a competence in metaphysics but on a rather less rarified conception of disciplinary history and practice. And while the analysis of rhetoric in non-literary texts is valid and can produce an effective political critique, the conceptual conflation of reason and rhetoric can act only to the detriment of rigorous and coherent argument. The theorists who continue to present conceptual oppositions as pernicious ideological reifications and recruit deconstruction to projects designed to alter material practices in the humanities should be challenged.

Bibliography

Adorno, Theodor W. and Max Horkheimer, *Dialectic of Enlightenment*, trans. John Cumming (London: Verso, 1979).

Ainley, Patrick, *Degrees of Difference: Higher Education in the 1990s* (London: Lawrence & Wishart, 1994).

Allen, Jeffner and Iris Marion Young (eds), *The Thinking Muse: Feminism and Modern French Philosophy* (Bloomington and Indianapolis: Indiana University Press, 1989).

Allot, Miriam, *Novelists on the Novel* (London: Routledge & Kegan Paul, 1965).

Ammann, Daniel, *David Lodge and the Art-and-Reality Novel* (Heidelberg: Winter, 1991).

Anderson, Perry, editorial, *New Left Review* 52 (1968), 1–8.

———, 'Socialism and Pseudo-Empiricism', *New Left Review* 35 (1966), 2–42.

Angus, Ian, 'Learning to Stop: A Critique of General Rhetoric' in Angus and Langsdorf, pp. 175–211.

——— and Lenore Langsdorf (eds), *The Critical Turn: Rhetoric and Philosophy in Postmodern Discourse* (Carbondale and Edwardsville: Southern Illinois University Press, 1993).

The Complete Works of Aristotle, ed. Jonathan Barnes (Oxford: Princeton University Press, 1984).

Aristotle's De Anima Books II and III, trans. D.W. Hamlyn (Oxford: Clarendon, 1968).

Arnold, Matthew, *Culture and Anarchy*, ed. J. Dover Wilson (Cambridge: Cambridge University Press, 1960).

Ashcroft, Bill, abstract, 'Post-Colonial Literatures and the Contemporary', *Literature and the Contemporary* (University of Hull, 1994).

Auden, W.H., *Collected Shorter Poems* 1927–1957 (London: Faber, 1966).

Auerbach, Erich, *Mimesis: The Representation of Reality in Western Literature*, trans. Willard R. Trask (New York: Doubleday Anchor, 1957).

Austen, Jane, *Mansfield Park* (Harmondsworth: Penguin, 1966).

Jane Austen's Letters, 3rd edn, ed. Deirdre Le Faye (Oxford: Oxford University Press, 1995).

Backus, Guy, *Iris Murdoch: The Novelist as Philosopher, the Philosopher as Novelist; 'The Unicorn' as a Philosophical Novel* (Berne: Lang, 1986).

Bannet, Eve Tavor, *Structuralism and the Logic of Dissent: Barthes, Derrida, Foucault, Lacan* (London: Macmillan, 1989).

Barnes, Jonathan, *Aristotle* (Oxford: Oxford University Press, 1982).

Barthes, Roland, *Image-Music-Text*, trans. Stephen Heath (London: Fontana, 1977).

———, *Mythologies*, trans. Annette Lavers (London: Paladin, 1973).

Baudry, Jean-Louis et al., 'La Révolution ici maintenant', *Tel Quel* 34 (1968), 3–4.

Beebee, Thomas O., *The Ideology of Genre: A Comparative Study of Generic Instability* (University Park: Pennsylvania State University Press, 1994).

Bell, Pearl K., 'Games Writers Play', *Commentary* 71, 2 (1981), 69–73.

Belsey, Catherine, *Critical Practice* (London: Methuen, 1980).

Bennett, Tony, *Formalism and Marxism* (London: Methuen, 1979).

Bennington, Geoffrey, *Legislations: The Politics of Deconstruction* (London: Verso, 1994).

——— and Jacques Derrida, *Jacques Derrida* (London: University of Chicago Press, 1993).

Bergonzi, Bernard, *David Lodge* (Plymouth: Northcote House, 1995).

———, *Exploding English: Criticism, Theory, Culture* (Oxford: Clarendon, 1990).

Bérubé, Michael, *Public Access: Literary Theory and American Cultural Politics* (London: Verso, 1994).

Birkett, Jennifer, 'The Implications of Etudes Féminines for Teaching' in Wilcox et al., pp. 204–13.

Bloom, Harold (ed.), *Iris Murdoch* (New York: Chelsea House, 1986).

———, *The Western Canon: The Books and School of the Ages* (London: Harcourt Brace, 1994).

——— et al., *Deconstruction and Criticism* (London: Routledge & Kegan Paul, 1979).

Booth, Wayne C., *The Rhetoric of Fiction*, 2nd edn (London: Penguin, 1987).

Bowen, John, 'Practical Criticism, Critical Practice: I.A. Richards and the Discipline of "English"', *Literature and History* 13, 1 (1987), 77–94.

Bradbury, Malcolm, *Dr Criminale* (London: Penguin, 1993).

Brooke-Rose, Christine, 'A Conversation with Christine Brooke-Rose', interview by Maria del Sapio Garbero in D'haen and Bertens, pp. 101–20.

———, *Thru* (London: Hamilton, 1975).

Brooks, Cleanth, 'Irony as a Principle of Structure' in Rylance, pp. 37–47.

——— and Robert Penn Warren, *Modern Rhetoric*, shorter 3rd edn (New York: Harcourt Brace Jovanovich, 1972).

Brown, Gordon, 'The Politics of Potential: A New Agenda for Labour' in Miliband, pp. 113–22.

Brown, Lee B., 'Philosophy, Rhetoric, and Style', *The Monist* 63, 4 (1980), 425–44.

Bruns, Gerald L., 'Writing Literary Criticism', *The Iowa Review* 12, 4 (1981), 23–43.

Brydon, Diana, 'Commonwealth or Common Poverty?: The New Literatures in English and the New Discourse of Marginality' in *After Europe: Critical Theory and Post-Colonial Writing*, ed. Stephen Slemon and Helen Tiffin (Sydney: Dangaroo, 1989), pp. 1–16.

Byatt, A.S., *Degrees of Freedom: The Early Novels of Iris Murdoch*, 2nd edn (London: Vintage, 1994).

Bybee, Michael D., 'Logic in Rhetoric – And Vice Versa', *Philosophy and Rhetoric* 26, 3 (1993), 169–90.

Cain, William E., *The Crisis in Criticism: Theory, Literature, and Reform in English Studies* (London: Johns Hopkins University Press, 1984).

———, 'The Crisis of the Literary Left: Notes toward a Renewal of Humanism' in *After Poststructuralism: Interdisciplinarity and Literary Theory*, ed. Nancy Easterlin and Barbara Riebling (Evanston: Northwestern University Press, 1993), pp. 127–40.

Calvino, Italo, *If on a Winter's Night a Traveller*, trans. William Weaver (London: Picador, 1982).

Cascardi, Anthony J. (ed.), *Literature and the Question of Philosophy* (London: Johns Hopkins University Press, 1987).

Cixous, Hélène, *'Coming to Writing' and Other Essays*, trans. Sarah Cornell et al., ed. Deborah Jenson (London: Harvard University Press, 1991), pp. 58–77.

———, 'An Exchange with Hélène Cixous', interview by Verena Andermatt Conley in *Hélène Cixous: Writing the Feminine* by Verena Andermatt Conley, expanded edn (London: University of Nebraska Press, 1991), pp. 129–61.

———, 'The Laugh of the Medusa', trans. Keith Cohen and Paula Cohen in Marks and de Courtivron, pp. 245–64.

——— and Catherine Clément, *The Newly Born Woman*, trans. Betsy Wing (Manchester: Manchester University Press, 1986).

——— et al., 'Conversations with Hélène Cixous and members of the Centre d'Etudes Féminines' in Sellers (1988), pp. 141–54.

Connor, Steven, 'Aesthetics, Pleasure and Value' in *The Politics of Pleasure: Aesthetics and Cultural Theory*, ed. Stephen Regan (Buckingham: Open University Press, 1992), pp. 203–20.

————, *The English Novel in History: 1950–1995* (London: Routledge, 1996).

————, *Postmodernist Culture: An Introduction to Theories of the Contemporary* (Oxford: Blackwell, 1989).

————, *Theory and Cultural Value* (Oxford: Blackwell, 1992).

Conradi, Peter J., *Iris Murdoch: The Saint and the Artist*, 2nd edn (London: Macmillan, 1989).

————, 'The Metaphysical Hostess: The Cult of Personal Relations in the Modern English Novel', *ELH* 48 (1981), 427–53.

Corbett, Edward P.J., *Classical Rhetoric for the Modern Student* (New York: Oxford University Press, 1965).

Cordner, Christopher, 'F.R. Leavis and the Moral in Literature' in Freadman and Reinhardt, pp. 60–81.

Court, Franklin E., 'The Social and Historical Significance of the First English Literature Professorship in England', *PMLA* 103, 5 (1988), 796–807.

Cullen, Barry, '"I thought I had provided something better": F.R. Leavis, Literary Criticism and Anti-Philosophy' in Day, pp. 188–212.

Culler, Jonathan, *On Deconstruction: Theory and Criticism After Structuralism* (London: Routledge & Kegan Paul, 1983).

————, 'Poststructuralist Criticism', *Style* 21, 2 (1987), 167–80.

————, *Saussure* (London: Fontana, 1986).

————, *Structuralist Poetics: Structuralism, Linguistics and the Study of Literature* (London: Routledge & Kegan Paul, 1975).

Currie, Dawn and Hamida Kazi, 'Academic Feminism and the Process of De-radicalization: Re-examining the Issues', *Feminist Review* 25 (1987), 77–98.

Currie, Gregory, *The Nature of Fiction* (Cambridge: Cambridge University Press, 1990).

Curti, Lidia, 'What is Real and What is Not: Female Fabulations in Cultural Analysis' in *Cultural Studies*, ed. Lawrence Grossberg, Cary Nelson and Paula A. Treichler (London: Routledge, 1992), pp. 134–53.

Danto, Arthur C., 'Philosophy as/and/of Literature' in Cascardi, pp. 3–23.

Dasenbrock, Reed Way (ed.), *Redrawing the Lines: Analytic Philosophy, Deconstruction and Literary Theory* (Minneapolis: University of Minnesota Press, 1989).

Davidson, Donald, 'What Metaphors Mean', *Critical Inquiry* 5 (1978), 31–47.

Davidson, Harriet, 'The Logic of Desire: The Lacanian Subject of *The Waste Land*' in Davies and Wood, pp. 55–82.

Davies, Ioan, *Cultural Studies and Beyond: Fragments of Empire* (London: Routledge, 1995).

Davies, Tony and Nigel Wood (eds), *The Waste Land* (Buckingham: Open University Press, 1994).

Davis, Lennard J., *Factual Fictions: The Origins of the English Novel* (New York: Columbia University Press, 1983).

Day, Gary (ed.), *The British Critical Tradition: A Re-evaluation* (London: Macmillan, 1993).

Deleuze, Gilles and Félix Guattari, *What Is Philosophy?*, trans. Hugh Tomlinson and Graham Burchell (New York: Columbia University Press, 1994).

Derrida, Jacques, *Acts of Literature*, ed. Derek Attridge (London: Routledge, 1992).

————, 'Deconstruction and the Other', interview by Richard Kearney in *Dialogues with Contemporary Continental Thinkers*, ed. Richard Kearney (Manchester: Manchester University Press, 1984), pp. 105–26.

————, *A Derrida Reader: Between the Blinds*, ed. Peggy Kamuf (London: Harvester, 1991).

————, 'In Discussion with Christopher Norris', *Deconstruction* II, ed. Andreas C. Papadakis (London: Academy Editions, 1989), pp. 7–11.

————, *Dissemination*, trans. Barbara Johnson (London: Athlone, 1981).

————, 'Geslecht II: Heidegger's Hand', trans. John P. Leavey, Jr in Sallis, pp. 161–96.

————, *Glas*, trans. John P. Leavey, Jr and Richard Rand (London: University of Nebraska Press, 1986).

————, *Of Grammatology*, trans. Gayatri Chakravorty Spivak (London: Johns Hopkins University Press, 1974).

————, 'Letter to a Japanese Friend', trans. David Wood and Andrew Benjamin in Wood and Bernasconi, pp. 1–5.

————, 'Limited Inc abc . . .', trans. Samuel Weber, *Glyph* 2 (1977), 162–254.

————, 'Living On: Border Lines' in Bloom et al., pp. 75–176.

————, *Margins of Philosophy*, trans. Alan Bass (London: Harvester Wheatsheaf, 1982).

————, *Memoires for Paul de Man*, trans. Cecile Lindsay et al., revised edn (Oxford: Columbia University Press, 1989).

————, *Positions*, trans. Alan Bass (London: Athlone, 1987).

————, *The Post Card: From Socrates to Freud and Beyond*, trans. Alan Bass (London: University of Chicago Press, 1987).

————, 'The Principle of Reason: The University in the Eyes of Its Pupils', trans. Catherine Porter and Edward P. Morris, *Diacritics* 19 (1983), 2–21.

————, 'Spectres of Marx', *New Left Review* 205 (May/June 1994), 31–58.

————, 'The Time of a Thesis: Punctuations', trans. Kathleen McLaughlin in *Philosophy in France Today*, ed. Alan Montefiore (Cambridge: Cambridge University Press, 1983), pp. 34–50.

————, *The Truth in Painting*, trans. Geoff Bennington and Ian McLeod (London: University of Chicago Press, 1987).

————, *Writing and Difference*, trans. Alan Bass (London: Routledge, 1978).

The Essential Descartes, ed. Margaret D. Wilson (New York and Scarborough: Meridian, 1969).

The Philosophical Works of Descartes I, trans. E. Haldane and G.R.T. Ross, 2nd edn (Cambridge: Cambridge University Press, 1931).

D'haen, Theo and Hans Bertens (eds), *British Postmodern Fiction* (Amsterdam: Rodopi, 1993).

Dickstein, Morris et al., 'The State of Criticism: The Effects of Critical Theories on Practical Criticism, Cultural Journalism, and Reviewing', *Partisan Review* 48, 1 (1981), 9–35.

Dipple, Elizabeth, *Iris Murdoch: Work for the Spirit* (London: Methuen, 1982).

————, *The Unresolvable Plot: Reading Contemporary Fiction* (London: Routledge, 1988).

Dixon, John, *A Schooling in 'English': Critical Episodes in the Struggle to Shape Literary and Cultural Studies* (Milton Keynes: Open University Press, 1991).

Doody, Margaret Ann, *A Natural Passion: A Study of the Novels of Samuel Richardson* (Oxford: Clarendon, 1974).

Dutton, Denis, 'Why Intentionalism Won't Go Away' in Cascardi, pp. 194–209.

Eagleton, Terry, *The Crisis in Contemporary Culture* (Oxford: Clarendon, 1993).

————, 'A Culture in Crisis', *The Guardian* (27 November 1992).

————, 'Discourse and Discos: Theory in the space between culture and capitalism', *TLS* (15 July 1994), pp. 3–4.

————, *Literary Theory: An Introduction* (Oxford: Blackwell, 1983).

————, interview by Catherine Bennett, *The Guardian* (15 August 1991).

————, *Marxism and Literary Criticism* (London: Methuen, 1976).

————, 'Is Theory what other people think?', review of *The Practice of Reading* by Denis Donoghue, *TLS* (29 January 1999), p. 27.

Easthope, Antony, 'Can literary journalism be serious?', *TLS* (20 May 1994), p. 14.

————, *Literary into Cultural Studies* (London: Routledge, 1991).

————, *Wordsworth Now and Then: Romanticism and Contemporary Culture* (Buckingham: Open University Press, 1993).

Eaves, T.C. Duncan and Ben D. Kimpel, *Samuel Richardson: A Biography* (Oxford: Clarendon, 1971).

Eco, Umberto, *The Role of the Reader: Explorations in the Semiotics of Texts* (Bloomington: Indiana University Press, 1984).

Edmundson, Mark, *Literature Against Philosophy, Plato to Derrida: A Defence of Poetry* (Cambridge: Cambridge University Press, 1995).

Elam, Diane, *Feminism and Deconstruction: Ms. en Abyme* (London: Routledge, 1994).

Elias, Amy J.,' Meta-mimesis?: The Problem of British Postmodern Realism' in D'haen and Bertens, pp. 9–31.

Eliot, George, *Middlemarch* I (London: Dent, 1930).

Eliot, T.S., *Selected Essays* (London: Faber & Faber, 1932).

Selected Prose of T.S. Eliot, ed. Frank Kermode (London: Faber & Faber, 1975).

Ellis, Steve, '*The Waste Land* and the Reader's Response' in Davies and Wood, pp. 83–104.

Emck, Katy, 'Fear of floating', review of *The Skull of Charlotte Corday and other Stories* by Leslie Dick, *TLS* (17 November 1995), p. 26.

Ermarth, Elizabeth Deeds, 'The Crisis of Realism in Postmodern Time' in Levine, pp. 214–24.

Evans, Colin, *English People: The Experience of Teaching and Learning English in British Universities* (Buckingham: Open University Press, 1993).

Everman, Welch D., *Who Says This?: The Authority of the Author, the Discourse, and the Reader* (Carbondale and Edwardsville: Southern Illinois University Press, 1988).

Fairlamb, Horace L, *Critical Conditions: Postmodernity and the Question of Foundations* (Cambridge: Cambridge University Press, 1994).

Fekete, John (ed.), *Life After Postmodernism: Essays in Value and Culture* (London: Macmillan, 1988).

Felman, Shoshana, 'Madness and Philosophy or Literature's Reason', *Yale French Studies* 52 (1975), 206–28.

————, *What Does a Woman Want? Reading and Sexual Difference* (London: Johns Hopkins University Press, 1993).

Felperin, Howard, *Beyond Deconstruction: The Uses and Abuses of Literary Theory* (Oxford: Clarendon, 1985).

Ferrell, Robyn, 'Xenophobia: At the Border of Philosophy and Literature' in Freadman and Reinhardt, pp. 142–61.

ffrench, Patrick, *The Time of Theory: A History of Tel Quel (1960–1983)* (Oxford: Clarendon, 1995).

Fielding, Henry, *Joseph Andrews*, ed. R.F. Brissenden (Harmondsworth: Penguin, 1977).

————, *Tom Jones*, ed. R.P.C. Mutter (Harmondsworth: Penguin, 1966).

Fischer, Michael, 'Does Deconstruction Make Any Difference?' in *The Textual Sublime: Deconstruction and Its Differences*, ed. Hugh J. Silverman and Gary E. Aylesworth (Albany: State University of New York Press, 1990), pp. 23–30.

Fish, Stanley, *Is There a Text in This Class?* (London: Harvard University Press, 1980).

————, *Professional Correctness: Literary Studies and Political Change* (Oxford: Clarendon, 1995).

Forster, E. M., *Aspects of the Novel* (London: Edward Arnold, 1927).

Foster, Hal, '(Post)modern Polemics', *New German Critique* 33 (1984), 67–79.

The Foucault Reader, ed. Paul Rabinow (Harmondsworth: Penguin, 1984).

Foucault, Michel, *The History of Sexuality: An Introduction*, trans. Robert Hurley (Harmondsworth: Penguin, 1981).

————, *Madness and Civilization: A History of Insanity in the Age of Reason*, trans. Richard Howard (London: Tavistock, 1967).

Fowler, Alastair, *Kinds of Literature: An Introduction to the Theory of Genres and Modes* (Oxford: Clarendon, 1982).

Fraser, W.R., *Reforms and Restraints in Modern French Education* (London: Routledge & Kegan Paul, 1971).

Freadman, Richard and Lloyd Reinhardt (eds), *On Literary Theory and Philosophy: A Cross-Disciplinary Encounter* (London: Macmillan, 1991).

Frith, Simon, 'Literary Studies as Cultural Studies: Whose Literature? Whose Culture?', *Critical Quarterly* 34, 1 (1992), 3–26.

Frow, John, *Cultural Studies and Cultural Value* (Oxford: Clarendon, 1995).

Frye, Northrop, *Anatomy of Criticism: Four Essays* (London: Penguin, 1990).

Gasché, Rodolphe, 'Infrastructures and Systematicity' in Sallis, pp. 3–20.

Giddens, Anthony, *Beyond Left and Right: The Future of Radical Politics* (Oxford: Polity, 1994).

Giroux, Henry A., 'Academics as Public Intellectuals: Rethinking Classroom Politics' in *PC Wars: Politics and Theory in the Academy*, ed. Jeffrey Williams (London: Routledge, 1995), pp. 294–307.

———— et al., 'The Need for Cultural Studies: Resisting Intellectuals and *Oppositional* Public Spheres', *Dalhousie Review* 64, 2 (1984), 472–86.

Golden, James L. and Joseph J. Pilotta (eds), *Practical Reasoning in Human Affairs: Studies in Honour of Chaïm Perelman* (Dordrecht: Reidel, 1986).

Graff, Gerald, 'The Future of Theory in the Teaching of Literature' in *The Future of Literary Theory*, ed. Ralph Cohen (London: Routledge, 1989), pp. 250–67.

Gramsci, Antonio, *Letters From Prison*, trans. Lynne Lawner (London: Cape, 1975).

Gray, John, 'On to the New Left?', review of *Arguments for a New Left* by Hilary Wainwright, *TLS* (8 April 1994), p. 29.

Griswold, Charles, 'Style and Philosophy: Plato's Dialogues', *The Monist* 63, 4 (1980), 530–46.

Grize, Jean-Blaise, 'To Reason While Speaking' in Meyer (1989), pp. 37–48.

Guy, Josephine M. and Ian Small, *Politics and Value in English Studies: A Discipline in Crisis?* (Cambridge: Cambridge University Press, 1993).

Haber, Honi Fern, *Beyond Postmodern Politics: Lyotard, Rorty, Foucault* (London: Routledge, 1994).

Hall, Stuart, 'Brave New World', *Marxism Today* 32 (February 1988), 24–7.

————, editorial, *New Left Review* 1 (1960), 1–3.

————, 'The Emergence of Cultural Studies and the Crisis of the Humanities', *October* 53 (1990), 11–23.

Harper, Philip Brian, *Framing the Margins: The Social Logic of Postmodern Culture* (Oxford: Oxford University Press, 1994).

Harpine, William D., 'Can Rhetoric and Dialectic Serve the Purposes of Logic?', *Philosophy and Rhetoric* 18, 2 (1985), 96–112.

Hartman, Geoffrey, 'Critical Practice and Literary Theory', interview by Vijay Mishra, *Southern Review* 18, 2 (1985), 189–200.

————, *Criticism in the Wilderness: The Study of Literature Today* (London: Yale University Press, 1980).

————, *Saving the Text: Literature/Derrida/Philosophy* (London: Johns Hopkins University Press, 1981).

Hartsock, Nancy, 'Foucault on Power: A Theory for Women?' in *Feminism/Postmodernism*, ed. Linda J. Nicholson (London: Routledge, 1990), pp. 157–75.

Havercamp, Anselm, 'Deconstruction is/as Neopragmatism: Preliminary Remarks on Deconstruction in America' in *Deconstruction is/in America: A New Sense of the Political*, ed. Anselm Havercamp (London: New York University Press, 1995), pp. 1–13.

Hawkes, Terence, *Metaphor* (London: Methuen, 1972).

————, *Structuralism and Semiotics* (London: Methuen, 1977).

Hebdige, Dick, *Subculture: The Meaning of Style* (London: Methuen, 1979).

Hegel, G.W.F., *Aesthetics: Lectures on Fine Art* II, trans. T.M. Knox (Oxford: Clarendon, 1975).

Hegel's *Logic*, trans. William Wallace (Oxford: Clarendon, 1975).

Hekman, Susan J., *Gender and Knowledge: Elements of a Postmodern Feminism* (Oxford: Polity, 1990).

Henze, Donald, 'The Style of Philosophy', *The Monist* 63, 4 (1980), 417–24.

Hidalgo, Pilar, 'Cracking the Code: The Self-Conscious Realism of David Lodge', *Revista Canaria de Estudios Ingleses* 8 (1984), 1–12.

Hoggart, Richard, *Speaking to Each Other* (II): *About Literature* (London: Chatto & Windus, 1970).

————, *The Uses of Literacy* (Harmondsworth: Penguin, 1958).

————, *The Way We Live Now* (London: Chatto & Windus, 1995).

————, 'Why I Value Literature' in *The Critical Moment* (London: Faber, 1964), pp. 31–9.

hooks, bell, *Feminist Theory: From Margin to Centre* (Boston: South End, 1984).

Hoy, David Couzens and Thomas McCarthy, *Critical Theory* (Oxford: Blackwell, 1994).

Huggan, Graham, 'Decolonizing the Map: Post-Colonialism, Post-Structuralism and the Cartographic Connection' in *Past the Last Post: Theorizing Post-Colonialism and Post-Modernism*, ed. Ian Adam and Helen Tiffin (London: Harvester Wheatsheaf, 1991), pp. 125–38.

Hughes, H. Stuart, *Consciousness and Society: The Reorientation of European Social Thought, 1890–1930* (Brighton: Harvester, 1979).

Humm, Peter, Paul Stigant and Peter Widdowson (eds), *Popular Fictions: Essays in Literature and History* (London: Methuen, 1986).

Hunter, Lynette, *Rhetorical Stance in Modern Literature: Allegories of Love and Death* (London: Macmillan, 1984).

Hutcheon, Linda, *Narcissistic Narrative: The Metafictional Paradox* (London: Methuen, 1984).

————, *The Politics of Postmodernism* (London: Routledge, 1989).

Inglis, Fred, *Cultural Studies* (Oxford: Blackwell, 1993).

Irigaray, Luce, 'This Sex Which Is Not One' in Marks and de Courtivron, pp. 99–106.

James, Henry, *Partial Portraits* (London: Macmillan, 1888).

Jameson, Fredric, 'Postmodernism, or the Cultural Logic of Late Capitalism', *New Left Review* 146 (1984), 53–92.

Jensen, Hal, 'In quotation marks', review of *Marked for Life* by Paul Magrs, *TLS* (3 November 1995), p. 23.

J.F., review of *Margery Kempe* by Robert Glück, *TLS* (17 November 1995), p. 28.

Johnson, Barbara, *The Critical Difference: Essays in the Contemporary Rhetoric of Reading* (Baltimore: Johns Hopkins University Press, 1980).
————, 'Rigorous Unreliability', *Critical Inquiry* 11 (1984), 278–85.
Johnson, Christopher, *System and Writing in the Philosophy of Jacques Derrida* (Cambridge: Cambridge University Press, 1993).
Johnson, Deborah, *Iris Murdoch* (Brighton: Harvester, 1987).
Joyce, James, *A Portrait of the Artist as a Young Man* (Harmondsworth: Penguin, 1960).
Kamuf, Peggy, *The Division of Literature, or the University in Deconstruction* (London: University of Chicago Press, 1997).
Kant, Immanuel, *The Critique of Judgement*, trans. James Creed Meredith (Oxford: Oxford University Press, 1980).
Kavanagh, Thomas M. (ed.), *The Limits of Theory* (Stanford: Stanford University Press, 1989).
Kellman, Steven G., 'Under the Net: The Self-Begetting Novel' in Bloom (1986), pp. 95–103.
Kellner, Douglas, 'Toward a Multiperspectival Cultural Studies', *Centennial Review* 36, 1 (1992).
Kenny, Michael, *The First New Left: British Intellectuals After Stalin* (London: Lawrence & Wishart, 1995).
Kermode, Frank, 'Old wine in new bottles', *The Guardian* (23 February 1996).
Kettle, Arnold, *An Introduction to the English Novel* I, 2nd edn (London: Hutchinson, 1967).
Kijinski, John L., 'Securing Literary Values in an Age of Crisis: The Early Argument for English Studies', *English Literature in Translation* 31, 1 (1988), 38–52.
Kimball, Roger, 'Taboo, or not taboo, that is the question', *The Guardian* (27 April 1996).
————, 'The Treason of the Intellectuals and "The Undoing of Thought"' in Kramer and Kimball, pp. 3–12.
Kintz, Linda, 'In-Different Criticism: The Deconstructive "Parole"' in Allen and Young, pp. 113–35.
Kirwan, James, *Literature, Rhetoric, Metaphysics: Literary Theory and Literary Aesthetics* (London: Routledge, 1990).
Klein, Julie Thompson, *Interdisciplinarity: History, Theory, and Practice* (Detroit: Wayne State University Press, 1990).
Kramer, Hilton, 'Studying the Arts and Humanities: What Can Be Done?' in Kramer and Kimball, pp. 74–81.
———— and Roger Kimball (eds), *Against the Grain: The New Criterion on Art and Intellect at the End of the Twentieth Century* (Chicago: Dee, 1995).
Kristeva, Julia, *The Kristeva Reader*, ed. Toril Moi (Oxford: Blackwell, 1986).
Kuehl, John, *Alternative Worlds: A Study of Postmodern Antirealistic American Fiction* (London: New York University Press, 1989).
Kuhns, Richard, *Literature and Philosophy: Structures of Experience* (London: Routledge & Kegan Paul, 1971).
Lacan, Jacques, *Ecrits: A Selection*, trans. Alan Sheridan (London: Tavistock, 1977).
Ladrière, Jean, 'Logic and Argumentation' in Meyer (1989), pp. 15–35.
Lamarque, Peter, 'Narrative and Invention: The Limits of Fictionality' in *Narrative in Culture: The Uses of Storytelling in the Sciences, Philosophy, and Literature*, ed. Christopher Nash (London: Routledge, 1990), pp. 131–53.
Lamarque, Peter and Stein Haugom Olsen, *Truth, Fiction, and Literature: A Philosophical Perspective* (Oxford: Clarendon, 1994).
Lazere, Donald, 'Cultural Studies: Countering a Depoliticized Culture' in Newfield and Strickland, pp. 340–60.

Leavis, F.R., *The Common Pursuit* (Harmondsworth: Penguin, 1963).

──────, *Education and the University: A Sketch for an 'English School'* (London: Chatto & Windus, 1943).

──────, *Revaluation: Tradition and Development in English Poetry* (Harmondsworth: Penguin, 1972).

Leavis, Q.D., *Fiction and the Reading Public* (London: Chatto & Windus, 1932).

Leitch, Vincent B., *Cultural Criticism, Literary Theory, Poststructuralism* (Oxford: Columbia University Press, 1992).

Lemon, Lee T. and Marion J. Reis (eds), *Russian Formalist Criticism: Four Essays* (London: University of Nebraska Press, 1965).

Levin, Richard, 'The New Interdisciplinarity in Literary Criticism' in *After Poststructuralism: Interdisciplinarity and Literary Theory*, ed. Nancy Easterlin and Barbara Riebling (Evanston: Northwestern University Press, 1993), pp. 13–43.

Levine, George, 'Looking for the Real: Epistemology in Science and Culture' in Levine, pp. 3–23.

──────── (ed.), *Realism and Representation: Essays on the Problem of Realism in Relation to Science, Literature, and Culture* (Madison: University of Wisconsin Press, 1993).

Lévi-Strauss, Claude, *Structural Anthropology I* (Harmondsworth: Penguin, 1968).

Lie, Sissel, 'Pour une Lecture Féminine?' in Wilcox et al., pp. 196–203.

Lipking, Lawrence I., 'The Practice of Theory', *ADE Bulletin* 76 (Winter 1983), 22–9.

Lodge, David, *After Bakhtin: Essays on Fiction and Criticism* (London: Routledge, 1990).

──────, *How Far Can You Go?* (Harmondsworth: Penguin, 1981).

──────, *Language of Fiction: Essays in Criticism and Verbal Analysis of the English Novel*, 2nd edn (London: Routledge & Kegan Paul, 1984).

────── (ed.), *Modern Criticism and Theory: A Reader* (London: Longman, 1988).

──────, *The Modes of Modern Writing: Metaphor, Metonymy, and the Typology of Modern Literature* (London: Edward Arnold, 1983).

──────, *The Novelist at the Crossroads: And Other Essays on Fiction and Criticism* (London: Ark, 1986).

──────, 'The Novelist Today: Still at the Crossroads?' in *New Writing*, ed. Malcolm Bradbury and Judy Cooke (London: Minerva, 1992), pp. 203–15.

──────, *Working with Structuralism: Essays and Reviews on Nineteenth- and Twentieth-Century Literature* (London: Routledge & Kegan Paul, 1981).

Logan, Marie-Rose, 'Graphesis . . .', *Yale French Studies* 52 (1975), 4–15.

Lombardo, Patrizia, 'Cultural Studies and Interdisciplinarity', *Critical Quarterly* 34, 3 (1992), 3–10.

Lukács, Georg, *The Meaning of Contemporary Realism*, trans. John and Necke Mander (London: Merlin, 1962).

Lynn, Steven, *Texts and Contexts: Writing About Literature with Critical Theory* (New York: HarperCollins, 1994).

Lyotard, Jean-François, *Libidinal Economy*, trans. Iain Hamilton Grant (London: Athlone, 1993).

──────, *The Postmodern Condition: A Report on Knowledge*, trans. Geoff Bennington and Brian Massumi (Manchester: Manchester University Press, 1984).

MacCabe, Colin, 'Cultural Studies and English', *Critical Quarterly* 34, 3 (1992), 25–34.

──────, 'Towards a Modern Trivium: English Studies Today', *Critical Quarterly* 26 (1984), 69–82.

MacLeod, Donald, 'Top universities threaten £3,000 fees', *The Guardian* (3 June 1996).

Magnus, Bernd, Stanley Stewart and Jean-Pierre Mileur, *Nietzsche's Case: Philosophy as/and Literature* (London: Routledge, 1993).
de Man, Paul, *Allegories of Reading: Figural Language in Rousseau, Nietzsche, Rilke, and Proust* (New Haven: Yale University Press, 1979).
————, *Blindness and Insight: Essays in the Rhetoric of Contemporary Criticism*, 2nd edn (London: Routledge, 1983).
————, 'The Epistemology of Metaphor', *Critical Inquiry* 5 (1978), 13–30.
————, *The Resistance to Theory* (Manchester: Manchester University Press, 1986).
————, 'The Resistance to Theory' in Lodge (1988), pp. 355–71.
————, 'Semiology and Rhetoric' in *Textual Strategies: Perspectives in Post-Structuralist Criticism*, ed. Josué V. Harari (Ithaca: Cornell University Press, 1979).
Marks, Elaine and Isabelle de Courtivron (eds), *New French Feminisms: An Anthology* (London: Harvester Wheatsheaf, 1981).
Martz, Louis L., 'The London Novels' in Bloom (1986), pp. 39–57.
Marx, Karl, *Capital: A Critical Analysis of Capitalist Production* I, trans. Samuel Moore and Edward Aveling, ed. Frederick Engels (London: Lawrence & Wishart, 1961).
Marx's *Grundrisse*, trans. David McLellan (St Albans: Paladin, 1973).
Marx, Karl and Frederick Engels, *Collected Works* VI (London: Lawrence & Wishart, 1976).
————, *Collected Works* X (London: Lawrence & Wishart, 1978).
————, *Collected Works* XXXVIII (London: Lawrence & Wishart, 1982).
————, *The German Ideology*, ed. C.J. Arthur (London: Lawrence & Wishart, 1970).
McGann, Jerome J., *The Beauty of Inflections: Literary Investigations in Historical Method and Theory* (Oxford: Clarendon, 1988).
McHale, Brian, *Constructing Postmodernism* (London: Routledge, 1992).
————, *Postmodernist Fiction* (London: Routledge, 1987).
McRobbie, Angela, *Postmodernism and Popular Culture* (London: Routledge, 1994).
Melberg, Arne, *Theories of Mimesis* (Cambridge: Cambridge University Press, 1995).
Mews, Siegfried, 'The Professor's Novel: David Lodge's Small World', *MLN* 104, 3 (1989), 713–26.
Meyer, Michel, *From Logic to Rhetoric* (Amsterdam: Benjamins, 1986).
————, *Rhetoric, Language, and Reason* (University Park: Pennsylvania State University Press, 1994).
———— (ed.), *From Metaphysics to Rhetoric* (London: Kluwer, 1989).
Miliband, David (ed.) *Reinventing the Left* (Oxford: Polity, 1993).
Mitchell, Julian, 'Truth and Fiction' in *Philosophy and the Arts* (London: Macmillan, 1973), pp. 1–22.
Murdoch, Iris, *An Accidental Man* (London: Triad/Granada, 1979).
————, 'Against Dryness' in Bloom (1986), pp. 9–16.
————, *The Black Prince* (London: Chatto & Windus, 1973).
————, *Bruno's Dream* (St Albans: Triad, 1977).
————, *A Fairly Honourable Defeat* (Harmondsworth: Penguin, 1972).
————, *The Fire and the Sun: Why Plato Banished the Artists* (Oxford: Clarendon, 1977).
————, *The Green Knight* (London: Penguin, 1994).
————, *Jackson's Dilemma* (London: Chatto & Windus, 1995).
————, *The Nice and the Good* (St Albans: Triad/Panther, 1977).
————, 'The Novelist as Metaphysician', *The Listener* (16 March 1950).
————, *Nuns and Soldiers* (Harmondsworth: Penguin, 1981).
————, *The Philosopher's Pupil* (Harmondsworth: Penguin, 1984).

————, *Sartre: Romantic Rationalist* (London: Bowes & Bowes, 1953).

————, *The Sea, The Sea* (London: Triad/Panther, 1980).

————, *The Sovereignty of Good* (London: Routledge & Kegan Paul, 1970).

————, 'Iris Murdoch on Natural Novelists and Unnatural Philosophers', interview by Bryan Magee, *The Listener* (27 April 1978), 533–5.

————, *Under the Net* (London: The Reprint Society, 1955).

Newfield, Christopher and Ronald Strickland (eds), *After Political Correctness: The Humanities and Society in the 1990s* (Oxford: Westview, 1995).

Newton, K.M. (ed.), *Theory into Practice: A Reader in Modern Literary Criticism* (London: Macmillan, 1992).

———— (ed.), *Twentieth-Century Literary Theory: A Reader* (London: Macmillan, 1988).

Nietzsche, Friedrich, *Thus Spake Zarathustra: A Book for All and None*, trans. Thomas Common, 6th edn (London: Allen & Unwin, 1932).

Nietzsche, Friedrich, *The Will to Power: An Attempted Transvaluation of All Values* I, trans. Anthony M. Ludovici (London: Foulis, 1909).

Norris, Christopher, *The Deconstructive Turn: Essays in the Rhetoric of Philosophy* (London: Methuen, 1983).

————, *The Contest of Faculties: Philosophy and Theory After Deconstruction* (London: Methuen, 1985).

————, *Derrida* (London: Fontana, 1987).

————, *Deconstruction and the Interests of Theory* (London: Pinter, 1988).

————, *Deconstruction: Theory and Practice* (London: Methuen, 1982).

————, 'Philosophy as Not Just a "Kind of Writing": Derrida and the Claim of Reason' in Dasenbrock, pp. 189–203.

————, *What's Wrong with Postmodernism: Critical Theory and the Ends of Philosophy* (London: Harvester, 1990).

————, 'Reason, Rhetoric, Theory: Empson and de Man' in Day, pp. 153–69.

Nussbaum, Martha Craven, '"Finely Aware and Richly Responsible": Literature and the Moral Imagination' in Cascardi, pp. 169–91.

O'Connor, Patricia J., 'Iris Murdoch: Philosophical Novelist', *New Comparison* 8 (1989), 164–76.

Ommundsen, Wenche, 'Sin, Sex, and Semiology: Metafictional Bliss and Anxiety in the Novels of David Lodge', *J. Australasian Universities Lang. and Lit. Assoc.* 73 (1990), 123–40.

Orwell, George, *Collected Essays, Journalism and Letters* (London: Secker & Warburg, 1980).

Paglia, Camille, *Vamps and Tramps* (London: Penguin, 1995).

Palmer, D.J., *The Rise of English Studies: An Account of the Study of English Language and Literature from its Origins to the Making of the Oxford English School* (London: Oxford University Press, 1965).

Parrinder, Patrick, *The Failure of Theory: Essays on Criticism and Contemporary Fiction* (Brighton: Harvester, 1987).

————, 'Having Your Assumptions Questioned: A Guide to the "Theory Guides"' in *The State of Theory*, ed. Richard Bradford (London: Routledge, 1993), pp. 127–44.

'Patten to abolish NUS closed shop', *The Guardian* (8 October 1992).

Pelling, Henry, *The British Communist Party: A Historical Profile* (London: Black, 1958).

Perelman, Chaïm, 'Formal Logic and Informal Logic' in Meyer (1989), pp. 9–14.

Petrey, Sandy, *Speech Acts and Literary Theory* (London: Routledge, 1990).

Pinkney, Tony, '*The Waste Land*, Dialogism and Poetic Discourse' in Davies and Wood, pp. 105–34.

The Collected Dialogues of Plato, ed. Edith Hamilton and Huntington Cairns (Princeton: Princeton University Press, 1961).

Plato's *Phaedo*, trans. David Gallop (Oxford: Clarendon, 1983).

Plato's *Phaedrus*, trans. R. Hackforth (Cambridge: Cambridge University Press, 1952).

The Republic of Plato, trans. F.M. Cornford (Oxford: Clarendon, 1941).

Plotnitsky, Arkady, 'Interpretation, Interminability, Evaluation: From Nietzsche Toward a General Economy' in Fekete, pp. 120–41.

Preziosi, Donald, 'Between Power and Desire: The Margins of the City' in Weber, pp. 237–53.

Pykett, Lyn, *Engendering Fictions: The English Novel in the Early Twentieth Century* (London: Edward Arnold, 1995).

Reading, Russell J., 'Can Cultured Reading Read Culture?: Toward a Theory of Literary Incompetence', *Tulsa Studies in Women's Literature* 10, 1 (1991), 67–77.

Rice, Philip and Patricia Waugh (eds), *Modern Literary Theory: A Reader* (London: Edward Arnold, 1989).

Richards, I.A, *The Philosophy of Rhetoric* (London: Oxford University Press, 1936).

————, *Principles of Literary Criticism*, 2nd edn (London: Routledge & Kegan Paul, 1960).

————, *Science and Poetry* (London: Kegan Paul, Trench, Trubner, 1935).

Richardson, Samuel, *Pamela* I (London: Dent, 1962).

Ricoeur, Paul, *The Rule of Metaphor: Multi-Disciplinary Studies of the Creation of Meaning in Language*, trans. Robert Czerny (London: Routledge & Kegan Paul, 1978).

'The Rise of Theory – a Symposium', *TLS* (15 July 1994), p. 13.

Rorty, Richard, *Consequences of Pragmatism: (Essays: 1972–1980)* (Brighton: Harvester, 1982).

————, 'Deconstruction and Circumvention', *Critical Inquiry* 11 (1984), 1–23.

————, 'Towards a liberal Utopia', interview by Martyn Oliver, *TLS* (24 June 1994), p. 14.

————, 'Two Meanings of "Logocentrism": A Reply to Norris' in Dasenbrock, pp. 204–16.

Rosmarin, Adena, 'Theory and Practice: From Ideally Separate to Pragmatically Joined', *The Journal of Aesthetics and Art Criticism* 43, 1 (1984), 31–40.

Rushdie, Salman, *Midnight's Children* (London: Pan, 1982).

Russell, Bertrand, *History of Western Philosophy*, 2nd edn (London: Unwin, 1979).

Rylance, Rick (ed.), *Debating Texts: A Reader in Twentieth-Century Theory and Method* (Milton Keynes: Open University Press, 1987).

Sage, Lorna, 'The Pursuit of Imperfection: Henry and Cato' in Bloom (1986), pp. 111–19.

————, review of *Jackson's Dilemma* by Iris Murdoch, *TLS* (29 September 1995), p. 25.

————, *Women in the House of Fiction: Post-War Women Novelists* (London: Macmillan, 1992).

————, 'The Women's Camp', *TLS* (15 July 1994), p. 11.

Said, Edward W., *Culture and Imperialism* (London: Vintage, 1994).

Sallis, John (ed.), *Deconstruction and Philosophy: The Texts of Jacques Derrida* (London: University of Chicago Press, 1987).

de Saussure, Ferdinand, *Course in General Linguistics*, trans. Wade Baskin, ed. Charles Bally and Albert Sechehaye (London: Owen, 1959).

Schrag, Calvin O. and David James Miller, 'Communication Studies and Philosophy: Convergence Without Coincidence' in Angus and Langsdorf, pp. 126–39.

Searle, John R, 'Reiterating the Differences: A Reply to Derrida', *Glyph* 1 (1977), 198–208.

Seaton, James, *Cultural Conservatism, Political Liberalism: From Criticism to Cultural Studies* (Ann Arbor: University of Michigan Press, 1996).

Selden, Raman, *Criticism and Objectivity* (London: Allen & Unwin, 1984).

————, *Practising Theory and Reading Literature: An Introduction* (London: Harvester Wheatsheaf, 1989).

———— (ed.), *A Theory of Criticism From Plato to the Present: A Reader* (London: Longman, 1988).

Sellers, Susan (ed.), *Writing Differences: Readings from the Seminar of Hélène Cixous* (Milton Keynes: Open University Press, 1988).

————, 'Learning to Read the Feminine' in Wilcox et al., pp. 190–95.

Shiach, Morag, *Hélène Cixous: A Politics of Writing* (London: Routledge, 1991).

Shklovsky, Victor, 'Art as Technique' in Lemon and Reis, pp. 3–24.

————, 'Sterne's Tristram Shandy: Stylistic Commentary' in Lemon and Reis, pp. 25–57.

Sim, Stuart, *Beyond Aesthetics: Confrontations with Poststructuralism and Post-modernism* (London: Harvester Wheatsheaf, 1992).

Simons, Jon, *Foucault and the Political* (London: Routledge, 1995).

Singer, Linda, 'True Confessions: Cixous and Foucault on Sexuality and Power' in Allen and Young, pp. 136–55.

Smallwood, Philip, *Modern Critics in Practice: Critical Portraits of British Literary Critics* (London: Harvester Wheatsheaf, 1990).

Smith, Barbara Herrnstein, *Contingencies of Value: Alternative Perspectives for Critical Theory* (London: Macmillan, 1988).

Smithson, Isaiah, 'Introduction: Institutionalizing Culture Studies', in *English Studies/Culture Studies: Institutionalizing Dissent*, ed. Isaiah Smithson and Nancy Ruff (Urbana and Chicago: University of Illinois Press, 1994), pp. 1–22.

South Bank Show, prod. David Thomas, ITV (29 September 1991).

Spear, Hilda, *Iris Murdoch* (London: Macmillan, 1995).

Spender, Dale, 'Women and Literary History' in *The Feminist Reader: Essays in Gender and the Politics of Literary Criticism*, ed. Catherine Belsey and Jane Moore (London: Macmillan, 1989), pp. 21–33.

Spivak, Gayatri Chakravorty, 'French Feminism Revisited' in *Feminists Theorize the Political*, ed. Judith Butler and Joan W. Scott (London: Routledge, 1992), pp. 54–85.

————, *The Post-Colonial Critic: Interviews, Strategies, Dialogues*, ed. Sarah Harasym (London: Routledge, 1990).

————, 'Poststructuralism, Marginality, Postcoloniality and Value' in *Literary Theory Today*, ed. Peter Collier and Helga Geyer-Ryan (Cambridge: Polity, 1992), pp. 219–44.

Stanton, Domna C., 'Difference on Trial: A Critique of the Maternal Metaphor in Cixous, Irigaray, and Kristeva' in Allen and Young, pp. 156–79.

Staten, Henry, 'The Secret Name of Cats: Deconstruction, Intentional Meaning, and the New Theory of Reference' in Dasenbrock, pp. 27–47.

Sterne, Laurence, *The Life and Opinions of Tristram Shandy, Gentleman*, ed. Graham Petrie (Harmondsworth: Penguin, 1967).

Stevenson, Randall, 'Postmodernism and Contemporary Fiction in Britain' in *Postmodernism and Contemporary Fiction*, ed. Edmund J. Smyth (London: Batsford, 1991), pp. 19–35.

Tallack, Douglas (ed.), *Literary Theory at Work: Three Texts* (London: Batsford, 1987).

174 CHALLENGING THEORY

Tallis, Raymond, *In Defence of Realism* (London: Edward Arnold, 1988).
————, *Not Saussure: A Critique of Post-Saussurean Literary Theory* (London: Macmillan, 1988).
Taylor, Mark C. (ed.), *Deconstruction in Context: Literature and Philosophy* (London: University of Chicago Press, 1986).
Thompson, E.P., 'Revolution', *New Left Review* 3 (1960), 3–9.
Todd, Richard, 'Confrontation Within Convention: On the Character of British Postmodernist Fiction' in *Postmodern Fiction in Europe and the Americas*, ed. Theo D'haen and Hans Bertens (Amsterdam: Rodopi, 1988), pp. 115–25.
Turnell, Martin, 'Literary Criticism in France (I), *Scrutiny* 8 (September 1939), 167–83.
————, 'Literary Criticism in France (II)', *Scrutiny* 8, (December 1939), 281–98.
Turner, Graeme, *British Cultural Studies: An Introduction* (London: Unwin, 1990).
Turner, Jenny, 'Words never fail him', *The Guardian* (29 April 1995).
Tyson, Lois, 'Teaching Deconstruction: Theory and Practice in the Undergraduate Literature Classroom' in *Practicing Theory in Introductory College Literature Courses*, ed. James M. Cahalan and David B. Downing (Urbana: National Council of Teachers of English, 1991), pp. 227–38.
Varsava, Jerry A., *Contingent Meanings: Postmodern Fiction, Mimesis, and the Reader* (Tallahassee: Florida State University Press, 1990).
Veeser, H. Aram (ed.), *The New Historicism Reader* (London: Routledge, 1994).
Warner, Martin, *Philosophical Finesse: Studies in the Art of Rational Persuasion* (Oxford: Clarendon, 1989).
Watson, George, *British Literature since 1945* (London: Macmillan, 1991).
Watt, Ian, *The Rise of the Novel: Studies in Defoe, Richardson, and Fielding* (London: Penguin, 1963).
Waugh, Patricia, *Harvest of the Sixties: English Literature and its Background 1960 to 1990* (Oxford: Oxford University Press, 1995).
————, *Metafiction: The Theory and Practice of Self-Conscious Fiction* (London: Methuen, 1984).
Weber, Samuel (ed.), *Demarcating the Disciplines: Philosophy Literature Art* (Minneapolis: University of Minnesota Press, 1986).
Weedon, Chris, *Feminist Practice and Poststructuralist Theory* (Oxford: Blackwell, 1987).
————, Andrew Tolson and Frank Mort, 'Introduction to Language Studies at the Centre' in *Culture, Media, Language: Working Papers in Cultural Studies, 1972–79*, ed. Stuart Hall et al. (London: Hutchinson, 1980), pp. 177–85.
Wellek, René, 'Literary Criticism and Philosophy', *Scrutiny* 5, 4 (1937), 375–83.
Widdowson, Peter, 'The Anti-History Men: Malcolm Bradbury and David Lodge', *Critical Quarterly* 26, 4 (1984), 5–31.
Wilcox, Helen et al. (eds), *The Body and the Text: Hélène Cixous, Reading and Teaching* (London: Harvester, 1990).
Williams, Raymond, *Marxism and Literature* (Oxford: Oxford University Press, 1977).
Wimsatt, Jr, W.K. and Monroe C. Beardsley, 'The Intentional Fallacy' in W.K. Wimsatt, Jr, *The Verbal Icon: Studies in the Meaning of Poetry* (Kentucky: University of Kentucky Press, 1954).
Winchester, James J., *Nietzsche's Aesthetic Turn: Reading Nietzsche after Heidegger, Deleuze, Derrida* (Albany: State University of New York Press, 1994).
Wittgenstein, Ludwig, *Tractatus Logico-Philosophicus* (London: Routledge & Kegan Paul, 1922).
Wolf, Naomi, *Fire With Fire: The New Female Power and How It Will Change the Twenty-first Century* (London: Chatto & Windus, 1993).

Wood, David, 'Following Derrida' in Sallis, pp. 143–60.
————, 'Différance and the Problem of Strategy' in Wood and Bernasconi, pp. 63–70.
———— and Robert Bernsconi (eds), *Derrida and Différance* (Evanston: Northwestern University Press, 1988).
Woolf, Virginia, *Collected Essays* II, ed. Leonard Woolf (London: Hogarth, 1966).
Wordsworth, Ann, 'Derrida and Foucault: Writing the History of Historicity' in *Post-Structuralism and the Question of History*, ed. Derek Attridge, Geoff Bennington and Robert Young (Cambridge: Cambridge University Press, 1987), pp. 116–25.
Yarbrough, Stephen R., *Deliberate Criticism: Toward a Postmodern Humanism* (London: University of Georgia Press, 1992).
Young, Robert J.C., *Torn Halves: Political Conflict in Literary and Cultural Theory* (Manchester: Manchester University Press, 1996).

Index